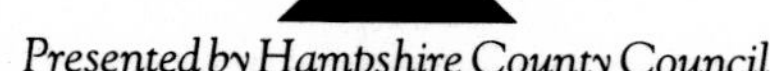

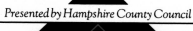

on the occasion of its Centenary.

A CALENDAR OF NEW FOREST DOCUMENTS
The Fifteenth to the Seventeenth Centuries

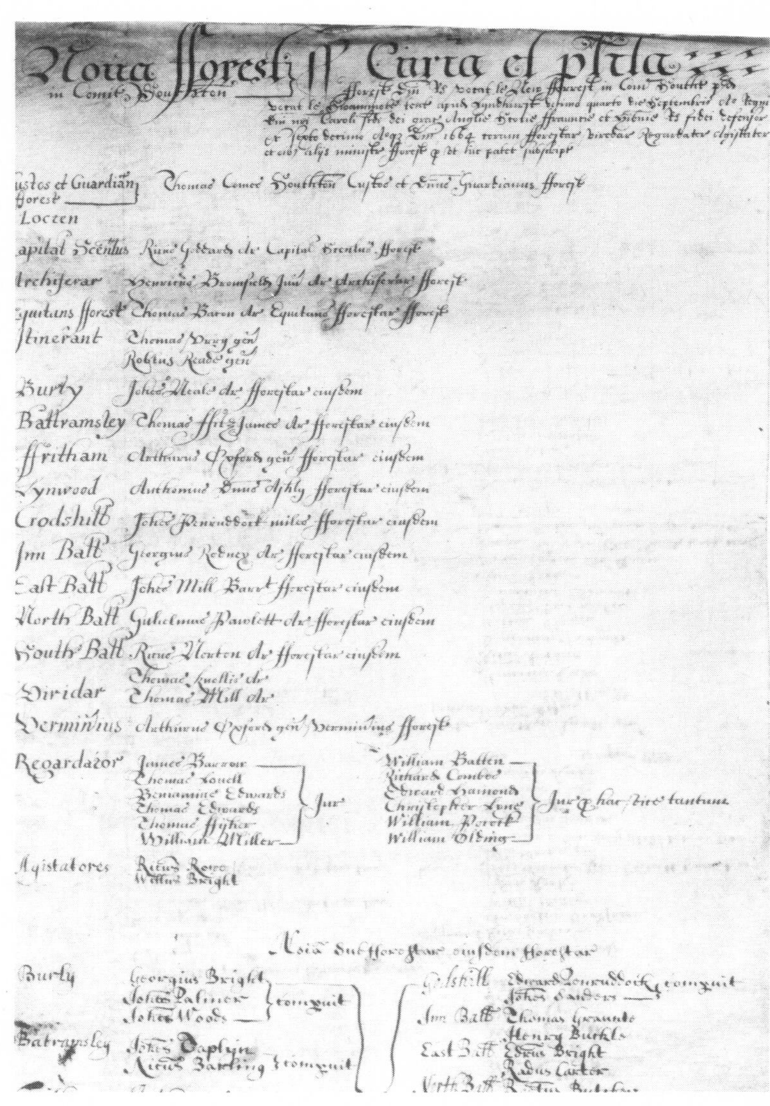

Noua fforesta ss' Curia et placita
in Comit' Southton

fforest Dni Regis vocat le New fforest in Com Southt pdict vocat le Swainmote tent apud Lyndhurst ... quarto die Septembris Anno Regni dni nri Caroli Secundi dei gratia Angliae Scotiae ffranciae et Hiberniae Rex fidei defensor etc Sextodecimo Anoq Dni 1664 coram fforestar Viridar Regardator Agistator et aliis ministris fforest q ut hic patet subscript

Custos et Guardian fforest — Thomas Comes Southton Custos et Dnus Guardianus fforest

Locten

Capital Senescall — Ricus Goddard Ar Capital Senescall fforest

Archiferar — Henricus Bromfield Jun Ar Archiferarius fforest

Equitans fforest — Thomas Baron Ar Equitans fforestar fforest

Itinerant — Thomas Dury gen; Robtus Reade gen

Burly — Johes Neale Ar fforestar eiusdem

Battramsley — Thomas ffitz James Ar fforestar eiusdem

ffritham — Arthurus Oxford gen fforestar eiusdem

Lynwood — Anthonius Dnus Ashly fforestar eiusdem

Godshill — Johes Penruddock miles fforestar eiusdem

In Ball — Georgius Rodney Ar fforestar eiusdem

East Ball — Johes Mill Bart fforestar eiusdem

North Ball — Gulielmus Pawlett Ar fforestar eiusdem

South Ball — Ricus Norton Ar fforestar eiusdem

Viridar — Thomas Knollis Ar; Thomas Mill Ar

Verminius — Arthurus Oxford gen Verminius fforest

Regardator — James Barrow, Thomas Lovell, Beniamine Edwards, Thomas Edwards, Thomas ffisher, William Miller — Jur; William Batten, Richard Combe, Edward Hamond, Christopher Long, William Perrett, William Elding — Jur p hac vice tantum

Agistatores — Ricus Rowe; Willus Bright

Noia Subfforestar eiusdem fforestar

Burly — Georgius Bright, Johes Palmer, Johes Woods — comparuit

Batramsley — Johes Daplyn, Ricus Barling — comparuit

Godshill — Edward Penruddock comparuit; Johes Sanders

In Ball — Thomas Grante; Henry Buckle

East Ball — Edwus Bright; Radus Carter

North Ball — Robtus Butcher

Roll of Swainmote Court of the New Forest, 1664

Hampshire Record Series Volume V

A CALENDAR OF NEW FOREST DOCUMENTS

The Fifteenth to the Seventeenth Centuries

Edited by D. J. Stagg

HAMPSHIRE RECORD OFFICE for
HAMPSHIRE COUNTY COUNCIL, 1983

ISBN 0 906680 02 6

Produced by Alan Sutton Publishing Limited
and Printed in Great Britain

Contents

Illustrations

Preface

The opinion is widely held that forest law was near obsolete by the late 16th century. From the documentary evidence available for the New Forest, and also by a more critical and objective examination of the writings of John Manwood, the present work attempts to put forward an alternative opinion that forest law remained effective until the mid 17th century.

The argument for the early desuetude of the forest laws has been largely derived from a superficial reading and uncritical acceptance of the writings of Manwood, and in particular the removal from context and misunderstanding of his words: "And also that very little, or nothing, as yet is extant concerning the Laws of the Forest . . ."[1] This has been taken as referring to the disuse of forest law at the time when Manwood was writing, but in fact it is nothing more than a justification of the need for a published work on forest law. Further confusion has arisen from his statement: "But now of late within these hundred years, there have been very seldom any justice seat at all kept for forests"[2], but here Manwood is dealing with the renting of assarts and purprestures by the chief justice of the forest, and not of the day to day offences such as were dealt with by the deputy forest justices.

Once a misconception has arisen it tends to be magnified by subsequent writers and a good example of this occurs in connection with forest law in the seventeenth century. Gardiner, who has been described as the most trustworthy of nineteenth century historians,[3] in commenting upon the decision to hold a forest eyre in 1634 states that: "the Earl of Holland, was Chief Justice in Eyre, and was thus officially empowered to investigate all malpractices in the administration of the forests", and although he goes on to describe as monstrous the claim that the perambulations of Edward I should be declared invalid thus extending the forest laws to areas previously disafforested, he does not suggest that this represented a general reintroduction of the forest laws.[4] Unfortunately this is not made clear by Holdsworth, who, writing a quarter of a century later, states: "But though, at the end of the sixteenth century, the forest laws were rapidly becoming obsolete, the financial embarrassments of Charles I caused an attempt to revive them in the earlier part of the seventeenth century".[5] This is only true for areas which had been disafforested, and does not apply to areas such as the New Forest which had always been subject to the forest laws. Petit-Dutaillis, published in 1915, fell even further into the trap using the words: "When, under Elizabeth, John Manwood took up his pen to write the 'Treaties and Discourse of the Lawes of the Forrest', it was in the hope of reviving laws of which 'verie little or nothing' remained. James I and Charles I tried to recall them to life . . ."[6] A noteworthy dissenter from the accepted viewpoint has been Hammersley who wrote that in 1632 "the laws themselves may have been old-fashioned but were still widely known and respected".[7]

The text of the present volume comprises documents associated with forest courts held for the New Forest between 1487 and 1494, in 1634 and 1635, and between 1660 and 1670, together with various grants of forest rents made between 1608 and 1631. Additional material, either published elsewhere or considered unsuitable for the present volume, includes a few short inquests held towards the end of the reign of Edward III,[8] records of the election of verderers between 1366 and 1485,[9] and various regarders' certificates made during the reigns of Elizabeth and James I.[10] Of more interest and importance are the "Orders and Rules of the New Forest",[11] which can be dated to 1534, and an associated commentary upon the Charter of the Forest, which may be of the same date. It is also known that details of an attachment court held in 1607 and of a justice seat held in 1622 were contained in the Court Books of the New Forest,[12] but these have unfortunately been lost. For other forests the documentary records are similarly sparse. In Dean there is some evidence for justice seats having been held in 1407–8, 1432–3, and in 1436, and of swainmotes in 1435–6, 1566–70, 1601–6, and 1623–5.[13] During the reign of Henry VII forest eyres were held in Essex,[14] in Pickering,[15] and in Wiltshire.[16] In Northamptonshire an eyre was held in the reign of Henry VIII, and there in the late sixteenth century the swainmote still manifested a real vitality.[17]

Due to the fragmentary nature of the surviving court records it is difficult to demonstrate the continuity of forest law between the fourteenth and the seventeenth centuries, but for those forests where records have been published the overall picture is not of disuse and ignorance of the forest laws, but rather of the chance survival of records of insufficient importance to merit permanent retention. Certainly there is ample evidence to support Hammersley's contention that the forest law was widely known and respected prior to the forest eyres instigated by Charles I, but there is the possibility that this could have been the result of a reawakened interest in the forests following the publication of Manwood's "Treatise", and certainly some of the court procedures appear to have been modified in the light of Manwood's opinions. However the holding of swainmotes in Northamptonshire in the late sixteenth century, in Dean at the start of the seventeenth century, and in the New Forest in 1607, all suggest the continued holding of forest courts irrespective of Manwood's influence.

In addition to the light thrown upon forest law, the documents contain information upon more general matters. In the late fifteenth century there are the occasional references to the felling of oak and beech for ship or house building [**158,207**], but the majority of the proceedings deal with deer, and this confirms that the primary importance of the Forest was still as a game reserve at this time. There is a somewhat sad reference to the killing of deer in anticipation of the coronation of Edward V [**154**], arranged for the 4th May 1483 but never to take place because of the usurpation of the crown by Richard III, who to achieve this brought down large forces from the north.[18] This was noted in the Forest by the killing of 500 deer by the northern men and servants of king Richard [**157**]. There are undated references to visits by the king [**150,156**], and by the queen and prince [**149**], probably Anne the wife of Richard III and prince Edward, but conceivably Elizabeth wife of Henry VII and prince Arthur. More deer were killed for the coronation of Henry VII in 1485 [**155**].

Also of interest are the various terms used in the description of deer [see Glossary], and the method used in hunting. In essence this was for the deer to be driven by beaters to a "standing" convenient to the huntsman, this being the purpose for driving deer into the park [**150,156**] before the king's visit. An explanation of the word "stable" is contained in the Orders and Rules, it being the duty of the residents to help bring the deer "to such places as the kings majesty may take his pleasure, and the same people shall compass and stand in a stable until such time as the hunting be done". A more detailed description of this method of hunting is contained in Crawford's article on "Medieval Forests".[19] In contrast most of the poaching seems to have been with greyhounds, although some deer were shot with bows and arrows, and others were taken with snares, the various offenders including servants of the foresters **[58]**, and several churchmen. It was actually a priest who was accused of killing one of the yeomen of the king's hunt with his greyhounds **[253]**.

In the seventeenth century deer were still being taken with bows and arrows, with dogs, and with snares, and guns were also being used, but the work of the forest courts was no longer dominated by venison offences. Instead the emphasis had changed to timber production and in consequence a large proportion of court cases were now for vert offences, the majority of these having been committed by the foresters who continued to lop branches for the deer to browse upon the leaves and bark, by custom the wood being a perquisite of the forester. No doubt Gabriel Lapp, the woodward, also had custom on his side in the taking of dotard trees and stubbs for his own benefit **[460–475]**. In a different class were the timber merchants and shipwrights found guilty of stealing very large numbers of oak and beech trees **[457–459]**, and also the number of local residents who from time to time carried off a tree.

Many other forest offences were also brought before the courts, these including the making of purprestures or illegal enclosures, the construction of buildings, the taking of turf for fuel, and the depasturing of sheep and unringed pigs. At the swainmote held in 1635 a large number of presentments were concerned with the placing of bee-hives on the Forest, this involving the construction of small enclosures to protect the hives, and in at least one instance this appears to have been planted as an orchard for the benefit of the bees **[691]**.

However the greatest value of the later documents is perhaps in the information provided upon the inhabitants of the Forest, their status or occupation, and their landholdings. In that the various lists of officials, freeholders, and jurors, span the period of the Civil War and Commonwealth, and also the outbreaks of plague in 1665 and 1666 in Southampton,[20] there appears a remarkable degree of continuity. Additional information upon land tenancies is provided by the various seventeenth century rentals of purprestures and other crown lands **[1559–1717]**, but as it was the practice to grant or sell the rents only for a limited period, in consequence the lands listed may have been included in earlier rentals and are not necessarily recent encroachments as for example Rollstone, said to have been rented in 1317–8 [**1669**], or Priestcroft [**1592, 1674**] which was an old enclosure in 1276.[21]

A matter of considerable historical interest is the statement made by the grand jury in 1670 that "from time out of mind the commoners have had common pasture for their cattle throughout the fence month, this under consideration of a fixed annual rent called Month Money received and accepted by his majesty and his predecessors" [**1519**], this providing confirmation of an earlier claim contained in the Orders and Rules A.D. 1537 that the forest vills "be at a certain rent for cattle going in the Forest the Month time, which was purchased of old time". Payments of "month money" continued to be included in forest rents at least until the mid 19th century,[22] but its purpose had been forgotten, and indeed the 1698 Act[23] specifically excluded the Fence Month from the period allowed for common grazing.

Among the more miscellaneous matters contained in the documents is the stealing of lead from the roof of a hunting lodge [**152**], and the different charges to be made for the pasture of a working or a non-working horse [**210**]. It is also of interest to find a number of occupational surnames, presumably hereditary by the late 15th century, where the holder still followed the same trade, for example Richard Fletcher, a fletcher [**33**], Ellis and Giles Bouchier, both butchers [**24,85**], Richard Chapman, a mercer [**28**], and Roland Sadeler, a saddler [**10**].

Acknowledgements

This book represents a continuation of the work commenced in "New Forest Documents AD 1244–1334", the majority of the present work having been done at that time, and for this reason the acknowledgements contained therein apply equally to the present volume. In particular my gratitude is due to Miss Margaret Cash who since her retirement has continued as general editor of the Hampshire Record Series, to the present archivist and staff of the Hampshire Record Office, and to the New Forest District Council for their generous contribution towards the purchase of photo-copies of the included documents.

Crown-copyright records in the Public Record Office appear by permission of the Controller of Her Majesty's Stationery Office; and Duchy of Lancaster copyright records by permission of the Chancellor and Council of the Duchy of Lancaster.

Introduction

1 THE DOCUMENTS

All the documents here published are preserved in the Public Record Office and have not been previously published with the exception of the swainmote roll for 1662 [**929–983**] which was included by Lewis,[24] and the perambulation of 1670 which has been variously published in 1776,[25] in 1789,[26] and in 1811 by Lewis.

The earliest of the documents, those relating to the forest proceedings of 1487–94 are included among twelve bundles of forest proceedings (D.L.39) contained in the records of the Duchy of Lancaster. It is not clear why this should be as there is no obvious connection between the New Forest and the Duchy, and we can only be thankful that they have survived. However apart from four swainmote rolls, the other thirty five documents are of a very fragmentary nature, many of them consisting of no more than a slip containing a single presentment, and their relationship is far from certain. In the calendar these have been arranged in what appeared to be a fairly logical order, but anomalies did occur as for instance the names of the justices [**168**], in association with an incomplete presentment and two sureties, and perhaps this should be regarded as an endorsement rather than a heading.

By contrast the documents of 1634–5 present no problems. They are contained in a distinct class of Chancery records (C.99) consisting mainly of claims made in the reign of Charles I before the justices in eyre, and associated documents such as swainmote rolls and grants of land. The claims for common rights (C.99/41), and their subsequent enrolments (C.99/42–47), have little bearing upon the later history of forest law and have been excluded from the present volume, but it is hoped to make a detailed study of these documents at some future date, and to make a proper comparison with the claims for 1670 which have previously been published.[27]

The records of 1660–70 are to be found among the Forest

Proceedings of the Treasury of the Receipt of the Exchequer (E.32). The most interesting of these must be the paper notebook of the clerk to the 1670 forest eyre (E.32/176) in that it so clearly demonstrates the day to day workings of the eyre. Contained in the same class are the originals (E.32/179–81) of the published claims of common rights made in 1670. There appears no obvious reason why these documents were retained by the Exchequer rather than by the Chancery as in 1635.

To complete the present collection of New Forest documents various seventeenth century grants of forest rents have been included. Four of these are contained in the class of Chancery records described above, the other two being taken from the enrolments contained in the Patent Rolls (C.66).

The majority of the court records were written in Latin, but many of the subsidiary documents were in English, also it was not uncommon for the scribe, perhaps at a loss to find the precise Latin equivalent, to give the more descriptive words in both languages as for example *cablicie anglice browsewood* [**908**].

2 FOREST LAW IN 1670

The accession of Edward III in 1327 has been accepted as marking the end of the long struggle for disafforestation and a turning point in forest history.[28] Since the time of Magna Carta, and probably before, the extent of the forests had provided continual grounds for complaint in that estates situated within forests were subject to the liabilities, constraints, and interferences of forest law. The Articles of the Barons, Magna Carta, the Charter of the Forest, and the Petititon of the Barons at Oxford, were all concerned with the extent of the forests, with disafforestation, and with the introduction of more restricted boundaries. On various occasions, either as the result of political pressure or in return for financial and military aid, new perambulations had been made of the forests, but there is little evidence that any resulting revisions of forest boundaries were introduced before 1299–30, and even these were to be revoked in 1306. Further grounds for complaint were the non-observance of the judicial procedures established by the Charter of the Forest and the Ordinance of 1306. Among the first deeds of the new reign were confirmations of the Charter of the Forest and of the forest boundaries as established in the time of Edward I, also the reenactment and extension of the judicial procedures of the Ordinance of 1306, and these measures appear to have largely settled the long standing grievances. Subsequently "such complaints as were heard in parliament related to abuses of the system itself".[29]

In 1327 the general framework of forest law was in accordance with the measures enacted by the Charter of the Forest, the Ordinance of 1306, and the Statute of 1327, these consisting largely of provisions against the excesses and abuses of the foresters and other officials of the forest. The principal precepts were that persons living outside the forest were not required to attend the forest courts unless indicted for an offence,[30] and were not to be oppressed by the foresters;[31] that offenders of vert or venison could only be summarily detained if taken during the commitment of the offence, otherwise detention could only be imposed after indictment in the proper form;[32] that attachments of vert and venison were to be viewed every forty days by the foresters and verderers, and the findings to be enrolled by the verderers for subsequent presentment before a justice of the forest;[30] that the proper form of indictment was for offences of vert and venison to be presented by the foresters at the following swainmote before all the forest officers, for the truth of the presentment to be determined by jurors living in the locality of the alleged offence, and for the findings to be confirmed and sealed by all the officers;[31] that forest offences could only be sentenced by a justice of the forest, that offenders were to be fined and only if unable to pay the fine could be held in prison for a year and a day, and subsequently to be required either to find sureties for their future good behaviour or to abjure the realm;[30] that a forest justice or his deputy had the right of taking fines and amercements for forest offences except when a forest eyre was anticipated;[31] that wardens or keepers of forests were not to act as forest justices;[32] and that judgements were to be reserved for the forest eyre.[32] It is the last of these that is the most difficult to reconcile with known forest procedures, and the most probable explanation is that at the time of the Statute it had already been decided to hold forest eyres in all forests. Certainly between 1327 and 1337 forest eyres were held in a very large number of forests.[33]

The forest eyres held at the commencement of the reign of Edward III followed a period of civil unrest, as also did those held early in the reign of Henry VII. For the New Forest, and for most other forests, no forest eyres have been recorded between these two occasions, and the impression given is that the forests continued to function quietly and smoothly with little outside interference. Such legislation as was enacted appears to have been designed to protect the forest dwellers rather than the forest. The Statute of Purveyors AD 1350[34] instructed that foresters and keepers of forests should not gather sustenance, victuals, nor other things by right of office, unless freely given or of ancient right, but it is doubtful to what extent this could have been enforceable. In 1369 an amnesty was announced for forest offences, except for those which had been committed by forest officers or by sellers of wood,[35] it being stated that this had been demanded by the commons and granted in return for help given. From the date of the amnesty, the 11th June, this help could have been in connection either with Edward's resumption on the 3rd June of the title of king of France, or alternatively in anticipation of the recommencement of the war with France.

Grounds for speculation are also provided by the Statute of 1383,[36] this providing that no jury should be compelled by any officer of the forest to travel from place to place against their will, nor should they be constrained to reach verdicts against their consciences, and that they should deliver their verdict where they received their charge. As this was at a time when it was held that after having been sworn a jury should not eat or drink until a verdict was reached,[37] one is presented with the possibility of hungry and travel-stained juries before this date. The Statute continues with a reiteration that forest officers should observe correct procedures in the detention and indictments of offenders [c.4].

The next legislation of importance is the Statute of 1540[38] which authorised the making of deputies by justices of forests. "Forasmuch as it is much doubted whether the king's justices of his forests . . . may lawfully make or depute any deputy or deputies . . . for the avoiding of which ambiguity and doubt . . . from henceforth all and every the justice or justices of the king's forests . . . shall make, assign, depute, and appoint as many deputy or deputies . . . as . . . shall be thought convenient; which deputy and deputies so appointed shall have like power and authority to do and execute all things concerning the king's forests . . ."

In 1640, no doubt in consequence of the recently held forest eyres, was passed an Act to determine the Meets and Bounds of the Forests.[39] An attempt had been made to re-establish the forest boundaries as at the time of Edward I and as confirmed by Edward III, these bounds being more extensive than those "commonly known and formerly observed, to the great grievance and vexation of many persons having lands adjoining . . ." This Act limited the bounds of the forests to those commonly known in the 20th year of James I [1622–3], and made void any presentments to the contrary made since that date. Furthermore no place was to be adjudged a forest except where a justice seat, swainmote, or attachment court had been held, or verderers elected, or a regard held, within the sixty years prior to the reign of Charles I, i.e. since 1565.

3 THE FOREST COURTS

The fundamentals of forest law, as detailed in the previous chapter, were comparatively straightforward. In practice the majority of offences were concerned either with the poaching of deer or the stealing of timber, and the treatment of offenders varied with the circumstances. When an offender was taken while committing an offence, depending upon the seriousness and nature of the offence, he could either be released upon the provision of sureties or bail, or he could be detained until trial. Such offenders would appear at the attachment or swainmote court, where the foresters would make presentments of alleged offences, and these would be examined by a jury. The preliminary hearings were conducted by the verderers, as also were inquisitions into offences where the culprit was unknown. By tradition the verderers had authority to pass sentence for minor offences worth less than 4d., but the findings in more serious cases would be enrolled for subsequent sentencing by a forest justice. It is probable that the verderers also supervised the arrangements for sureties or bail. Presentments could also be made by other forest officers and by the jurors, this procedure also applying before the forest justices where a larger jury would be empanelled [**125–130**]. The most specialised form of jury was the regard, the regarders having a detailed list of headings to be enquired into, these being known as the chapters of the regard [**1543**].

These procedures were derived from the Forest Charter of 1217 and the Statute of 1327, and although they may appear to involve a certain degree of duplication of responsibilities, under the circumstances it would be difficult to devise a more practical and effective system. The detection and reporting of offences required the local knowledge of the foresters and underforesters, but they were the very people who had the greatest opportunity to carry out such crimes and also sufficient local authority and power to make detection difficult. It is obviously of significance that so much of the early legislation deals with abuses by the foresters. Similarly the wardens or keepers of the forests were not above suspicion as is shown by the edict of 1327 that in future the chief wardens were not to be forest justices. The overlap between the duties of forest officers, the involvement of jurors, and the responsibility of outside officials for the sentencing of offenders and general supervision of judicial and administrative matters, were all necessary components if the forests were to be managed in a proper manner.

There has been considerable confusion over the number and purpose of forest courts and their responsibilities. The Forest Charter of 1217 [para. 8] provided for the holding of three swainmotes in the year, namely fourteen days before Michaelmas [the 14th September] to deal with agistment matters, about Martinmas [11th November] to deal with the pannage of pigs, and fourteen days before the feast of St. John the Baptist [the 9th June] in connection with the fawning time of the deer. On the latter occasion only the foresters and verderers were required to attend, but at the other two swainmotes the agisters were also present. Elsewhere [para. 16] the Charter makes provision that the foresters and verderers should meet every forty days to view any attachments of vert and venison. Those attached would attend, the foresters would make their presentments, and these would be enrolled and sealed for subsequent determination by a justice of the forest. Nearly one hundred years later the Ordinance of 1306 instructed that offences of vert and venison should be presented at the next swainmote. Manwood took this to mean two distinct courts, an Attachment Court held for the enrolment of attachments and a Swainmote Court at which the attachments would be "proved" by jurors. It is now generally accepted that these were one and the same court, the name of swainmote at some early time having been transferred to the attachment court of the Forest Charter. It may well be that as foresters and verderers were required to attend both the earlier swainmotes and the attachments, the practice may have grown up of holding them at the same time whenever possible, and their separate identities lost.

Further confusion has arisen from Manwood's mistaken belief that before the Statute of 1540 ". . . it seemeth that the justices of the forest could not make a deputy or lieutenant to execute their place or office . . ." As an example of the appointment of a deputy justice after this date he quotes a writ from Thomas Lovell, justice itinerant of all forests, to John de Vere, earl of Oxford and keeper of Essex forest, in which Lovell orders an appearance before himself or his deputy *(coram me aut locum meum tenente)*.[40] Unfortunately for Manwood's claim, as Lovell was appointed in 1510 and John de Vere died in 1513, the writ actually demonstrates the existence of a deputy justice prior to the statute of 1540. It is perhaps a comment upon Manwood's editorial methods that the same writ is contained in the unpublished "Explanatory Notes upon the Charter of the Forest",[41] but here the opposite conclusion is reached that "It appeareth by the writ that the authority of the justice of the forest doth differ from the authority of the justices of the eyre, for the justices of the forest may take their deputies and lieutenants for to exercise their offices, and so cannot other justices." In the present documents the wording "before us or our deputies" is contained in the writ of 1488 from John Radcliffe to the earl of Arundel [**115**]. In the opinion of Holdsworth the justices of the forest "were allowed, and in fact obliged to do their work by deputies, appointed sometimes by the crown and sometimes by the justices. By the end of the fourteenth century all the duties of the justices were performed by these deputies . . ." This practice was given statutory validity by 32 Hen. 8 c.35.[42]

It was probably Manwood's failure to recognize the work of the deputy justices that lead him to write ". . . all the proceedings of the two other courts are as nothing before they do come to the justice seat of the forest to receive their judgement"[43] and elsewhere "But now of late within these hundred years, there have been very seldom any justice seat at all kept for forests".[44] By subsequent writers this has been taken to mean the failure of the forest system during the 16th century. In the words of Holdsworth "We have seen that the ordinary forest courts could do very little except present criminals at the eyre. It was at the eyre that they were punished; so that it might be said that the whole execution of the forest law depended upon the regular holding of the eyre. But by the end of the sixteenth century eyres were seldom held . . . The desuetude of the eyre meant, in fact, the collapse of the whole system".[45]

"The forest eyre was a court called into being by the king's letters patent appointing justices to hear and determine pleas of the forest in a particular county or group of counties".[46] Such visitations by justices in eyre were so infrequent as to make negligible any impact upon the day to day course of forest justice, and elsewhere the author has suggested that the work of the forest eyre must be compared with that of the general eyre.[47] The records of the forest eyres contained not only a review of judicial cases and the completion of any outstanding business, but also exhaustive enquiries into all matters of forest management and administration. Largely this comprised matters of an administrative or financial nature, and for this reason the eyre rolls were returned to the Exchequer where their preservation has served to distract attention from the importance of the work done by deputy justices, and of whom few records have survived.

The Ordinance of 1306 stated that the justice or his deputy should have the right of taking fines and amercements for forest offences except when a forest eyre was anticipated, this being an identical procedure to the suspension of the work of minor courts upon the proclamation of the holding of a general eyre.[48] As a function of the eyre was to check upon the work of the local courts, then this embargo would have been necessary to prevent the carrying out of corrective measures before the arrival of the chief justice. This is no doubt the explanation of the requirement of the Statute of 1327 that judgements were to be reserved for the forest eyre, it then being the intention to instigate forest eyres to deal with the dishonesty and corruption of the forest officials, this being referred to in the preamble to the statute.

A special type of forest inquisition was recognised by Turner and termed by him a 'general inquisition'. These were held in the presence of a justice of the forest or his deputy, and heard all types of offences against forest law, but, in the opinion of Turner, sentencing was reserved for a forest eyre. In the documents these were sometimes called swainmotes, but were not held on the dates designated in the Charter of the Forest, but were "probably held at such times as were convenient to the justice of the forest or his deputy".[49] Forest pleas of a similar description have been recognised for the New Forest, and from these it is quite evident that the justices were appointed to both hear and determine cases, i.e. in legal terms to bring to a conclusion, and to do full and swift justice. That this was done is shown by the penalties imposed upon offenders.[50]

It may be that the work of the deputy forest justices has largely passed unnoticed because of the paucity of documentary record. This was because the work of the forest justices differed from that of other justices in that their main task was the sentencing of offenders, these having already been found guilty in the swainmote court, and for this reason the only record of the forest justice is frequently no more than a marginal annotation of the swainmote roll giving the amount of the fine or detail of any other sentence imposed. However with intervals of over one hundred and fifty years between the recorded visitations of the chief justices of the forest in eyre, there is no other way in which the forest system could have continued to function.

It is only by chance that we know of the justice seat held at Lyndhurst on the 19th September 1622, in that a genealogist made notes of names contained in the now lost New Forest Court Books.[51] It is also by chance, in that the swainmote rolls have been preserved because of their association with the 1635 forest eyre, that we have a record of the justice seat held in 1634 [**343**]. The main work of this justice seat would have been the sentencing of offenders found guilty at the preceding swainmote [**304–341**], but there were also a small number of cases from swainmotes held between 1626 and 1631 [**373–378**], and the implication must be that the bulk of the cases from these swainmotes had already been dealt with at justice seats held prior to that of 1634.

For that matter the forest eyres have also left comparatively little in the form of documentation. That for 1488 has not previously been noted in New Forest literature, its records are fragmentary and their collation uncertain, the only definite references to the forest eyre being the writs of summons [**115,125**] and an isolated heading [**168**]. However the presence of the three jointly appointed chief justices of the forest in circuit assize can scarcely be termed anything other than a forest eyre. For the eyre of 1635 there is little record other than the writ of summons to the deputies of the earl of Holland [**259**], and the claims of common rights made on this occasion.[52] In themselves the sentences annotated on the swainmote roll of 1635 [**457–726**] are completely anonymous although undoubtedly imposed by the eyre court. For the 1670 eyre we are more fortunate in having what appears to be the record of sir John Shaw, the clerk to the eyre [**1450–1518**], also the returns by the grand jury [**1519–1538**], and by the regarders [**1542–1558**]. Elsewhere the claims of common rights have been published.[53]

4 MANWOOD'S TREATISE

John Manwood, a barrister of Lincoln's Inn, is best known for his book entitled "A Treatise and Discourse on the Laws of the Forest

. . ." published in 1598 and reprinted with additions in 1615 after his death. This enlarged edition was reprinted in 1665 and a complete rearrangement appeared in 1717. An earlier work entitled "A Brief Collection of the Laws of the Forest . . ." had been printed in 1592 for private circulation, this unfortunately being little known because of its rarity. However the two works comprise a complementary study, although some amount of duplication was unavoidable, the first book dealing with the fundamentals of forest law, the statutes, courts, and officers of the forest, while the second book dealt with matters of a peripheral nature such as the beasts of the forest, of venison and vert, hawking and hunting, agistment, purlieus, etc.

In the 1615 edition of the "Treatise" the editor attempted to combine the two works by the addition of material taken from the "Brief Collection", this amounting to the inclusion of the texts of the various statutes and ordinances, and by the addition of five extra chapters, the added material being described on the title page as ". . . the Statutes of the Forest, a Treatise of the several offices of Verderers, Regarders, and Foresters, and the Courts of Attachments, Swainmote, and Justice Seat of the Forest . . ." An accompanying editorial note reads "The materials of whatsoever is now added, are all the first authors without alteration, gathered from the remains of his first work and reduced to the order you see, with this care that there is nothing there of substance omitted but what was largely before uttered by the author in his second Treatise." No doubt this editing was carried out with some care, but by retaining the "Treatise" as it was written, while at the same time greatly reducing and rearranging the "Brief Collection", the unfortunate result has been to obscure the importance of Manwood's earlier work, to completely destroy its coherence, and more damagingly has placed undue emphasis upon matters of lesser importance and of a peripheral nature.

The most serious misunderstanding that has arisen is the belief that "very little or nothing" remained of the forest laws at the time of Manwood. This is not the suggestion contained in Manwood's earlier book, but rather that the laws were being too lightly enforced. In the words of his preface: "So that now at this day, although the laws of the forest are of themselves very mild, gentle, and merciful laws towards the subjects of this realm, over that they have been in times past, yet notwithstanding, we do at this present live under the government of so gracious and merciful a queen that her clemency in the execution of those laws is much more greater than the favour and clemency of the laws themselves." It is not until his second book that we read in the dedication to Charles, lord Howard, that "And seeing that so many do daily commit such heinous spoils and trespasses therein, that the greatest part of them are spoiled and decayed: And also that very little, or nothing, as yet is extant concerning the Laws of the Forest, I thought it very necessary to collect this small Treatise, declaring therein the ways and means how to preserve and maintain the forests, together with the due punishment of such as shall be found offenders therein, to the intent that thereby men may the better know those laws wherein they so often offend . . ." In the following notes "To the Reader" Manwood's purpose is further expounded "First, the necessary use and common good that may arise . . . by the publishing of this treatise, in making the forest laws more certainly known than they were before, seeing that so few do know these laws and yet so many do fall into the danger thereof: Secondly . . . that the forest laws are grown clean out of knowledge in most places in this land, partly for want of use and partly by reason that there is very little or nothing extant of it *in any treatise by itself* . . . great injuries and wrongs have insued to many, and for want of the knowledge of these laws, many fond opinions of unlearned men, mere vanities and conceits, are taken and held for law, which are neither law nor reason." In essence Manwood is simply saying that as there had previously been no single book dealing with forest law, these laws were little understood, treated with contempt, and insufficiently enforced, this leading to the spoilation of the forests.

Manwood was not an original writer. In his own words "I have set down nothing for the which I have not called to warranty some one author or other . . . approving every argument by some lawful authority . . ." However this was insufficient to avoid contemporary criticism as it appears to have been with reference to Manwood that sir Edward Coke wrote ". . . beware to give credit to our new authors either vouching acts of parliament, book cases, or judgements in eyre, etc., for we have found many of them mistaken, vouched without warrant, or not understood . . ."[54]

5 COURT PROCEDURES IN THE NEW FOREST

Court procedures in the 15th century appear to have been in compliance with the requirements of the Ordinance of 1306 that offences of vert and venison were to be presented at the swainmote before all the forest officers, that the truth of the presentments was to be determined by jurors, and that the findings be confirmed and sealed by all the officers. An earlier requirement under the Charter of the Forest was that the findings should be enrolled by the verderers.

In the New Forest proceedings of 1487–94 the offences were presented by the foresters and other officers [**57–64,66–86**], these were proved by twelve jurors [**38**], and by the regarders [**88**], the proceedings being held before the verderers [**56**]. Numerous deletions occur in the presentments [**7,8,13,17, etc.**], and in that these relate to matters of evidence, it is probable that they are instances where a presentment was not accepted or "proved" by the jurors.

There has survived a copy of an interesting document entitled "The Orders and Rules of the New Forest" and dated to 1537.[55] This makes provision for the holding of attachment courts at intervals of three weeks at which the forest officers or their deputies should attend "and must make every man by himself what attachment of carts and other trespasses and offences done within the Forest from three weeks to three weeks". Fifteen days notice was to be given by the two verderers prior to the holding of a swainmote so that the "four men and the reeve of every township and all gentleman freeholders within the Forest shall appear there and be sworn before the verderers to enquire as they have in charge." Offenders taken either in the killing of deer, or accused before the verderers of offences of vert or venison, were to be detained in the "blindhouse", the king's prison in Lyndhurst which was used only for forest offences, until sureties were found for their subsequent appearance before the justices of the forest.

Modifications to these procedures occurred in the 17th century, presumably as a consequence of Manwood's "Treatise" upon forest law, and it is possible that he was directly involved in the New Forest as it is recorded that in 1608 Manwood was acting as a forest justice and was paid £30 10s for holding two justice sessions within the forests of Hampshire.[56] In the opinion of Manwood[57] it was requisite that presentments should follow the formula *"Presentatum est per forestarios et duodecim juratores, et convictum per viridarios"*, and closely similar the form adopted in the New Forest was: "It is presented by the foresters and other ministers of the forest and twelve jurors, and proved by the verderers". Both forms would appear to suggest that the establishment of guilt was the responsibility of the verderers rather than of the jurors, although it was accepted by Manwood that "if the jury do find that those presentments that the foresters have presented be true, then the offender against whom they are presented doth stand convicted thereof", and conviction by jurors was a requirement of the Ordinance of 1306.

A further example of Manwood's influence is in the date upon which the swainmote court was held. It has been noted above that in the 14th century they were not being held upon the days specified in the Charter of the Forest, these being the 9th June, the 14th September, and about the 11th November. Of the four New Forest swainmotes known from the late 15th century only one, that held on the 14th September 1489, conformed with these dates, the other three being held on the 9th February 1487, the 29th July 1488, and the 10th December 1494. In the 17th century, in marked contrast, swainmotes known for 1626, 1629, and 1631 were all held on the 14th September, in 1634 on the 15th September (the 14th having fallen on a Sunday), and in 1635 on the 9th June. From 1660–7 and in 1669 swainmotes were also held on the 14th September, a second swainmote in 1666 on the 9th November, and that of 1668 on the 9th June. The swainmote of 1670 was also held on the 9th June with adjournment to the 27th June [**1542**], and presumably to the 19th August [**1539–1541**]. Additional swainmotes were recorded in the New Forest Court Books, the great majority of these having been held on the 14th September for various years between 1670 and the termination of the extracts in 1722. Elsewhere it is recorded that swainmotes continued to be held annually on the 14th September at least until 1828.[58]

The only information to have survived from the justice seat held at Lyndhurst on the 19th September 1622 is the names of the forest officers and regarders, and certain of the tithing men, freeholders, and jurors.[59] For the justice seat of 1634 we are more fortunate in that the names of the justices are also recorded, these being sir Richard Tychborne a deputy lieutenant of Hampshire; Robert Mason, presumably also the Steward of the Forest, who was a commissioner for oyer and terminer in Hampshire, the recorder of London, and who in 1597 had been a student at Lincoln's Inn and possibly a contemporary of Manwood; and Thomas Leigh, the lord of Testwood manor. No records of forest pleas being held before deputy justices in the New Forest are known after this date.

6 THE FOREST EYRE OF 1670

It has been said that the forest eyres held at the end of the seventeenth century were "*pro forma* only",[60] but in view of the number and severity of the sentences imposed this does not appear to have been the case with the New Forest eyre of 1670.

The preliminaries had begun in May when the earl of Oxford, chief justice in eyre, issued instructions that a regard of the forest should be made [**1542**]. The regard was a detailed enquiry into the overall state of forest management made periodically by twelve regarders, in effect a special form of jury, with the responsibility of furnishing the forest courts with answers to a number of specific questions, these being known as the chapters of the regard [**1543**]. In theory a regard of the forest was made every third year,[61] but in the seventeenth century the number of offences reported on the same dates appears to indicate that the custom was to carry out an inspection shortly before the holding of the annual swainmote court. As many of the presentments dealt with the cutting of browsewood, this being a standard practice of the foresters, it appears unlikely that these were self-accusations on the part of the foresters, but more probably were made by the regarders who were in attendance at each court.

In 1670 the regarders were sworn at the swainmote held on the 9th June, the court then being adjourned until the 27th June to allow time for the regard to be made. The court roll of this swainmote, although referred to in the present documents [**1492**], has not been preserved, but one would expect it to have continued the pattern of previous years and to have contained a number of presentments against foresters for the cutting of browsewood. In the regarders' roll it is stated that there had been great destruction and spoil in the king's woods, "but who made the same we do not know, saving only that the greatest spoils have been made by the foresters or keepers . . ." [**1553**]. However in reply to the question concerning "the defaults, negligences, and insufficiences of the foresters and woodwards and their underkeepers [**1543**], the regarders stated that "we have come so recently into office, we have nothing further to present" [**1556**]. This can not be a reference to a lack of knowledge on the part of the regarders as two of them had been in office for at least ten years, and two others had several years experience, so presumably the meaning must be that they had nothing further to present for the period since the holding of the swainmote.

On the 15th September 1670 the forest eyre opened at Lyndhurst and was immediately adjourned until Monday the 19th September at Winchester Castle. The first task was to check upon the necessary attendances and to impose fines upon various vills which were not fully represented and upon freeholders who had failed to attend [**1451**], also it is probable that the grand jury [**1519**] was sworn and commenced its' deliberations on this day. The verderers were instructed to attend on the following morning, Tuesday the 20th, with their swainmote rolls and sentences were imposed upon offenders found guilty in the rolls between 1660 and 1663 [**1452–1467**], although no penalties were imposed for offences committed prior to the Act of Indemnity of the 25th April 1660. The first case determined, that of Henry Browne [**1452**], is contained in the roll for 1660 [**839**] and clearly demonstrates the procedure of annotating the swainmote roll with the sentence imposed by the forest eyre, although in this particular case there appears some disagreement as to whether the fine was £4 or £6, with the actual amount paid of £10 10s appearing to comprise a fine of £5, the value of the cart and draught animals £5, and the value of the stolen tree 10s. However it is not unusual for some arithmetical disagreement to occur.

The following day, Wednesday the 21st, the court dealt first with the swainmote roll for 1664. No evidence of conviction had been entered [**1098**], and it subsequently appeared that due to the negligence of the understeward, Ferdinand Knapton, the roll had been transcribed with blanks, and for this he was fined £100 and dismissed from office [**1486**]. It was ordered that process should be made out against the persons presented in the swainmote roll, but no further action was to be taken [**1468**], and no fines were entered on the swainmote roll. The eyre then went on to sentence offenders from the swainmote rolls of 1665 to 1668 [**1469–1479**], following this with the appointment of regarders, and with claims of common rights [**1484**]. The following day, the 22nd, deficiencies were found in the swainmote roll for 1669, presumably further negligence on the part of Ferdinand Knapton, and this roll was returned to the lord warden [**1491**]. The same day the 1670 swainmote roll was also found to be insufficient, and the following day, Friday the 23rd, affidavits were sworn by the verderers and regarders as to irregularities in the conduct of this swainmote [**1539–1541**], and it was ordered that any evidence against persons presented in the 1670 swainmote roll should be passed to the grand jury [**1495**].

There is no record of any action being taken by the grand jury in respect of the 1670 swainmote roll, and by this time its original task had been completed as on the Friday the eyre court had begun to issue processes against offenders convicted by the grand jury [**1499**]. Most of the offences dealt with by the jury related either to offenders living outside the forest or to offences committed on private land within the forest, the attendance of such offender being enforced by means of a *venire facias* issued by the forest eyre [**1502,1505**]. On the Saturday was read the regarders' roll which had been delivered to the swainmote on the 27th June [**1501**], but no action appears to have been taken regarding the offences reported therein, and the presumption must be that these presentments were already contained in the 1670 swainmote roll. The forest eyre was to continue on the Monday and Tuesday of the following week dealing with miscellaneous matters such as the issue of further writs of *venire facias*, claims of common rights, the appointment of regarders, and various petitions for the reduction of fines. All these matters were concluded on the 27th September, the court then being adjourned until the 23rd March 1671, but never continued.[62]

7 FOREST LAW AFTER 1670

It has been stated that by the end of the 17th century the forest law and the old machinery of forest courts had become anachronisms because by then the forests were more valued for their timber than for sport.[63] In itself this is insufficient reason to account for the disuse of the forest laws as the same authority also notes that the forest law was valued in that it enabled measures to be taken for the preservation of timber. The Dean Forest Act of 1667[64] provided for the reafforestation of the whole Forest "forasmuch as by former experience it hath been found that nothing did more conduce to the raising, increase and preservation of timber and wood within the said wastes than the execution of the forest laws . . . the said 11,000 acres so to be inclosed as all other the waste lands aforesaid shall be and are hereby reafforested, and shall from henceforth be governed by forest law and put under the regard of the forest . . . and that all articles and agreements . . . concerning the . . . disafforestation shall be henceforth void . . . and to that end new elections shall be made forthwith . . . of all verderers, regarders, and other officers of and for the governing of the said Forest . . ." No such measure was necessary in the New Forest where disafforestation had not occurred, but an Act of 1698[65] for the provision of timber inclosures specifically preserved the forest laws, and at the same time increased the responsibility of the verderers and of the swainmote court.

The immediate reason for the collapse of forest law was because justice seats ceased to be held. In the words of an understeward of the New Forest "a material alteration has necessarily taken place with regards to the jurisdiction of the verderers, for when the proceedings of the courts in which they presided ceased to be rendered efficient by the judgement of the chief justice in eyre, trials in the swainmote became useless and were discontinued".[66]

There appears no obvious reason why the employment of deputy forest justices was discontinued, but conceivably it could have been connected with the progressive transfer of influence and responsibility from the Crown to the Exchequer. In 1542 the post of Surveyor General of Crown Woods had been created, this appointment being made by the Exchequer, with responsibilities for the production, preservation, and sale of timber. By a judicial decision of c.1603 the king's appointed officers, these comprising the forest justices, the wardens or keepers, and the foresters, were responsible for the venison and the vert, this to include all manner of trees, but the lord treasurer and the court of Exchequer had the power to sell wood, trees, and coppice for the profit of the Crown, this arrangement subsequently becoming known as the *divisum imperium*.[67] Continuous controversy and friction was to ensue, the foresters no doubt opposing the loss of their time honoured perquisites and profits arising from the disposal of waste timber, and from this was largely derived the money for the underforesters' wages. At the same time the sale of timber and renting of coppices by the Exchequer was equally damaging to the forests. A Commission of Enquiry of 1609 had reported that "nothing has ensued but expense of money and spoil of timber trees . . . the coppices never well finished nor at all preserved . . ."[68]

Presumably it was as a result of complaints made by the Surveyor of Crown Woods that presentments were made against the foresters in 1634–5 for the cutting of browsewood, this being to provide winter feed for the deer [**315–331, 487–489, etc.**], small fines being imposed. It was a different matter in 1660–1670 when the majority of presentments concerned the foresters and very heavy fines were imposed [**908–917, etc.**]. This may well have lessened any incentive on the part of the forest officers for the holding of forest pleas. At the same time the reprinting in 1665 of Manwood's "Treatise" probably reinforced the opinion that the forest laws were already obsolete, and the appointment in 1673 of James, duke of Monmouth, as chief justice of the forests had reduced this key post to a sinecure.

Under the forest laws the verderers had lacked the necessary authority to impose sentence, with the exception that under the 1287 Assize of William de Vescy[69] it was claimed that they could deal with vert offences of less than 4d value. In the New Forest this was changed by the 1698 Act for the Increase and Preservation of Timber[65] under which the verderers were given powers to impose fines of up to £5, and to commit an offender to prison for up to three months or until payment of the fine, for offences concerning the breaking of timbr inclosures, the burning of heather or fern, the destruction of covert, and the stealing of wood. It is probable that the "destruction of covert" was used to cover grazing offences, and the digging of gravel and marl, etc.

There was no provision for the sentencing of venison offences, but these could be dealt with under statute law, the penalties in this way generally being more severe than those under forest law, and eventually increasing to fines of up to £50 for hunting deer in an uninclosed area, and transportation for seven years for hunting within an inclosure.[70] Similarly the hearing of timber offences under forest law appears to have ceased with the passing of the Preservation of Timber Acts of 1765–6,[71] these providing penalties up to transportation for a third offence. In that these provided "a speedier and more effectual punishment" the forest courts "have been still less frequently held, and their powers less exerted",[72] and the New Forest Act of 1808[73] actually instructed that breakers of timber inclosures should be dealt with under 6 Geo.3, c.48.

Further powers whereby all unlawful inclosures, purprestures, encroachments, and tresspasses whatsoever were to be inquired into in the court of attachments, were given to the New Forest verderers under the Act of 1800 for the better preservation of Timber in the New Forest,[74] with powers to impose fines of up to £10, but these provisions were not to come into force until after the completion of a plan of the Forest, and as the plan was never completed, further legislation was needed before these powers were eventually introduced in 1810.[75] Also in 1800 the verderers had been given powers to enquire into the conduct of the underforesters. These powers were extended in 1812 so that the verderers were to enquire into the conduct and behaviour of the regarders, underforesters, underkeepers, or other officers, also the maximum penalty for unlawful enclosures, purprestures, encroachments, and trespasses was increased to £20.[76] In 1819 an Act for regulating Common of Pasture in the New Forest [77] provided a series of fixed penalties for the illegal depasturing of stock, and in 1829 a consolidating Act[78] while repealing the Act of 1812 reincluded the powers given to the verderers under the earlier Act with respect to unlawful enclosures, etc., and to enquire into the conduct of forest officers.

In certain areas the verderers were very uncertain of their authority, in particular in matters regarding the depasturing of sheep, these not being specifically mentioned in the 1819 Act; also in the cutting of turf, peat, heath, and furze; and in the taking of mould, gravel, and soil. Apparently some years before 1828 a man had refused to pay a fine imposed for such an offence, "in consequence of which the Court ordered him to be imprisoned until the fine was paid and he was accordingly detained for some time at Lyndhurst, but on his threatening to bring an action for false imprisonment, the verderers (doubting their authority to enforce payment of the fine) consented to discharge the offender and the matter was compromised with by the understeward."[79]

In attempts to resolve these and other problems the verderers sought legal opinion in 1828 and again in 1849. That of the Attorney and Solicitor General in 1828 was that there could be a good prescription for depasturing sheep, and that sheep illegally depastured could be dealt with under the 1819 Act; but that the cutting of peat, etc., and the carrying away of leaf mould, gravel, etc., were not "trespasses" as intended by the Acts of 1800 and 1812, and in such matters the verderers were unable to impose fines of their own authority. In the subsequent opinion of 1849 it was considered that "covert" included furze, heath, and fern, in that these plants afforded cover for beasts of the forest, and therefore could be dealt with under the Act of 1698; but that the taking away of mould or soil were not "trespasses" within the meaning of the consolidating Act of 1829.

The New Forest Act of 1877[80] materially changed both the constitution and the responsibilities of the verderers, but continued their authority to enquire into all unlawful inclosures, purprestures, encroachments, and trespasses, but with the penalty for such offences limited to a fine of £10. At the same time the verderers were to retain such powers and jurisdiction as were "by any law, statute, or custom directed, authorised, or empowered to punish, do, exercise, or perform." Additional powers were granted for the making of byelaws to regulate the exercise of common rights.

This remained the situation until 1971 when much early legislation was repealed under the Wild Creatures and Forests Law Act.[81] This included the Charter of the Forest, the Customs and Assize of the Forest, and the Ordinances of Edward I, and much subsequent legislation including the New Forest Acts of 1698, 1800, 1808, 1810, 1819, and 1829, but retaining the Act of 1877 and more recent legislation.

References to Introduction

1 John Manwood, *A Treatise of the Lawes of the Forest,* edition 1615, Dedication
2 Ibid., cap.9/3, f.69
3 Dictionary of National Biography — S.R. Gardiner (1829–1902)
4 S.R. Gardiner, *The Personal Government of Charles I, 1628–1637*, vol. 2, 1877, pp. 73–6
5 Sir William Holdsworth, *A History of English Law,* vol. 1, edition 1969, p. 105
6 Charles Petit-Dutaillis, *Studies and Notes Supplementary to Stubbs' Constitutional History,* edition 1923, p. 245
7 George Hammersley, History, vol. 45, 1960, p. 85, *The Revival of the Forest Laws under Charles I*
8 P.R.O. (Public Record Office) E.32/310–1
9 Calendar of Close Rolls, various entries
10 P.R.O. E.101/142 (12–20), E.101/143 (1–2), E.101/147 (7–17), E.101/536 (30–5)
11 P.R.O. F.20/47, *The Orders and Rules of the New Forest AD 1537,* published in Hants. Field Club New Forest Section, Rep. No. 13, 1974
12 Rev. A.W. Stote, *Extracts from the Court Rolls of the New Forest,* Ms Notebook, Soc. of Genealogists Ac 29232
13 Cyril Hart, *The Verderers and Forest Laws of Dean,* 1971, pp. 90–3
14 William Richard Fisher, *The Forest of Essex,* 1887, p. 110
15 Robert Bell Turton, North Riding Record Society, N.S. vol. 1, 1894, p. 139, *The Honor and Forest of Pickering*
16 R. Grant, Victoria County History, Wiltshire, vol. 4, 1959, p. 400, *Royal Forests*
17 Philip A.J. Pettit, Northants Record Society, vol. 23, 1968, p. 24, *The Royal Forests of Northamptonshire*
18 E.F. Jacob, Oxford History of England, vol. 6, 1961, pp. 154–7, *The Fifteenth Century 1399–1485*
19 O.G.S. Crawford, The Cornhill Magazine, N.S. vol. 54, 1923, pp. 469–76, *Mediaeval Forests*
20 Rev. J. Silvester Davies, *A History of Southampton,* 1883, pp. 495–9
21 D.J. Stagg, Hampshire Record Series, vol. 3, 1979, p. 81, entry 126, *A Calendar of New Forest Documents AD 1244–1334*
22 *Report of the Royal New and Waltham Forest Commission,* 1850, p. 16

23 Statute 9 & 10 Will. III c.36, *An Act for the Increase and Preservation of Timber in the New Forest,* AD 1698
24 Percival Lewis, *Historical Inquiries concerning Forests and Forest Laws,* 1811, pp. 178–203
25 Anon., *An Abstract of all the Claims on the New Forest 1670,* 1776, pp. 197–202
26 *The Fifth Report of the Commissioners of Woods, Forests, and Land Revenues of the Crown,* dated 22nd July 1789, Appendix No. 4
27 *Abstract of Claims preferred at a Justice Seat held for the New Forest AD 1670,* Eyre and Spottiswoode, 1853
28 Charles Petit-Dutaillis, op. cit., p. 232
29 May McKisack, Oxford History of England, vol. 5, 1959, p. 208, *The Fourteenth Century 1307–1399*
30 *The Charter of the Forest*, AD 1217, William Stubbs, *Select Charters*, 9th edition, 1962, pp. 344–8
31 Ordinance 34 Edward I, s.5, *Ordinatio Foreste,* AD 1306
32 Statute 1 Edward I, s.1, c.8, *How he shall be used that is taken for any Offence in the Forest,* AD 1327
33 Nellie Neilson, *The English Government at Work 1327–36,* vol. 1, 1940, p. 413, *The Forests,* general editors J.F. Willard and W.A. Morris
34 Statute 25 Edward III, s.5, c.7, *Statute of Purveyors,* AD 1350
35 Statute 43 Edward III, c.4, *The King's General Pardon to all men of Vert and Venison,* AD 1369
36 Statute 7 Ric. II, c.3, *A Jury for a Trespass within the Forest shall give their Verdict where they received their Charge*; c.4, *None shall be taken or imprisoned by the Officers of the Forest without Indictment,* AD 1383
37 Sir William Holdsworth, op. cit., p. 319
38 Statute 32 Hen. VIII, c.35, *The Justices of Forests to make Deputies,* AD 1540
39 Statute 16 Car. I, c.16, *Act to determine the Meets and Bounds of the Forests,* AD 1640
40 John Manwood, op. cit., cap. 24/2, f. 233
41 P.R.O. F.20/47, *Explanatory Notes upon the Charter of the Forest*
42 Sir William Holdsworth, op. cit., p. 95
43 John Manwood, op. cit., cap. 21/1, f. 188
44 Ibid., cap. 9/3, f. 69
45 Sir William Holdsworth, op. cit., p. 104
46 G.J. Turner, Selden Society Publications, vol. 13, 1901, pp. l–lxxv, *Select Pleas of the Forest*
47 D.J. Stagg, op. cit., pp. 15–18
48 Sir William Holdsworth, op. cit., p. 266
49 G.J. Turner, op. cit., pp. xlii–l
50 D.J. Stagg, op. cit., pp. 16–17
51 Rev. A.W. Stote, op. cit.
52 P.R.O. C.99/41–7
53 *Abstract of Claims etc.*, op. cit.
54 Sir Edward Coke, Fourth Institute, f. 320
55 *Orders and Rules of the New Forest AD 1537,* op. cit.
56 *Calendar of State Papers Domestic,* 26th March 1608

57 John Manwood, op. cit., cap. 23/6, f. 224
58 Mr. Daman, *Observations relative to the Jurisdiction of the Verderors of the New Forest,* 1828, Ms. Hampshire Record Office
59 Rev. A.W. Stote, op. cit.
60 Sir William Holdsworth, op. cit., p. 106
61 *The Charter of the Forest,* op. cit.
62 Mr. Daman, op. cit.
63 Sir William Holdsworth, op. cit., p. 106
64 Statute 19 & 20 Car. II, c.8, *Dean Forest Act,* AD 1667
65 Statute 9 & 10 Will. III, c.36, op. cit.
66 Mr. Daman, op. cit.
67 William Nelson, *Manwood's Treatise of the Forest Laws,* 4th edition, 1717, p. 371
68 C.R. Tubbs, Forestry, vol. 37, no. 1, 1964, p. 100, *Early Encoppicements in the New Forest*
69 *Assize of William de Vescy AD 1287,* G.J. Turner, op. cit., pp. 62–4
70 Statute 16 Geo. III, c.30, s.27 & 42 Geo III, c.107, s.1, *For the punishment of such persons as shall kill or destroy deer,* AD 1775–6, 1801–2
71 Statute 6 Geo. III, c.36 & c.48, s.1, *Acts for the Preservation of Timber,* AD 1765–6
72 *The Fifth Report etc.,* op. cit., p. 223
73 Statute 48 Geo. III, c.72, *New Forest Act,* AD 1808
74 Statute 39 & 40 Geo. III, c.86, *Act for the better preservation of Timber in the New Forest,* AD 1800
75 Statute 50 Geo. III, c.116, *An Act to extend the term of the 39 & 40 Geo. III,* AD 1810
76 Statute 52 Geo. III, c.161, *Act to grant Leases,* AD 1812
77 Statute 59 Geo. III, c.86, *Act for regulating the Right of Common of Pasture in the New Forest,* AD 1819
78 Statute 10 Geo. IV, c.50, s.100 & 102, *Act to Consolidate Laws relating to Woods and Forests,* AD 1829
79 Mr. Daman, op. cit.
80 Statute 40 & 41 Vict., c.121, *Act to amend the administration of the law relating to the New Forest,* AD 1877
81 Statute Eliz. II, 1971, c.47, *Wild Creatures and Forest Laws Act*

Editorial Methods

In general court documents are by nature concise and present little opportunity for further condensation, but where a standard formula is repeatedly used, e.g. "It is presented by the foresters and other ministers of the forest and the twelve jurors, and proved by the verderers . . .", or ". . . more for his own advantage than for the necessary forage of the king's beasts", or ". . . to the destruction of the king's beasts and great harm of the forest and damage of the king, and against the laws and assizes of the forest", such phrases have been included only for the first of a series of similar presentments. However much repetition occurs in the various grants, and here the information calendared has been restricted to essential information of the lands concerned, areas, values, and tenants.

Italic type and round brackets have been used for individual words or phrases taken direct from the manuscript either where the wording appears of particular interest or where the meaning is uncertain, but the round brackets have been omitted in instances where no translation has been possible. Italic type has also been used for references to documents and membranes.

Process additions, interlineations, and marginations have been indicated by the use of angle brackets, this occurring in particular where sentencing information has been added to the original presentment. Square brackets have been used to indicate explanatory matter and any extraneous words or phrases inserted to clarify the text.

In the text the original spelling has been retained for all surnames, but for most place-names the modern spelling has been substituted except where an early spelling appears of particular interest or has been previously unrecorded, or where identification has not been possible.

In the index all spellings which appear in the calendar have been cross-referenced to the most acceptable version, place-names and topographical surnames being grouped under the modern place-name spelling. More caution has been exercised with the later surnames these being grouped only where they appear to be variants of a single form. Where possible different persons of the same name have been separately indexed, but if it has not been possible to determine whether one or more individual is involved, as for instance identical names appearing at different dates in the seventeenth century, such references have been indexed under one entry.

List of Documents Calendared

EXCHEQUER T.R., FOREST PROCEEDINGS (E.32)

CHANCERY, FOREST PROCEEDINGS (C.99)

C.99/50	Grant to Thomas Ely and George Merreil made 27th May 1609	1597–1650
C.99/55	Grant to John Foyle made 29th May 1609	1651–1658

CHANCERY, ENROLMENTS OF PATENT ROLLS (C.66)

C.66/1790	Grant to Edward Savage and Andrew Mundey made 2nd June 1609	1659–1667
C.66/1995	Grant to Thomas Ely and Nicholas Lucye made 13th June 1613	1668–1670

CHANCERY, FOREST PROCEEDINGS (C.99)

C.99/48	Grant to John Chamberlain made 21st May 1631	1671–1717

The Calendar

DL.39/2/12

m.1

1 ‹New Forest› A Swainmote held there on Friday 9th February 1487

2 Henry Erlesman, the forester of the bailiwick of Battramsley, attends and he presents that on the 24th June 1485[1] William Holcombe, a gentleman recently of Lymington, had entered the New Forest at Lady Hill within the said bailiwick, and with greyhounds had taken and killed a buck, one of the king's beasts, and he had carried away the flesh without permission or warrant.

[1] Dated to the 2nd year of Richard III, but as the regnal year ended on the 25th June, it is possible that 1484 was intended, thus placing this entry in chronological order with those following.

3 Also that on the 4th September 1484 the same William had entered the forest at Rhinefield, and with greyhounds had killed two of the king's beasts, namely a pricket and a doe, without warrant.

4 Also that on the 2nd October 1484 the same William with greyhounds had taken and killed a doe at *Le Leyne* in the same bailiwick, and had carried away the flesh without warrant.

5 Also that on the 4th November 1485 the same William had entered the forest near *Le Hurst* in the same bailiwick, and with greyhounds had killed a doe and had carried away the flesh without warrant.

6 Also that on the 7th January 1486 the same William had entered the forest as far as *Le Leyne*, and with greyhounds had killed two of the king's beasts, namely a doe and a young hind *(hynnulum)*, and carried away the flesh without permission or warrant.

7 Also that on the 13th September 1486 the same William had entered the forest near Hinchelsea in the same bailiwick, and with greyhounds had taken and killed a buck, and had carried away the flesh without warrant or permission.[1]

[1] This entry has been deleted.

8 Also that on the 17th December 1486 the same William had entered the forest as far as *Le Hurst*, and with greyhounds had killed a doe, and had carried away the flesh without warrant.[1]

[1] This entry has been deleted.

9 Also that on the 24th October 1484 William Johnson, a chaplain recently of Lymington, had entered the forest as far as Rhinefield, and with greyhounds had killed a doe without warrant.

10 Also that on the 10th December 1485 Walter Peny, a husbandman recently of Walkford, and Roland Sadeler, a saddler recently of Milton, had entered the same bailiwick and with a greyhound had killed a doe without warrant.

11 Also that on the 11th August 1486 Walter Bedell, a yeoman recently of Bisterne, had entered the forest as far as *?Fyvoc'* within the same bailiwick, and with greyhounds had killed a doe, and had carried away the flesh without permission or warrant.

12 Also that on the 12th January 1487 William Rengeborne,[1] a gentleman recently of Parley, and Thomas Westbury, a gentleman recently of Christchurch, had entered the forest as far as Rhinefield, and with greyhounds had killed three of the king's beasts, namely a hind and two does,[1] and they had carried away the flesh without permission or warrant.

[1] The name William Rengeborne and the reference to two does have been deleted.

13 Also that on the 11th January 1487 the same William and Thomas had entered the forest as far as *Sewersbury*, and with greyhounds had killed a doe, and had carried away the flesh without permission or warrant.[1]

[1] This entry has been deleted.

14 Also that on the 17th September 1484 Henry Smyth, Robert Bowman, Ralph Imberson, and Robert Welles, all yeoman and recently of Bisterne, had entered the forest as far as Rhinefield, and both with greyhounds and with bows and arrows had killed four of the king's beasts, namely a staggard and three does, and they had carried away the flesh without permission or warrant.

15 ‹Vert›. Also that on the 16th January 1487 John Holebroke, husbandman recently of Downton [in Hordle], had entered the forest as far as Wootton Wood, and had cut down a green oak worth 4d., and with his cart had carried it away without permission or warrant against the assize of the forest.

16 Also that on the 12th January 1487 John Pekenett junior, husbandman recently of Battramsley, had entered the forest as far as *Seweresbury*, and had cut and carried away green thorns worth 2d. without permission against the assize of the forest.

17 Also that on the 14th December 1486 Thomas Smyth, husbandman of Ripley, had entered the forest as far as Wootton Wood, and had cut down and carried away a green oak worth [value omitted] without permission or warrant.[1] ‹Not known›.

[1] This entry has been deleted.

18 Edward Berkeley esquire, forester of the bailiwick of Burley, attends by William Foule and Richard Marlowe his deputies, and he presents that during the first and second years of the reign of king Richard III [1483–5] John Hoton esquire, recently of Bisterne, and Robert Vasy, Henry Smyth, Richard Imberson, Thomas Lokkewode, Ralph Imberson, and Robert Wellys, all yeomen and recently of Bisterne, had entered the forest at various times and at various places within the said bailiwick, and both with greyhounds and with bows and arrows they had killed two harts *(cervos)*, eight hinds *(cervas)*, forty bucks, one hundred does, and forty young hinds, and they had carried away the flesh without warrant.

19 Also that on the 13th May 1486 Nicholas Filioll, a gentleman recently of Fordingbridge, had entered the forest near to Burley Lodge, and with greyhounds had killed a doe, and had carried away the flesh without permission or warrant.

20 Also that on the 7th June 1486 Walter Bedell, a yeoman recently of Bisterne, had entered the forest at *Sandhurst* in the bailiwick of Burley and with greyhounds had taken and killed a buck, and had carried away the flesh without permission or warrant.

21 Also that on the 17th June 1486 the same Walter had entered the forest as far as *Floddon* in the same bailiwick, and had killed a doe and carried away the flesh without warrant.

22 Also that on the 16th December 1486 William Holcombe, a gentleman recently of Lymington, had entered the forest near *Trendeleyford* in the bailiwick of Burley, and with greyhounds had killed a doe without permission or warrant.

23 John Capelyne, forester of the East Bailiwick, attends and he presents that on the 10th January 1487 John Faunt, a vagabond recently of Beaulieu, had entered the East Bailiwick and with greyhounds had taken and killed a doe, and had carried away the flesh without permission or warrant.

24 Also that on Thursday 29th June 1486 Giles Bouchier, a butcher of Southampton, had entered the forest near Denny in the East Bailiwick, and with greyhounds had taken and killed a young hind ‹two young hinds›, and had carried away the flesh without permission or warrant.

25 Also that on the 4th July 1486 Walter Bedell, a yeoman of Bisterne, and Thomas Whiteby, a tailor of Beaulieu, had entered the forest near Woodfidley in the East Bailiwick, and with greyhounds had killed a sore, and had carried away the flesh without permission or warrant.

26 Thomas Alwyn and Thomas Fulfan, rangers *(forestarii itinerantes)*, attend and they present that on the 24th November 1485 Thomas Rypon, yeoman recently of Plaitford, had entered the forest as far as Bentley in the bailiwick of Fritham, and with greyhounds had killed a doe, and had carried away the flesh without permission or warrant.

27 Also that on the 10th June 1485 Thomas Gaylpryn, a labourer recently of Canterton, with a bow and arrow had shot and killed a buck at the end of the king's road called Canterton Lane in the North Bailiwick, and had carried away the flesh without warrant.[1]

[1] This entry has been deleted.

28 Also that on the 7th September 1484 Thomas Northe, a yeoman, and Richard Chapman, a mercer, both recently of Fordingbridge, had entered the forest as far as Palmers Slough *(Palmereslose)*, and they had killed a buck and a doe, and had carried away the flesh without permission or warrant.

29 ‹Vert›. Also that on the 3rd December 1484 John, the rector of Dibden church, had entered the forest and cut down and carried away a large green beech at Ipley in the East Bailiwick without permission or warrant against the assize of the forest.

30 Robert Mour', bowbearer, attends and presents that on the 5th January 1487 Thomas Rypon, a yeoman recently of Plaitford, had entered the forest as far as Bramble Wood in the North Bailiwick, and with greyhounds had killed a doe, and had carried away the flesh without permission or warrant.

31 Also that on the 8th December 1486 John Calcayne, a yeoman recently of Romsey, had entered the North Bailiwick and with greyhounds had killed a doe and a young hind, and had carried away the flesh without permission or warrant.

32 Peter Pocok, forester of the In Bailiwick, attends and presents that on the 14th January 1486 William Holcombe, a gentleman of Lymington, had entered the forest as far as Huntley Bank in the said bailiwick, and with greyhounds had killed a doe and three young hinds, and had carried away the flesh without permission or warrant.

33 Also that on the 4th December 1485 the same William Holcombe and Richard Fletcher, a fletcher recently of Lymington, had entered the forest as far as *La Estyate* [East Gate] in the In Bailiwick, and with greyhounds had killed a doe without permission or warrant.

34 Also that on the 26th February 1486 William Thorner, a labourer recently of Lymington, had entered the forest as far as Whitley in the In Bailiwick, and with greyhounds had killed a young hind, and had carried away the flesh without permission or warrant.

35 Also that on the 17th June 1485 John Porchett, a baker, and William Johnson, chaplain, both of Lymington, had entered the forest as far as the said Whitley, and with greyhounds had killed a doe, and had carried away the flesh without permission or warrant.

36 Also that on the 4th July 1485 Robert Wellyfed, a yeoman recently of Bisterne, had entered the forest as far as Coxlease in the In Bailiwick, and with a bow and arrow had wounded and killed a buck, and had carried away the flesh without permission or warrant.

37 ‹Twelve Freemen›
John Canterton, John Symmys, John Skudemo', William Cook senior, Thomas Hertesbury, Nicholas Rawlyne, Richard Draper, Richard Whitehede, Robert Traas, Thomas White, Henry Knyght, John Elyott, the jurors attend.

38 ‹Verdict›. And they affirm to be true all and each thing presented above by the said foresters, and nothing other than all well presented at this day.

m.1d

39 John Pocok, the forester of Fritham Bailiwick, attends and presents that on the 20th October 1485 William Edmond, singleman recently of Ringwood, had entered the forest as far as *Stonewode* in the said bailiwick, and with greyhounds had killed two young hinds, and had carried away the flesh without permission or warrant.

40 Also that in the months of November, December, and January 1485–6 the same William Edmond had entered the forest at various times and places, namely at Acres Down and Ocknell in the said bailiwick, and with greyhounds he had killed four young hinds, and had carried away the flesh without warrant or permission.

41 Also that on the 25th July 1486 Henry Grene, yeoman recently of Burgate, had entered the forest as far as Fritham and with a bow and arrow had wounded and killed a buck, and had carried away the flesh without warrant or permission.

42 John Buysshopp, the forester of Linwood Bailiwick, attends and presents that on the 1st May 1486 Thomas Lancaster, a yeoman recently of Ellingham, had entered the forest as far as Roe in the bailiwick of Linwood, and with greyhounds had killed a doe, and had carried away the flesh without permission or warrant.

43 John Pyper, forester of the North Bailiwick, attends and presents that on the 15th January 1487 William Dalle and Nicholas Pugeon, both butchers and recently of Romsey, had entered the North Bailiwick and with greyhounds had killed one of the king's beasts, without permission or warrant.

44 Also that on the 20th July 1486 John Andrew junior, a husbandman of Cadnam, had entered the North Bailiwick and with a bow and arrow had wounded and killed a sore without warrant.

45 Richard Markes, forester of the South Bailiwick, attends and presents that on the 10th August 1485 William Holcombe, a gentleman recently of Lymington, had entered the forest as far as Ironshill in the said bailiwick, and with greyhounds had killed a buck and a sore, and had carried away the flesh without warrant or permission.

46 Also that on the 10th January 1487 the same William had entered the forest as far as Moon Hill in the South Bailiwick and had cut down and carried away a large oak worth 12d [changed from 6d] without warrant.

47 Also that on the 28th May 1486 William Seler, a fuller *(touker)* recently of Beaulieu, at *Le Lutton* in the South Bailiwick with greyhounds had killed a doe, and had carried away the flesh without permission or warrant.

48 Also that on the 29th October 1486 the same William Seler, and Thomas Whytebye, a tailor recently of Beaulieu, with others unknown had entered the forest as far as *Gueyseley* in the South Bailiwick, and had killed a buck with a bow and arrow, and a doe with greyhounds, without warrant or permission.

49 Also that on the 1st July 1486 John a Brigge, a shoemaker recently of Beaulieu, at various places within the South Bailiwick had killed six young hinds with greyhounds, and had carried away the flesh without warrant.

50 Also that on the 8th December 1486 the same John a Brigge with others unknown had entered the forest as far as *Gueyseley* in the said bailiwick, and with greyhounds had killed a doe, and had carried away the flesh without permission or warrant.

51 Also that on the 6th January 1487 John Faunt, a vagabond recently of Beaulieu, at Woodfidley in the South Bailiwick had killed a doe with greyhounds, and had carried away the flesh without warrant.

52 Also that on the 2nd February 1486 John Bokelond, a baker recently of Beaulieu, with greyhounds had killed a doe in the South Bailiwick, and had carried away the flesh without warrant or the permission of any officer of the king.

53 ‹Regarders›. John Rumsye senior, Charles Ryngwode, Walter Fletcher, John Ede, John Dudelesfold, John Lowen, James Ede, James White, William Colyer, Reginald Dollyng, Geoffrey Lord, Henry Blake, Edmund Hosey, the jurors attend.

54 ‹Verdict›. Who say on oath that all the foresters have presented well and faithfully, and they affirm to be true all and each thing presented above. And furthermore they present that Richard Trew, a labourer recently of Beaulieu, and John de Lynne, a bucket maker recently of Pilley, in the year 1485–6 on many and various occasions had entered the land of the Abbot and Convent of Netley called Royden in the South Bailiwick, and they had placed strings and snares for taking and killing the king's beasts, without any authority. And nothing other to present this day.

55 The sureties of Walter Tradde, yeoman, of Beaulieu [are] Edmund Bremous a tailor of the parish of St. Olave in Silver Street in London, and John Fredsam esquire of the parish of St. Sepulchre in London, who have gone surety for William both for paying his fine to the king for a venison offence and for his future good behaviour. And by this each of the sureties are under pain of £5, and

Walter for himself under pain of £10, which they agree to raise from their goods and chattels and lands and tenements for the benefit of the king.

D.L.39/2/12

m.2

56 ‹New Forest› A Swainmote held before Sir Maurice Bargh' and Thomas Troys esquire, verderers, on the 29th July 1488

57 Thomas Alwyn and Thomas Fulfan, rangers, attend and present that on Thursday 28th June 1487 William Okeden of Ellingham and George Besyle of Fordingbridge, both gentlemen, and Robert Sadeler, a groom of Lymington, had entered the forest as far as Rhinefield in the bailiwick of Battramsley, and had killed three of the king's beasts and had carried away the flesh without permission or warrant.

58 Also that on the 24th August 1487 the said Robert Sadeler,[1] Robert Aylsworth[1] the servant of Richard Markes, and John Ederiche the servant of Thomas Jurdan had entered the forest as far as *Allysley* in the South Bailiwick, and had killed one of the king's beasts and carried away the flesh, etc.

[1] The names of Robert Sadeler and Robert Aylsworth have been deleted.

59 Also that on the 15th February 1488 the said Robert Sadeler and John Arnewode junior, a yeoman of Arnewode, had entered the bailiwick of Battramsley and had killed two of the king's beasts in Rhinefield and one in Goldsmiths Hill, etc.[1]

[1] This entry has been deleted.

60 Also that on Monday 2nd June 1488 Richard Hasard the vicar of Downton, and Roger Mapell and William Mapell, both yeoman of Downton, had killed a doe near Canterton in the North Bailiwick, and had carried away the flesh without warrant.

61 Also that on Wednesday 4th June 1488 the said vicar and Roger had entered the forest as far as Emery Down in the In Bailiwick, and they had killed a fecund doe and carried away the flesh etc.

62 Also that on the 6th December 1487 Henry Hugons, a gentleman of Standlynch in Wiltshire, with others unknown had entered the forest as far as Fritham, and in a close at that place had killed a sore, and had carried away the flesh without permission or warrant.

63 Also that on Monday 2nd June 1488 Henry Grene, a yeoman of Fordingbridge, had entered the forest as far as Bentley Coppice in the bailiwick of Fritham, and had killed a doe, and had carried away the flesh without permission or warrant.

64 Also that on Friday 27th June 1488 [Roger] Brereton[1] a gentleman, and Roger Mapell a yeoman, both of Downton, had entered the forest as far as Rhinefield, and had killed two of the king's beasts without permission or warrant.

[1] Name deleted.

65 ‹Twelve Freemen›. Robert Vyryng, James White, Robert Traas, Thomas Blake, William Cook senior, John Lylkebawde, Thomas Purse, William Palmer junior, Richard Draper, John Couper, Richard Pocok, William Colyer, the jurors attend. ‹Verdict›. And they affirm to be true all and each thing presented above, and nothing other presented at this day.

66 Henry Erlesman, the forester of Battramsley, attends and presents that on the 2nd November 1487 Roland Whytyng a saddler and Robert Kyng a husbandman, both of Milton, had entered the forest as far as *Potteresbeche* in the bailiwick of Battramsley, and with greyhounds had killed a doe, and had carried away the flesh without permission or warrant.

67 Also that on the 30th January 1488 William Holcombe, a gentleman of Lymington, had entered the forest as far as *Rymethornes* in the said bailiwick, and with greyhounds had killed a doe, and the flesh he had himself carried without permission or warrant.

68 Also that on the 13th October 1487 John Holebroke, a mercer of Lymington, with greyhounds had killed a fawn at Hurst in the said bailiwick, and had carried away the flesh without permission or warrant.

69 Also that on the 1st June 1488 the said William Holcombe had killed a buck at Hincheslea in the said bailiwick, and he had carried away the flesh without permission or warrant.

70 Also that on the 6th February 1488 Robert Norton, a yeoman of Charford, and Henry Grene, a yeoman of Fordingbridge, with greyhounds had killed a doe at *Sandehurste* in the said bailiwick, and they had carried away the flesh without permission or warrant.

71 Also that on the 8th January 1488 Thomas Westbury a gentleman and Robert Welles a yeoman, both of Christchurch, with greyhounds had killed a doe at *Seweresbury* in the said bailiwick, and had carried away the flesh without permission or warrant.

72 Richard Marlow, the deputy of Sir Edward Berkeley the forester of Burley, presents that on Tuesday 22nd April 1488 Henry Tracy, a yeoman recently of Laverstock in the county of Wiltshire and servant of Sir Thomas Milborne, with greyhounds had taken and killed a doe within the bailiwick of Burley, and had carried away the flesh without permission or warrant.

73 Also that on Monday 28th April 1488 Andrew Welles, a gentleman recently of . . ., the son of Thomas Welles, with greyhounds had killed a buck in the said bailiwick, and had himself carried the flesh without permission or warrant.

74 Also that on the 16th May 1488 Thomas Sarusbury, a monk of Beaulieu Abbey, with greyhounds had taken and killed a buck in the same bailiwick, and had carried away the flesh without permission etc,[1]

[1] This entry has been deleted.

75 Also that on Sunday 18th May 1488 Thomas Westbury, a gentleman of *Cristbury* in Christchurch, with greyhounds had killed a doe within the same bailiwick, without permission or warrant.

76 Peter Pocok, the forester of the In Bailiwick, presents that on the 21st January 1488 William Holcombe, a gentleman of Lymington, and Charles Ryngwode,[1] a gentleman of Whiteparish in Wiltshire, and with greyhounds had killed a doe in Butts Lawn *(Buttes Launde)* in the said bailiwick, etc.

[1] Name deleted.

77 Also that on the 28th January 1488 William Westbury, a gentleman of Ringwood, and Robert Welles, a yeoman of Christchurch, with greyhounds had taken and killed two does in Lyndhurst Park within the In Bailiwick, and they had carried away the flesh without permission or warrant.

78 Also that on the 12th and 13th February 1488 John Rumsye senior,[1] esquire of Marchwood, William Holcombe a gentleman of Lymington, and John Holebroke a mercer of Lymington had killed a doe[2] in Lyndhurst Park, and had carried away the flesh without permission or warrant.

[1] Name deleted. [2] Altered from two does.

79 John Pyper, the forester of the North Bailiwick, attends and presents that on the 4th February 1487 William Hylles a labourer and William Calley a yeoman, both of Whiteparish, had entered the forest as far as Bramble Wood, and had killed a doe etc.

80 Also that on the 6th July 1488 Henry Hugons, a gentleman of Standlynch, and William Holmes, vicar of Salisbury cathedral church, with greyhounds had taken and killed a doe at Linwood within the said bailiwick, and had carried away the flesh without permission or warrant.

81 Also that on Sunday the 27th July 1488 Nicholas White, a husbandman of Merdon, with other unknown associates, had killed one of the king's beasts at Linwood without permission etc.

82 Also that on the 15th May 1488 William Waterman, a labourer of Bramshaw, with other unknown associates, with a prepositioned halter had taken and killed one of the king's beasts in Moore Close within the said bailiwick, and had carried away the flesh etc.

m.2d

83 John Capelyne, forester of the East Bailwick, attends and presents that on the 5th July 1487 Sampson Swete, a gentleman of Southampton, and [blank] Weston, a monk of Netley Abbey, had entered the forest as far as *Tweyfordys* in the said bailiwick, and had killed a stag and carried away the flesh without permission or warrant.[1]

[1] This entry has been deleted.

84 Also that on the 7th July 1488 Thomas Frenshe the servant of Thomas Lovell of Calmore had shot with a bow and arrow and had killed one of the king's beasts within the said bailiwick without permission or warrant.

85 Also that on the 29th June 1488 Ellis Bouchier, a butcher of Southampton had entered the said bailiwick and had killed a young hind and carried it away without permission or warrant.

86 Robert Mour', bowbearer, attends and presents that on the 27th August 1487 Richard Chestr', a labourer recently of Lymington, had killed a sore at *Stapeloke* in the South Bailiwick, and had carried away the flesh without permission or warrant.

87 The vills of Exbury and Lepe, Holbury and Langley, Hardley, Buttsash and Ipley, Baddesley, Warborne and Pilley, Battramsley and Wootton, Brookley and Brockenhurst, Burley, Godshill and Linwood, Canterton and Fritham, Minstead, and Lyndhurst and Bartley. The jurors attend but they present nothing because all well at this day.

88 ‹Regarders›. John Ede, Henry Knyght, John Symmys, Simon Marchaunt, John Blake, Thomas Lovell of Fritham, Peter Biddelcombe, William Houker, Richard Philipp' of Kingston, Nicholas Swetyngham, Robert Holmore, Richard Lorde, Richard Whitehede, Simon Knolles, William Cooke junior, the jurors attend.
‹Verdict›. And they affirm to be true all and each thing presented above and within by the prenamed foresters, and nothing other presented at this day.

m.3 [English]
89 The bailiff of Fritham presents that about or soon after the 6th January 1485 *(Epiphany)*, Robert Bulkeley esquire of Charford and William Kaylleway esquire of Rockbourne, in the bailiwick of Fritham with bows, arrows, and greyhounds killed in one day five fawns, a doe, and a pricket, and took and bore away the flesh of them, etc.

90 Also that on the 29th August 1486 the same William Kaylleway and Robert Bulkeley entered into the chief place of the said bailiwick, and with bows and greyhounds killed a sore and bore away the flesh.

91 Also that on the 20th June 1488 the same Robert Bulkeley and William Kaylleway, with Roger Mapull and William Mapull, both yeoman of Downton, entered the same bailiwick and killed a brocket and bore away the flesh.

92 Also that on the 10th July last past [?1488], William Cranborne in the chief place of the same bailiwick killed a tegge and bore away the flesh, and is a great harmer of deer all the year.

93 Also that on the 12th July last [?1488], John Audeley late of Wade killed a doe in the In Bailiwick and bore away the flesh.

94 Also that on the 3rd July last [?1488] in the fence month *(defens time)* the same John Audeley in the North Bailiwick killed a ?soaking doe [barren doe] and bore away the flesh.

95 Also that on the Saturday before Epiphany last [?4th January 1488], Henry Grene a yeoman of Fordingbridge killed a fat doe in the bailiwick of Fritham and bore away the flesh.

96 Also that Thomas Marde is a common harmer of deer.

97 A true list *(billa)* and it is affirmed in all by the Verderers and the Regarders.

m.4 [English]
98 Maurice Fyloll', a gentleman of Charford, and his company in the week before Midsummer 1487 killed a sore with greyhounds in the bailiwick of Burley, and the flesh carried away, etc.

99 Also in January 1488 the same Maurice killed a doe with greyhounds in the same bailiwick, and the flesh carried away, etc.

100 Also that on the 20th July 1487, Thomas Westbury a gentleman of Christchurch killed a buck with greyhounds in the said bailiwick, and the flesh carried away, etc.

101 Also that in January 1488 the same Thomas killed a doe with greyhounds in the same bailiwick.

102 Also that in the summer of the 2nd year of Henry VII [?1487], John Brereton squire, late of Bisterne, killed a buck and a sore in the same bailiwick.

103 Also in the winter season of the same year [1486/7] the same John killed a doe and a fawn.

104 Also that on Monday the 28th April 1488, [Andrew][1] Wellys killed a buck in the said bailiwick.[2] ‹Elsewhere›.

[1] Name omitted. [2] The entry has been deleted. [See entry **73**]

105 Also at various times Walter [Malyn] the parson of Bramshaw killed a buck and two does within Robert Barle Close[1] in Bramshaw, and the flesh carried away without permission, etc.

[1] Substituted for 'within the same bailiwick'.

106 Also that at various times Nicholas Fylyoll, a gentleman of Gorley, killed a buck and six does in various places[1] without warrant or permission etc.

[1] Substituted for 'within the said bailiwick'.

107 Also that at various times William Cramborne, a yeoman of Fordingbridge, killed a buck, two sores, and four does within the bailiwick of Fritham, and carried away the flesh without warrant or permission, etc.

108 Also that on the 15th August 1487, Thomas Starlyng a gentleman of *Allerholt* in Dorset killed a buck at Fritham.

109 Also that on the 2nd August 1488, Thomas Trusfeld of Wade, a servant of Sir James Awdeley, killed a buck at Mark Ash and carried him away, etc.

110 Also that the same day Roger Mapell and William Mapell, both yeoman of Downton, with others killed a buck at Bratley and carried away the flesh, etc.

m.4d
111 A true list and it is affirmed by the regarders and verderers.

m.5 [English]
112 Edward Mour the son of John Mour, a husbandman of Plaitford, on the 24th August 1485 with greyhounds killed a buck out of *Wythy Slade* in the bailiwick of Linwood, and carried him away without warrant or permission.

m.6 [English]
113 That at Candlemas [2nd February] Richard Knyght, a fuller of Ringwood, came with greyhounds and coursed in the bailiwick of Burley and killed a tegge.

m.7 [English]
114 William Parson and John Knollys, husbandmen of *Brow. . .oly* in the county of Hampshire, with their company on the 29th June 1483 killed two bucks.

[Circuit Assize held 16th August 1488]

DL.39/2/12

m.8

115 [Writ of Summons to the Keeper of the New Forest and his Deputy]

To Thomas earl of Arundel, keeper of the New Forest, and to sir Edward Berkeley his lieutenant.

Sir John Ratclyf, lord Fitzwater, and sir Reginald Bray, justices itinerant of all forests, parks, chases, and warrens of the lord king this side of the Trent, etc., to the keeper of the New Forest or his lieutenant, greetings. On the part of the lord king we command you to make appear before us or our deputies at Romsey on Saturday the 16th August next [1488], all the foresters, verderers, regarders, agisters, woodwards, and all other forest officers, who are holding or have held office since the last forest pleas to be held there, with their records since the said pleas. Also all the freeholders who have lands or tenements within the bounds of the forest. And from every vill within the forest four men and the reeve, and from every town twelve good and lawful men. Also to make appear all who have been attached, or have been convicted and are in custody or released to pledges, for offences of vert or venison since the last forest pleas, together with their sureties and pledges. Also all those who claim liberties or franchises within the forest, to show by what writ or franchise they have or claim, and by what warrant etc. Witnessed at Westminster on the 20th June 1488.

m.9

116 [List of Forest Officers, etc.] John Dudelesfold deputy lieutenant, Henry Rake riding forester, Thomas Alwyn and Thomas Witham rangers, Robert Mour bowbearer.

117 Thomas Jurdan forester of Burley, Henry Erlesman forester of Battramsley, John Pocok forester of Fritham, John Buysshopp forester of Linwood, Richard Northe forester of Godshill, Peter Pocok forester of the In Bailiwick, John Pyper forester of the North Bailiwick, John Capelyne forester of the East Bailiwick, Richard Markes forester of the South Bailiwick.

118 Sir Maurice Bargh and Thomas Troys esquire, the verderers.

119 John Capelyn woodward of Minstead, William Palmer woodward of Ipley.

120 There are no agisters.

121 Vills of Exbury and Lepe, Holbury and Langley, Hardley, Buttsash and Ipley, Baddesley, Warborne and Pilley, Battramsley and Wootton, Brookley and Brockenhurst, Burley, Godshill and Linwood, Canterton and Fritham, Minstead, Lyndhurst and Bartley. [Names of the jurors have been entered against the vills but are illegible].

122 None are attached, convicted, or detained in prison, nor released to sureties or pledges.

123 [Claimants of Liberties]. Abbot of Beaulieu, prior of Christchurch, prior of Breamore, prior of Mottisfont, keeper of Winchester College, lord Stourton, lord of Linwood, bishop of Winchester, dean and chapter of Salisbury cathedral.

m.10

124 Regarders of the New Forest and the Forest of Buckholt. Richard Reede esquire, John Pake esquire, William Tycheborne esquire, John Harryes esquire, Charles Ryngwod', John Rumsey senior, John Hamond, George Banbyrge, Walter Flecher, Maurice Legh, John Lewen, John Arnewode senior, John Rumsey junior, Thomas Jordan senior, Thomas Lovell, Henry Knyght, John Symmys, John Cott of Ibsley.

m.11

125 [Writ of Summons to John Tycheborne, sheriff of Hampshire]

To John Tycheborne sheriff of Hampshire. Sir John Ratclif, lord Fitzwater, and Reginald Bray, justices itinerant of all forests, parks, chases, and warrens of the lord king this side of Trent, etc., greetings. On the part of the lord king we command you to make appear before us or our deputies at Romsey on the 16th August next [1488], twenty four good and lawful men from each of the Hundreds within and about the New Forest to enquire and make known the truth on behalf of the king. And to proclaim in all public places within the county that all who have, or claim to have, liberties, franchises, privileges, or ancient profits within the forest are to appear before us or our deputies at the said day and place to show warrant. Witnessed at Westminster on the 20th June 1488.

m.12

126 New Forest Hundred. Thomas Baratt bailiff, Thomas Lovell of Bartley, Thomas Hertisber, James White, Robert Trace, Robert Holmor', Richard Whitehede, William White of *Slade*, John Auncell, John White of Pilley, John Holear, Henry Hobbys, John Andrew of Canterton, William Cole, Robert Veryng', Richard Lorde, Edward Swhetyngham, John Haylys, William Haylys, Robert Ston'.

m.13

127 Redbridge Hundred. Thomas Pedwyn bailiff, John Rumsey esquire, Walter Flecher, Thomas Lovell, Geoffrey Lord, John Newman, William Hokar, Thomas Hennyng, Richard Tarvar, John Tery of Totton, Richard Torver, William Kyng, John Warwyke, John Armenar, William Wallar, William James, Robert Terver, Walter Wyms.

m.14

128 Christchurch Hundred. Thomas Westbury bailiff, John Lewyn, John Ernewode, Robert Imberley, Nicholas Soper, Richard Tulse, Roland Whityng, William Colyer, Reginald Dollyng, Thomas Stephyn, Richard Ley, William Brownyng, John Averey, Thomas Smyth, William Sley, John Ernewode junior, Edward Lane, John Bulle senior.

m.15

129 Ringwood Hundred. Thomas Jourdayn junior bailiff, John Ede, John Wagge, Richard Pewyn, Thomas Purse, Thomas Lauverens, Richard Philippis, John Roggers, Henry Tele, John Serygge, Richard Gyly, John Franke, Peter Philippis, Peter Gose.

m.16

130 Fordingbridge Hundred. William Hurst bailiff, Henry Erlysman, Walter Poxwell, William Terell, John Pope, Richard Ashley, William Mew, John at Hyde, Richard Hurste, Richard Machyn,

Richard Sewall junior, John Collys, Thomas Nordyss, Thomas Moris, Ralph Elyng, William Howchyn, John Glosse, Thomas Pott', Simon Gordon, John Lockys of Ibsley, Thomas Sendy.

m.17

131 It is enquired for the king if sir James Audeley on the 21st June 1486 had entered the New Forest ‹outside, at Dibden in Purlieu› with bow, arrows, and greyhounds, had killed a stag,[1] and had carried away the flesh and hide without warrant.

[1] Substituted for hart.

132 Also if Richard Tervor, a yeoman of Marchwood, on the 26th July 1487 [had entered the forest within the parish of Eling and killed a great hart, and carried away the flesh and hide without warrant, etc.][1] ‹found a stag killed with an arrow at *Weswod*› which hart Richard had carried to sir James Audeley. ‹*We can not find who killed that deer*›.

[1] Deleted.

133 It is enquired etc. if the said sir James Audeley on the 12th December 1487 in the bailiwick of Fritham had killed a stag with bow and arrow, and greyhounds, and carried away the flesh and hide, etc.[1]

[1] Entry deleted.

134 Also if the said James on the 31st January 1488 had killed a hart with bow and greyhounds, and had carried away the flesh and hide.[1]

[1] Entry deleted.

135 Also if the said James on the 20th March 1488 had entered the East Bailiwick with bow and greyhounds, and had killed and carried away a stag.[1]

[1] Substituted for great hart.

136 Also if the said James on the 12th June 1488 [within the bounds of the forest][1] ‹outside, in the parish of Eling . . . Purlieu› with bow and greyhounds had killed [two great harts][1] ‹one hart›, and had carried away the flesh and hide.

[1] Deleted.

137 It is enquired for the king etc. if Gilbert Skory, husbandman of Brockenhurst, [William Sherde a yeoman of Beaulieu],[1] and Thomas Whitby a tailor of the same place, on the 17th July 1488 had entered the South Bailiwick and killed a doe ‹a sore› without warrant.

[1] Deleted.

138 Also if the same Gilbert had cut down two oaks in the forest.[1]

[1] Entry deleted.

139 Also if the same Gilbert on Friday the 30th May 1488 in the South Bailiwick with a bow had killed a doe ‹a pryket›, and had carried away the hide without warrant.

140 It is enquired for the king if John Rumsey junior on Wednesday 18th April 1487 had entered Lyndhurst Park with greyhounds and had killed a doe and a fawn without warrant, and took and carried away the flesh and hide.[1]

[1] Entry deleted.

141 Also if the same John in the North Bailiwick on Tuesday 24th April 1487 had killed a doe with greyhounds, and had taken and carried away the flesh and hide without warrant.[1]

[1] Entry deleted.

142 Also if the same John ‹Romesey› in *Northlond'* in the In Bailiwick on the 30th November 1486 had killed a doe without warrant, and had taken and carried away the flesh and hide.

143 Also if John Skudemor senior ‹deceased› of Gorley, with others unknown, had hunted by night in a close called Lyndhurst, and had disturbed the king's beasts.

144 Also if Gilbert Scory and John Grene had come at night in the South Bailiwick against the assize of the forest.[1]

[1] Entry deleted.

[The remainder of the membrane is in English]

145 Also enquire if John Howton' ‹deceased› and Robert Wasey ‹deceased› with others unknown in July 1483 at various times killed forty deer in the In Bailiwick.

146 Also the same year sir John Babyngton and master Dynham entered the In Bailiwick and killed sixteen deer without any warrant.

147 Also in the same year one Adsote ‹deceased› then being keeper of Hampton, with his servant, entered the forest in August and killed nine deer without warrant.

m.17d [English]

148 Also in June in the first year of the reign of the present king[1] [1486], sir John Cheyne killed two hinds in the In Bailiwick.

[1] Substituted for king Richard.

149 Also in the visit of the queen and the prince, in the In Bailiwick were killed eight male and rascal deer. Also when the Bishop of Winchester came were slain three bucks.

150 Against the king's coming there were driven out of the In Bailiwick into the park the number of four hundred [deer].

151 Also that Peter Pocok, the forester of the In Bailiwick, delivered his bill of hunting to John Ede which bill he understands is duly sealed John Ede is foreman of the inquest.[1]

[1] Entry deleted.

152 Also William Parson carried away two horse loads of lead of the covering of the queen's bower, the 19th day of February 1480. And the following night he carried away a load of lead of the covering of the same bower.[1]

[1] Entry deleted.

153 Also the said William on the 20th August 1479 met a thief in the forest with ?4 sheep, and took 3 sheep from him, and let him go with the remnant to Beaulieu.[1]

[1] Entry deleted.

154 Also that six harts and twenty fallow deer were slain when king Edward V should have been crowned.

155 Also six harts and fifteen bucks [were slain] at the coronation of king Henry VII.

156 Also against the king's coming down were driven seventeen [deer] to the New Park with a stable, out of three bailiwicks, that is to say the In Bailiwick, the South Bailiwick, and the East Bailiwick. Fifteen of the deer were slain and seven died by estimate.

157 Also in John Pocok's bailiwick during the reign of king Richard at various times were slain five hundred deer by the Northern men and servants of the king.

158 John Piper, forester of the North Bailiwick, comes and presents that Harry Palmer, the servant of Sir Reynold Bray, had felled in his bailiwick eighty eight oaks which were not principal timber for the making of the king's ships in Hampton, and thirty six beech for *scelying* and as necessary things, and all without warrant.

159 Also if Nicholas Fylol, a gentleman recently of Fordingbridge, on the 1st August 1486 with greyhounds slew a hart in the lodge of Burley.

m.18

160 ‹Sureties› of John Romsey junior, gentleman. John Holt a gentleman of Crondall, Robert Rike a servant of the king's court, Thomas Eston of *Puttenham* in Hampshire, who have gone surety for John Romsey both for paying his fine to the king for a venison offence which has been proved, and for his future good behaviour, each of the sureties being under pain of 40s, and John Romsey for himself under pain of £10, which each of them agrees to raise from his lands and chattels etc.

161 ‹Sureties› of William Holcombe ‹pardoned by the king› a gentleman of Lymington. Nicholas Compton and Henry Craford, gentlemen, David John a yeoman, and John Bedell a gentleman, all of London, who have gone surety for the said William both for his fine and his future good behaviour under pain of 100s. And William for himself under pain of £10. Which each of them agrees etc.

162 ‹Sureties› of John Breirton esquire of Bisterne. Roger Breirton, ?Lohes ApWilliam, Richard Battirsey, and John Launde, all gentlemen of Bishops Waltham, who have gone surety for John Breirton both for the fine and his future good behaviour under pain of £20. And John Breirton under pain of £40 etc.

163 ‹Sureties› of William Kaylway esquire of Rockborne. Robert Bulkeley esquire of Burgate, Maurice Filoll' gentleman of Charford, Nicholas Filloll' gentleman of Fordingbridge, and William Okeden gentleman of Ellingham, who have gone surety for the said William both for the fine and for his future good behaviour under pain of £10 each, and William for himself £20 etc.

164 ‹Sureties› of Robert Bulkeley esquire of Burgate. William Kayllwaye, Maurice Filoll, Nicholas Filoll, and William Okeden, who have gone surety for Robert's fine and future good behaviour, each under pain of £10, and Robert for himself £20 etc.

165 ‹Sureties› of Maurice Filoll. Robert Bulkeley, William Kayllwaye, Nicholas Fyloll, and William Okeden, who have gone surety for Maurice's fine and future good behaviour, each under pain of £10, and Maurice for himself £20 etc.

166 ‹Sureties› for Nicholas Fyloll. William Kaylwaye, Robert Bulkeley, Maurice Filoll, and William Okeden, who have gone surety for Nicholas' fine and future good behaviour, each under pain of £10, and Nicholas for himself £20 etc.

167 ‹Sureties› for William Okeden. William Kaylwaye, Robert Bulkeley, Maurice Filoll, and Nicholas Filoll, who have gone surety for William's fine and future good behaviour, as above.

m.19

168 New Forest. A Circuit Assize *(sessio in itinere)* held at Romsey on Saturday 16th August 1488 before sir John Ratclyf, lord Fitz Water, and sir Reginald Bray, justices itinerant of all the king's forests, parks, chases, and warrens this side of the Trent, and magistrates *(magistri)* to determine all premisses of statute of the said forest.

169 [Four men and the reeve].[1] John Coke of the vill of Minstead presents that John Capelyn woodward of Minstead [Blank].

[1] Deleted.

170 ‹Sureties› of Roger Mapell' yeoman of Downton. Robert White esquire of Farnborough in Surrey, Roger Brereton esquire of Downton, John Cokeson esquire of Dursley in Gloucestershire, and John Waller esquire of Groombridge in Kent, who have gone surety for the said Roger both for paying the fine to the king for the venison offence of which he is convicted, and also for his future good behaviour, each of the sureties being under pain of [Blank]. And Roger for himself under pain of [Blank], which each of them agrees to raise his lands, goods, and chattels, etc.

171 ‹Sureties› of William Mapelle yeoman of Downton. Robert White, Roger Brereton, John Cokeson, and John Waller, who have gone surety for William Mapelle both for the fine and his future good behaviour, as above.

m.20

172 ‹Warrants granted at that present Assize in the New Forest›

173 John Ratclyf etc., that it is delivered to sir Maurice Bargh and his associate, verderers of the New Forest.[1]

[1] Entry deleted.

174 John Radclyf etc., that it is delivered to Richard Rede esquire and his associates, regarders.[1]

[1] Entry deleted.

175 John Ratclif etc., that it is delivered to sir Edward Berkeley deputy lieutenant, one oak.

176 John Ratclif etc., that it is delivered to Thomas Jurdeyn junior, deputy to Edward Berkeley the forester of Burley, one oak and one beech.

177 John Ratclif etc., that it is delivered to William Ploufeld and his associates, clerks in the assize circuit, three *roboras* and three beech.

178 John Ratclif etc., that it is delivered to John Bisshop, forester of Linwood, one oak.

179 John Ratclif etc., that it is delivered to sir Maurice Barowyh and Thomas Troyes esquire, verderers of the New Forest, four *robora* and a buck.

180 John Ratclif etc., that it is delivered to Richard Rede and his associates, regarders of the New Forest, two *robora*, two beech, and two male deer.

181 John Ratclyf etc., that it is delivered to Robert Imberley, clerk to the Swainmote, one beech.

182 John Ratclyf etc., that it is delivered to Richard Marke, forester of the South Bailiwick, one oak.

183 John Ratcly etc., that it is delivered to Henry Erlesman, forester of Battramsley, one beech.

184 John Ratclif etc., that it is delivered to Richard Buison our deputy in our said office, in each bailiwick in the forest an oak, just as each of our deputies at each etc.

185 John Ratclif etc., that it is delivered to Nicholas Ticheborne, sheriff of Hampshire, a deer.

186 John Ratclif etc., that it is delivered to Henry Rake, riding forester, two oak and two beech.

187 John Ratclif etc., that it is delivered to Thomas Alwyn and Thomas Wulfan, rangers, to each of them a *robura* and a beech.

188 John etc., that it is delivered to Thomas Alwyn, receiver of the forest, one oak.

189 John etc., that it is delivered to John Duddelesfold, deputy lieutenant of the forest, one oak.

190 John etc., that it is delivered to Robert More, bowbearer, one *robura* and one beech.

191 John etc., that it is delivered to John Pocok, Richard North, Peter Pokok, and John Piper [and John Capelyn], foresters, to each of them an oak.

192 John etc., that it is delivered to John Coke, steward of the forest, two oaks.

193 Buckholt. ‹Warrants granted at that present Assize in Buckholt Forest.›

194 John Ratclif etc., that it is delivered to John Blake esquire, and to John Hamond, verderers, a beech to each of them.

195 John Ratclif etc., that it is delivered to William Ploufeld and his associates, clerks in the assize circuit, four beech.

m.21

196 Who are claiming Liberties. The abbot of Beaulieu appoints in his place Robert Dolyng, gentleman, he has a day the 15th St. Hilary etc.

197 The bishop of Winchester appoints in his place William Tichebourn', gentleman, and he has a day as above.

198 The prior of Christchurch appoints in his place John Calkyn his attorney, he has a day the 15th St. Hilary.

199 The prior of Breamore appoints in his place John Videan his attorney, and he has a day as above.

200 The prior of Mottisfont appoints in his place John Videan.

201 The keeper of Winchester College appoints in his place John Jakes.

202 Sir John Cheyne and Margaret his wife appoint in their place Michael Skyllyng their attorney, and they have a day the 15th Hilary at Westminster.

203 Richard Norton of Linwood appoints in his place William Tichebor'.

204 Ralph Stoure and Margaret his wife have a day the 15th Hilary for hearing their judgement upon showing exemplification.

205 The dean and chapter of Salisbury cathedral appoint in their place John Haptes, as above.

206 John Willer gentleman appoints in his place John Videan his attorney and he has a day the 15th St. Hilary.

m.22 [English]
207 By the king. Edward by the grace of God to our trusty and well beloved the Warden, Lieutenant, or Keeper of our New Forest, or to their deputy or deputies, greeting. For so much as our squire Edward Berkley mindeth to build beside the forest, we have granted him twenty oaks. Signed at Southampton the 19th December 1472.

m.23 [English]
208 By the king. To the right trusty and right well beloved cousin the earl of Arundel, warden of the new Forest, and to his lieutenant keeper there. We charge you that unto our right trusty and wellbeloved cousin the earl of Ormond, or unto the bringer of this in his name, you deliver twelve oaks from the bailiwick of Burley. Dated the 19th October 1486.

m.24
209 Henry by grace king of England etc. to sir John Radcliff, lord Fitz Walter, and sir Reginald Bray, justices itinerant . . . a pardon to Walter Bedell' . . . Signed at Westminster the 11th February 1491.

m.25 [English]
210 The regarders find that by ancient custom at a drift of the forest, the foresters should have 5d and no more for the pasture of any horse or mare that has been unshod for the year. And the pasture for a labouring beast, that shows any sign of labour, 1d and no more. And where the said keepers take 5d for a labouring beast, they be summoned by the court upon pain of 20s that no forester or walker do other than keep the ancient custom.

DL.39/2/12

m.26

211 ‹New Forest›. A Swainmote held on Tuesday 14th September 1489[1]

[1] Appears to be for 1490.

212 Robert Mour the bowbearer presents that on the 13th October 1489, Thomas Bruyne, husbandman of Wigley, at Paultons near to the forest had found, shot with an arrow, struck, and killed a hind, which had died at Bramblewood within the forest. And Thomas had taken and carried away the flesh without warrant or permission.

213 The rangers present that on the 18th May 1489, Thomas Sarusbury, a monk of Beaulieu Abbey, with greyhounds had killed, taken, and carried away one of the king's beasts in Breamore and another in Rhinefield, without permission or warrant.

214 Also they present that on the 24th July 1489 the same Thomas and William Buket, a merchant of New Salisbury, had entered the forest at Whitleyridge and with greyhounds had killed a buck, and had carried away the flesh without warrant or permission.

215 Also they present that in May 1489, Richard Hasard the vicar of Downton church, and William Mapell a yeoman of Downton, with greyhounds had killed two beasts at Studley, without warrant or permission.

216 Also they present that on the 9th November 1489, John Brereton esquire and Roger Brereton gentleman had entered the forest and with greyhounds had killed two beasts at Slufters, and had carried away the flesh without permission or warrant.

217 Also they present that on the 25th November 1489, Walter Malyne the rector of Bramshaw had found, shot with an arrow, struck, and killed a beast at *Hyndelys*, and had carried away the flesh without permission or warrant.

218 Also they present that on the 3rd July 1489, Elizabeth Bedyng a gentlewoman, John Newman a husbandman, and Stephen Houker a labourer, all of Newton Bury, had killed a beast in *La Lee* and had carried away the flesh without permission or warrant.

219 Also they present that on the 5th July 1489, Thomas Trusfeld yeoman of Totton, Thomas Marlow husbandman, and Richard James a labourer of Langley, had killed a beast at Halfpenny Herne, and had carried away the flesh without permission or warrant.

220 Also they present that on the 9th November 1489, the same Thomas and Thomas, and Thomas Lovell a yeoman of Calmore, had killed a beast at Costicles without permission or warrant.

221 Also they present that on the 10th May 1489, John Philippes a turner of Lyndhurst, and William Philippes his son, had killed a beast within the forest and had carried away the flesh without warrant.

222 Also they present that on the 20th June 1489 the same John and William had killed a beast within the forest and had carried away the flesh without warrant.

223 Also they present that on the 24th July 1489, Thomas Bruyne a husbandman of Wigley had entered the forest at Bramblewood and had shot with an arrow and killed a stag, and had carried away the flesh without permission or warrant.

224 Also they present that on the 13th October 1489, the same Thomas had shot with an arrow and wounded a hind at Wigley which had died within the forest, and he had taken and carried away the flesh without permission.

225 Also they present that on the 24th December 1488 the same Thomas had killed a sore in Linwood, and had carried away the flesh without permission or warrant.

226 Also they present that on the 24th July 1489, William Barry had killed a buck and a doe in *Ewer'* within the forest, and had carried away the flesh without permission or warrant.

227 The forester of the North Bailiwick presents that on the 2nd September 1489, Walter Malyn the rector of Bramshaw at Linwood in the said bailiwick had shot with an arrow and killed a sorel, and had carried away the flesh without permission or warrant.

228 Also they present that in 1488–9, Richard Lakes, a ?fawsett maker of Bramshaw, had taken and carried away a fawn he found in Linwood and Bramblewood.

229 Also they present that in the said month and year John Albrem *alias* John Arnewode junior of Marchwood had taken and carried away a hind calf he had found in Bartley Ford, without permission.

230 The forester of the South Bailiwick presents that on the 10th September 1489, Thomas Whitebye a yeoman of Beaulieu had killed a buck in the forest.

231 Also they present that on the 13th January 1489 the same Thomas, and Robert Freman a tanner of Beaulieu, with greyhounds had killed a buck in the same bailiwick, and had carried away the flesh without permission etc.

232 ‹The Regarders›. William Holcombe, Henry Knyght, John Ede, William Blake, Thomas Hendy . . ., William Colyer, Reginald Dollyng, John Andrews, Thomas Purse, Henry Hobbys, Simon Knolles, Richard Pocok, Simon Marchaunt, Nicholas Raulin, Nicholas Swetyngham, are sworn. And they affirm to be true all and each thing presented above and within.

DL.39/2/12

m.27 [English]

233 These be the presentments of the Swainmote of the New Forest held at Lyndhurst on the 10th December 1494

234 John Bysshopp the bailiff of Westlinwood presents that on Monday 31st March 1494, John Lane junior of Ringwood, with greyhounds killed a doe in Linford, and carried away the flesh without warrant or permission.

235 Also he presents that John Cole and John Curtyer of Lepe in a close called *Bottenhey* killed a red deer with a cord and carried away the flesh without warrant or permission.

236 Also he presents that before the 1st November 1493, John Cradde of Beaulieu killed a hind calf and carried away the flesh without warrant.

237 The bailiff of Burley presents that on the evening of the 14th September 1493, John Clerk of Minstead killed a doe in Bolderwood and carried away the flesh.

238 Also the said John Clerke and Thomas Newe on Sunday 29th June 1494 killed a buck and carried away the flesh without warrant or permission.

239 The keeper of the East Bailiwick presents that on the 20th August 1494, John Holehurste, a labourer of Beaulieu, in the said bailiwick killed a fallow stag and carried away the flesh without permission or warrant.

240 The bailiff of the South Bailiwick presents that Thomas Whytby, a tailor of Beaulieu, in 1493–4 entered the said bailiwick and killed a buck and carried away the flesh without warrant or permission.

241 The bailiff of Burley presents that on Tuesday 17th September 1493, William Okeden of Ellingham entered the said bailiwick and killed three deer, that is to say a buck, a sore, and a pricket, and carried away the flesh without warrant or permission.

242 Also he presents that the same day and year Walter [Malyn] the parson of Bramshaw with William Okeden entered the said bailiwick and killed a buck and two does, and carried away the flesh without warrant or permission of any keeper.

243 Also the bailiff of the North Bailiwick presents that on Friday 23rd August 1493, Richard Roke a labourer of Whiteparish entered the said bailiwick and with an arrow killed a pricket and carried away the flesh without warrant or permission.

244 Also he presents that on the 12th July 1494, John Irysshe, a husbandman of Downton, killed a hind with an arrow and carried away the flesh without warrant or permission. He is placed by the pledge of sir Maurice Barow and Richard Eliot.

245 Also he presents that on the 14th September 1493, William Mapull of Downton entered the said bailiwick and with greyhounds killed a buck and carried away the flesh without warrant or permission. He is placed by pledge, namely of the said Maurice Barow and Richard Eliot.

m.27d
246 Sureties of John Coole, husbandman of Exbury. Thomas Rok[1] yeoman of Eling, and William Grene, yeoman of Poole in Dorset. Who the 15th November 1496 at Westminster have gone surety for the said John, both for the fine and for his future good behaviour, etc.

m.28 [English]
247 Also that Richard Kymbrege of Marchwood killed two hind calves with his hounds in 1491–2.

m.29 [English]
248 Also that Thomas Lancaster, servant to John Coke of Ellingham, was taken in the bailiwick of Burley on the 12th February 1492 with a brace of greyhounds hunting by night contrary to the statute.

m.30 [English]
249 Also that in September 1492, Robert the prior of Christchurch killed a red deer with his bow in Hinton Close.
Also Carde, huntsman of the abbot of Beaulieu, killed a sorel the week before the 18th October.

Also the same Carde killed a hind calf with his hounds in Exbury the week before the 30th November.
Also Robert Kyng killed a red deer within John Collys bailiwick the week before the 24th August in the said year.

m.31 [English]
250 Also that sir William Holme, a priest of Salisbury, on Monday the 17th September 1492 with his greyhounds killed a sore in Fritham Bailiwick without leave of any keeper.

m.32 [English]
251 It is presented by an officer that Robert Dyer of Hordle, otherwise called Robert Foster, on the 15th October 1492, in Set Thorns in Battramsley Bailiwick felled and carried away twelve loads of green thorns.

m.33 [English]
252 Also that Edward Wellyby a priest on the 25th August 1492 with his greyhounds in the bailiwick of Fritham killed three bucks, a pricket, and a doe without permission or authority of any keeper.

m.34 [English]
253 John Pyper presents that on Saturday 25th August 1492, Edward Wellyby a priest recently of ..lton in Wiltshire, with his greyhounds killed one of the yeoman of the king's hunt.
Also William Regge[1] and John Lovejay entered the North Bailiwick and with their greyhounds killed three deer, that is to say two prickets and a tegge, without permission of any keeper.
Also on the 7th June 1493, Richard Carter yeoman of Beaulieu came to the bailiwick and took *aryder* and carried it away.

[1] Deleted.

m.35 [English]
254 The bailiff of Godshill presents that in the summer of the 8th year [1492–3], John Colens the bailiff of Godshill killed a buck, and a doe with an arrow and carried away the flesh without permission of any keeper.

m.36 [English]
255 On the 12th June 1493, Richard Carter yeoman of Beaulieu took a deer in the East Bailiwick and carried it away.

m.37 [English]
256 Also that on the 12th August 1493, John Rogers junior of Crow, struck and killed a buck with a broadhead [arrow] between Burley and Battramsley bailiwicks.

m.38 [English]
257 That the 10th January 1494, John Norys a butcher of Horton in Dorset was taken in Burley bailiwick hunting with four brace of greyhounds, hunting with persons unknown, against the statute.

m.39 [English]
258 That on the 20th December 1492, John Alver' junior of Crow was taken when going to stalk in the bailiwick of Burley. He was also taken whilst hunting in the same bailiwick on the 3rd February 1494.

C.99/53

259 Appointment of Deputies to Henry earl of Holland. Letters addressed to sir John Finch, chief justice of the Court of Common Pleas, and to sir John Bridgman, chief justice of the County Palatine of Chester

Trusty and well beloved, we greet you well. Whereas we have appointed a justice seat to be held for our forest called the New Forest, and also for our forests of Chute, Alice Holt and Woolmer, by our right trusty and well beloved cousin and counsellor Henry earl of Holland, chief justice and justice in eyre of all our forests, chases, parks, and warrens on this side of Trent, one of which justice seats for our said forest called the New Forest is to commence on the 24th day of August next at Lyndhurst in our county of Southampton, and the said justice seat for our said forest of Chute is to begin on the 22nd of the same month at Woodhouse, and for Alice Holt and Woolmer on the 20th at Binsted, and all the justice seats to be continued at the places named, or at any other place or places where our said chief justice shall think fit, until our affairs for these forests shall be settled according to our forest laws. We require you therefore, according to the trust and confidence we repose in your wisdom, learning and fidelity, to be there present and assistant to our said chief justice and justice in eyre, the better to advise him in such points of law as maybe fall out before him, that so the many abuses happening and increasing daily in these as in other forests for want of the due observance of our forest laws may be reformed. Given under our signet at our palace of Westminster the 16th day of June in the eleventh year of our reign [1635].

C.99/53

260 Certificate to the inhabitants of Lyndhurst

Henry earl of Holland, baron of Kensington etc., chief justice and justice in eyre of all his majesties forests, chases, parks, and warrens on this side of Trent, to the officers and ministers of the New Forest. It appears by certificate from the earl of Southampton, lord warden of the said forest, and by sir William Uvedall, lieutenant of the said forest, that license is required for diverse of the inhabitants of Lyndhurst, whose names are given in the certificate, to build stables and lodgings for the accomodation of his majesties attendants during the period of his stay there, [such work] not to disturb the game in the forest. His majesty has been pleased to give direction regarding this, and I do hereby authorise the said inhabitants of Lyndhurst, namely John Chamberlayne gent., Thomas White gent., Edward Fitchett gent., Henry Castilion gent., Hercules Turvile gent., Cheney Walbwe, James Elcombe, James Phillippes, Barger widow, Richard Stote, John Reynolds, William Elcombe, Richard Elcombe, Edward Bright, George Bright, James Brokenshawe, Phillip Veysey, William Wellen, [Blank] Gouldston, John Hibberd, James Waterman, John Mortying, John Lawrence, Walter Pyle, Thomas Bullocke, William Waterman, John Waterman, Richard Pococke, John Pococke, Anthony Buckle, James Barry, John Hardinge, Thomas Tilley, Richard Gascoigne, Thomas Phillippes, John Jewer, Edward Welsh, Anthony Jewer, Belfrey widow, John Buckler, and William Buckler, to erect and build such lodgings and stables as may be fit and requisite to receive and entertain and lodge his majesties train. Hereby requiring you, and whom it may concern, to permit and suffer the above named inhabitants so to do without let or hindrance, and this shall be sufficient warrant in that behalf. Given at Whitehall the 26th February 1634/5.

C.99/49

m.4

261 ‹The New Forest in the county of Southampton› Court called the Swainmote held at Lyndhurst on Monday 15th September 1634 before the foresters, verderers, regarders, agisters . . .
[the heading is badly damaged]

262	Keeper.	Thomas earl of Southampton, keeper and warden of the forest, is attending the king.
	Lieutenant.	Sir William Uvedale, lieutenant of the forest, is attending the king.
	Steward.	Robert Mason, armiger, steward of the forest, has appeared through Hercules Turvile, under forester.
	Bow Bearer.	John Kempe, armiger, bow bearer of the forest, has appeared.
	Riding Forester.	Cuthbert Bacon, armiger, riding forester of the forest, has appeared.
	Rangers.	Robert Knapton and Thomas Browne, gentlemen, have appeared but are presenting nothing.

263	Burley.	Philip earl of Pembroke and Montgomery, knight of the very noble Order of the Garter, lord of the king's chamber and a privy counsellor, forester, is perambulating attending the king.
	Battramsley.	Cuthbert Bacon, armitager, forester, has appeared.
	Fritham.	Arthur Oxford, gentleman, forester, is excused.
	Linwood.	Henry Hastings, armiger, forester, is excused.
	Godshill.	Sir Thomas Penruddocke, forester, has not appeared therefore in mercy 10s.
	Lyndhurst In bailiwick.	John Chamberlaine, armiger, forester, has appeared.
	East bailiwick.	Sir Richard Uvedale, forester, is excused.

	North bailiwick.	John Knight, armiger, forester, has appeared.
	South bailiwick	Michael Le Jeune, gentleman, forester, has appeared.
264	Verminer.	Henry Gifford, armiger, has appeared.
	Verderers.	Richard Goddard, armiger, and William Beeston, armiger, verderers.
265	Regarders.	William Battyn, gentleman, has appeared. Ambrose Ringwood, gentleman, has appeared William Gose, yeoman, has appeared. Andrew Hobbes, yeoman, has appeared. Michael Call, yeoman, is sick and in his place is sworn Walter Drue. Edward Skott, gentleman, has appeared. John Smith has appeared. William Coles has appeared. John Bannister has appeared. William Tyne, gentleman, has appeared. Richard Ingpen, gentleman, has appeared. Thomas Hyde, yeoman, is sick and in his place is sworn Richard Strong.
266	Agisters.	James Brockenshaw, yeoman, has appeared. William Rogers, yeoman, has appeared. Richard Stote is impotent and is excused.
	Riders.	Richard Gastin and Thomas Bullock have appeared.

267 Names of the under foresters

	Burley.	William Grove, gentleman, has appeared. Richard Wood is attending the perambulation. Henry Kymber, has appeared, and is presenting as is shown in the file. John Barlin is attending the perambulation.
268	Battramsley.	Nicholas Cluer has appeared, and is present-

ing as is shown in the file.
Henry Butler has appeared, and is presenting as is shown in the file.
William Rossiter is attending the perambulation.

269 Fritham.
Thomas Vennar has appeared, and is presenting as is shown in the file.
Thomas Clarke is attending the perambulation.
Nicholas Lawes is attending the perambulation.
Christopher Lawes has appeared, and is presenting as is shown in the file.
Richard Marsh is attending the perambulation.

270 Linwood.
Thomas Lacye senior has appeared.
William Lacye is attending the perambulation.
Thomas Lacye junior has appeared.
Lucas Larowse is attending the perambulation.

271 Godshill.
Francis Richardson has appeared, and is presenting as is shown in the file.
John Bramble has appeared.

272 In bailiwick.
John Call has appeared, and is presenting as is shown in the file.
Arthur Buckle has appeared, and is presenting as is shown in the file.

273 East bailiwick.
Edward Bright has appeared, and is presenting as is shown in the file.
John Bright is attending the perambulation.
John Oldinge has appeared.
Richard Dickman has appeared.

274 North bailiwick
George Bright junior has appeared, and is presenting as is shown in the file.

		Robert Butcher has appeared, and is presenting as is shown in the file.
		Stephen Warwick has appeared, and is presenting as is shown in the file.
		John Burden has appeared, and is presenting as is shown in the file.
275	South bailiwick.	George Bright senior has appeared and is presenting as is shown in the file.
		Thomas Rossiter has appeared and is presenting as is shown in the file.
		Henry Trippocke is attending the perambulation.
276	Woodward of the Forest.	Gabriel Lapp, armiger, woodward of the whole forest has appeared.
	Woodward of Minstead.	Michael Call senior, woodward of Minstead, is sick and therefore is excused.

277 Names of the vills, and the reeve and four men of each vill

	Vill of Exbury and Lepe.	Richard Wood, reeve John Tor James Ploughman William Dore Aubin Downer	sworn
278	Vill of Holbury and Langley	Nicholas Lambard, reeve John Amam William Weeld John Draper does not come therefore in mercy 5s	sworn
279	Vill of Buttsash and Hardley	John Cole, reeve William Collins John Selwood John Hardman William Thorpe	sworn
280	Vill of Pilley and	Zacharius Symond', reeve Christopher Hills	

	Warborne	Michael Ranstoe Richard Gifford John Elmes	sworn
281	Vill of Baddesley	Richard Jubber, reeve John Dobbins John Streete William Stark' Henry Wright	sworn
282	Vill of Battramsley and Wootton	James Elmes, reeve Thomas Younge James Deane Thomas Blake Thomas Wyat	sworn
283	Vill of Brock- enhurst and Brookley	John Henbist, reeve Thomas Norton Hugh Attlane Alexander Moore Ralph Gritnum	sworn
284	Vill of Godshill and Linwood	John Percye, reeve John Miles John Whitingstall William Newman John Amyes	sworn
285	Vill of Burley	William Anaor, reeve John Randole Stephen Purkis Edward Burges Thomas Randoll	sworn
286	Vill of Canter- ton and Fritham	Hugh Beckford, reeve Edmund Downer William Road' Robert Morris Andrew Taylor	sworn
287	Vill of	William Heale, reeve	

	Minstead	John Peirce senior Hugh Russell John Kinge Richard Goddin	sworn
288	Vill of Lyndhurst	John Stote, reeve Philip Vesye Bartholomew Stark' William Elcombe John Waterman	sworn
289	Vill of Bartley Regis and London Minstead	John Silver, reeve Robert Purkes James Purkes John Moulton Edward Sheperde	sworn

290 Names of the Freeholders of the New Forest

Exbury and Lepe

John Hills has not appeared, therefore in mercy 6s 8d
heir of Richard Cole, under age
Edmund Cole has appeared
Richard Moone has appeared
Stephen Palmer has appeared
Richard Moone has appeared
Richard Akeridge has appeared
West Fashion, gentleman, has appeared
Richard Cole …
… …
Stephen March, gentleman, is excused because he lives in the Isle of Wight
Sir Henry Compton is excused because he is not ?summoned *(som')*
Daniel Whitehead has appeared
Gilbert Pope is impotent, therefore he is excused
Richard Deane has appeared
William Hayward has appeared
John Kempe, armiger, has appeared
Richard Strong' has appeared

Richard Pittis, gentleman, has appeared
Richard Deane has appeared

m.4d

291 ?Buttsash ...
...
...

292 Hardley

Richard Pittis, gentleman, ...
Robert [Swayne] ...
John [Sansome] ...
George [Baskett] ...
Edmund [Brice] ...
Joan Thorpe, spinster, ...
heir of John Barton, under age
Nicholas Pescod ...
Henry Coomes ...
John Wadmore has appeared
John Brook' has appeared
Edward Keelinge has not appeared, therefore in mercy 5s.
John Tapper
John Harris

293 Pilley and Warborne

John Kempe, armiger, has appeared
Richard Knowles, gentleman, is sick
Simon Mist' is excused
William Goldwyer, gentleman, has appeared
Walter Drue has appeared
John Rickman has appeared
Jann' Turner, spinster
James Plowghman has appeared
George Carter has appeared
Christopher Hills has appeared
Thomas Boate has appeared
Richard Elmes has appeared
William Collins has appeared
Edmund Reeves has appeared

294 Baddesley

Henry Philpott, armiger, is excused

Walter Drue has appeared
Sir Henry Worsley, baronet, is excused
Thomas South, armiger, is excused
Richard Lyne, gentleman, has not appeared because he was not summoned
George Bright senior has appeared
William Kent has appeared
John Dobbins has appeared
Sir Henry Worsley, baronet, is excused
Ambrose Marsh is excused
John Streete has appeared

295	Battramsley and Wootton	Sir Francis Dowce is excused Sir Richard Tichborne, baronet, is excused Edward Skott senior, gentleman, has appeared Henry Tulce, gentleman, is excused because he lives outside the county John Penruddock, armiger, and William Goddard, gentleman, feoffees upon trust for William Goddard junior, are excused Sir William Mewis is excused because he lives in the Isle of Wight William Edwards has appeared James Elmes has appeared William Etheridge has appeared Edward Skott junior has appeared
296	Brockenhurst and Brookley	Robert Knapton, gentleman, has appeared Ralph Wilmott is excused Richard Draper has appeared John Emberley has appeared Robert Crooke is dead William Pitt is excused William Tapp has appeared Nicholas Hollyer has appeared Ralph Wilmott is excused Robert Uphill has appeared Thomas Norton has appeared Ralph Gretnum has appeared William Tapp has appeared

		Arthur Luke, gentleman, has appeared Ralph Gretnum has appeared Nicholas Hollyer has appeared Thomas Purdue has appeared
297	Burley	William Battin, gentleman, has appeared William Rogers has appeared John Nippered has appeared William Ovyat, gentleman, has appeared Christopher Lyne has appeared Joseph Coffyn has appeared John Warne is excused Christopher Garrett has appeared Henry Lyne senior, gentleman, is excused
298	Godshill and Linwood	Sir William Doddington is excused Richard Tucker has appeared Thomas Bradshaw has appeared John Aynell is excused by order of the eyre court William Gose has appeared Philip Rooke has appeared John Webb, armiger, has not appeared, therefore in mercy 6s 8d Edmund Okeden, armiger, has not appeared, therefore in mercy 6s 8d Edmund Weekes, gentleman, has not appeared, therefore in mercy 6s 8d
299	Canterton and Fritham	Sir Francis Dowce is excused Michael Call is sick and is excused Andrew Hobbs has appeared Roger Read' is excused John Bannister has appeared John Pinhorn' is under age Thomas Davis is under age Stephen Brownejohn has appeared Benjamin Edwards has appeared William Easton *alias* Mew has appeared Ann Knowell widow

300	London Minstead	Richard Goddard, armiger, has appeared Francis Raunger is excused John White has appeared John Crowcher has appeared John Robert', gentleman, is excused
301	Lyndhurst	Sir White Beconsawe Bartholomew Bulcley, gentleman, under age Henry Wiseman is outside the kingdom Lawrence Hyde, armiger, is excused James Elcombe is excused Walter Pyle has appeared William Hollowaye has appeared Robert Morris has appeared
302	Bartley Regis	Sir John Mill', baronet, is excused Richard Goddard, armiger Sir George Wrosley is excused Edmund White is excused Charles Lovell, gentleman, has appeared

303 Names of the Jurors for the lord king

William Hayward of Exbury, gentleman
Benjamin Edward' of Canterton, yeoman
Edmund Cole of Lepe, yeoman
Richard Deane of Exbury, yeoman
Edmund Brise of Langley, yeoman
John Dawson of the same, yeoman sworn
Henry Smith of Battramsley, yeoman
Thomas Lovell of Bartley Regis, yeoman
Robert Stryde of the same, yeoman
Richard Harris of the same, yeoman
Thomas Frinde of Minstead, yeoman

James Phillippes of Lyndhurst, yeoman
Thomas Corbyn of Baddesley, yeoman
George Carter *alias* Croker of Pilley, yeoman
John Rickman of the same, yeoman
John Nippered of Burley, yeoman sworn
John Scovell of Godshill, yeoman
Christopher Best of Linwood, yeoman

Thomas Hussye of Exbury, yeoman
Philip Rooke of Linwood, yeoman
Richard Cole of Lepe, yeoman

304 (1) It is presented by the foresters and other ministers of the forest and twelve jurors, and proved by the verderers, that Charles Stallenge recently of Laverstock in the county of Wiltshire, John Abarrowe recently of Ringwood, and Richard Shervile recently of Winterborne in the county of Wiltshire, gentlemen, and Edward Baines recently of Laverstock, and John Otrforde recently of Ringwood, grooms, on the 25th November 1633 entered the New Forest and then and there in a certain place called Melcombe Bottom [Milkham Bottom] in the bailiwick of Linwood were hunting with three greyhounds, and had put to flight, chased, and driven to death two deer, *anglice* a buck and a hart, to the destruction of the king's beasts and great harm of the forest and damage of the king, and against the laws and assizes of the forest. ‹Fine £20›. [See **406**]

m.5

305 (2) ... it is proved that ... recently of ...inge? ... in the night of the 26th August 1634 in a place called Barmore Throate [Balmer] in the South bailiwick was hunting, and had stalked *(pedetentavit)* with a horse, with a strung *(tensa)* crossbow and arrow ... ‹Fine £20›.

306 (3) ... it is proved that Richard Stote, yeoman, recently of Lyndhurst, on the 11th December 1633 had, and was in charge of, a pernicious *(nocivum)* dog at Lyndhurst, which dog in the night of the same day had hunted at a place called Low Meade within In bailiwick, and had put to flight and chased a deer ... ‹Fine £5› [See **403**]

307 (4) ... it is proved that Felix Lovell, yeoman, recently of Marchwood, is a common offender of venison and an abetter of venison offences throughout the forest, and in the night of the 23rd January 1634 he had and received in his house two unknown men with a greyhound, which men the same night in a place called Burned Heath in the East bailiwick had hunted, chased, and driven to death a brace of deer, and had then taken and carried off the flesh to the house of Felix ... ‹Fine £10 by warrant›.

308 (5) ... it is proved that Oliver Cowherd, yeoman, recently of

Holmore in the parish of Hale, on the last day of June 1633 in a place called Dryeleazue within Godshill bailiwick had hunted with a gun loaded with powder and shot, and had shot at the king's deer ... ‹Fine £20›. [See **407**]

309 (6)... it is proved that John Davis, carpenter, recently of Lyndhurst, on the 10th February 1634 at Emery Downe within the In bailiwick, had and kept in his house a crossbow and arrows ... ‹Fine 20 ?nobles›.

310 (7) ... it is proved that William Wheatley, husbandman, of Brockenhurst, on the 2nd February 1634 at Brockenhurst within the land of Robert Knapton, gentleman, had and was carrying in his hand a gun with intent to commit an offence and to kill the king's deer ... ‹Fine £10›.

311 (8) ... it is proved that William Wheatley on the 8th December 1633 and on various previous times, had perambulated the common land within the land of Robert Knapton with a gun loaded with powder and shot, and on the 8th December he was shooting at fowls ... ‹Fine £10›.

312 (9) ... it is proved that Thomas Huet, husbandman, recently of Pawletts Moor in the parish of Eling, on the 20th July 1634 in a place called Palsum within the bounds of the Guardian, Scholars, and Clerks of St. Mary's College near Winchester, was hunting with a gun loaded with powder and shot, with the intention of killing and evildoing to the king's beasts ... ‹Fine £10›. [See **730**]

313 (10) ... it is proved that John Archer, yeoman, recently of Brook, on the 25th May 1633 in a place near to Stirs Hedge and Brook Hedges within the North bailiwick, cut down and felled five timber trees worth 20s ... ‹Fine £10›.

314 (11) ... it is proved that Thomas Wyatt, husbandman, recently of Wootton, and George Stevens, husbandman, recently of Milton, on the 11th February 1634 in Wootton Coppice within Battramsley bailiwick, cut down and felled fifteen small stumps *(parvul' Caudices) anglice* stubs worth seven shillings ... ‹Fine ... ›.

315 (12) ... it is proved that George Bright senior, underforester, recently of Whitley Ridge Lodge in the South bailiwick, on the 20th March 1634 in the South bailiwick cut and lopped the branches of various trees for unlawful wood *(cablicio)*[1] worth 16s, more to sell for his own advantage than for the necessary forage of the king's beasts ... ‹Fine 5s›.

[1] *Cablicium* — the usual translation is windfall wood or brushwood, but in this context refers to browsewood.

316 (13) ... it is proved that Arthur Oxforde, gentleman, recently of Bolderwood Lodge, on the 20th March 1634 in the bailiwick of Fritham cut and lopped the branches of various trees for browsewood worth £6, more to sell for his own advantage than for the necessary forage ... ‹Fine £5›.

[Entries **317** to **322** follow the same formula as entry **316** and are of the same date]

317 (14) ... Thomas Rossiter, yeoman, underforester recently of Ladye Crosse Lodge ... in the South bailiwick ... browsewood worth 20s ... ‹Fine 20s›.

318 (15) ... Cuthbert Bacon, armiger, forester of Battramsley bailiwick ... browsewood worth £8 ... ‹Fine 20s›.

319 (16) ... Henry Butler, yeoman, underforester recently of Wilverly Lodge in Battramsley bailiwick ... browsewood worth £4 ... ‹Fine 20s›.

320 (17) ... Edward Bright, yeoman, underforester recently of Dynny Lodge in the East bailiwick ... browsewood worth 8s ... ‹Fine 2s›.

321 (18) ... John Oldinge, yeoman, underforester recently of Ashers Lodge in East bailiwick ... browsewood worth 8s ... ‹Fine 2s›. [See **781**]

322 (19) ... Stephen Warwicke, yeoman, underforester recently of Berkly Regis [Bartley Regis] in the North bailiwick on the 20th March 1634 cut and lopped six Colefyers *(Carbonar')* for browsewood worth 48s ... ‹Fine 20s›.

323 (20) ... Stephen Warwicke ... on the 11th November 1633 ... in the North bailiwick in places called Stubby Hatt, Halfepenny Hearne, and upon the water near to Halfpenny Herne, after the time of browsing *(frondation')* until the 1st May 1634, did browse *(frondidit)*, and cut and lopped the large branches of various trees, by estimation three Colefyers worth 15s ... ‹Fine 20s›.

324 (21) ... Arthur Buckle, yeoman, [underforester] in the In bailiwick, recently of Lyndhurst, on the 20th March 1634 in the In bailiwick cut and lopped the branches of various trees for browsewood worth 48s ... ‹Fine 5s›.

325 (22) ... Arthur Buckle, yeoman, underforester ... on the 20th March 1634 at Matley in the East bailiwick, cut and lopped part of an oak worth 5s without assignment on the pretence that it was lifeless ... ‹Fine 5s›.

m.5d

326 (23)... John Call, underforester, recently of Ironshill Lodge, on the 20th March 1634 within the In bailiwick, cut and lopped the branches of various trees for browsewood ... [document damaged]

327 (24) ... George Bright, yeoman, underforester, recently of Malwood Lodge, on the 20th March 1634 in the North bailiwick, cut and lopped the branches of various trees for browsewood ... ‹Fine 5s›.

328 (25) ... Nicholas Lawes, underforester, of Fritham Lodge in the bailiwick of Fritham, on the 20th March 1634 in Iware [Eyeworth] and Studley Head, cut and lopped the branches of various trees for browsewood, worth 8s, more to sell for his own his own advantage than for the necessary forage of the king's beasts ... ‹Fine ...›.

329 (26) ... Thomas Lacye, underforester, recently of Linwood, on the 20th March 1634 within the bailiwick of Linwood, cut hollies and thorns worth 10s, more to sell for his own advantage than ... ‹Fine 2s›.

330 (27) ... William Grove, gentleman, underforester recently of Homeslye Lodge [Holmsley], on the 20th March 1634 in the bailiwick of Burly, cut, felled, and lopped the branches of various trees, namely of oaks, hollies, and thorns, worth ..., of which many of the hollies and thorns were felled ... ‹Fine 5s›.

331 (28) ... Robert Butcher, underforester, recently of Bramshaw, on the 20th March 1634 in the North bailiwick, cut and lopped the branches of various trees for browsewood, worth 24s, ... ‹Fine 5s›.

332 (29) ... Robert Marks, husbandman, recently of Brockenhurst, on the 28th December 1633, in a place called Ramnar [Ramnor] in the South bailiwick, cut and felled fifty-two white and black thorns containing two cart loads *(vehes)* worth 20s, and a load of the same he took by his own waggon *(plaustro)* drawn by four horses worth £10 ... ‹Fine £10 and ...›.

333 (30) ... Robert Kymber, husbandman, recently of Hale, on the 11th February 1634 in a place called Bromehill [Broom Hill SU2614] within the North bailiwick, cut and felled an oak stump *(quercum Caudicem)* worth 5s ... ... ‹Fine 5s pardon ...› [See **408**]

334 (31) ... Christopher Stride, yeoman, of Minstead, on the 20th October 1633 within the bailiwick of Fritham, cut and lopped two cartloads of dry wood worth 4s ... ‹Fine 5s›. [See **411**]

335 (32) ... Benjamin Hancocke, tailor, recently of Lyndhurst, on the 8th September 1634 in a place called Lyndhurst Greene within the In bailiwick, made a purpresture and newly erected a dwelling house where no dwelling house was before ... ‹Fine £3›.

336 (33) ... Simon Husee, labourer, recently of Minstead, on the 1st June 1633 in a place called Shave in the North bailiwick, and enclosed [land] with a hedge ... ‹Fine 40s. Let it be thrown down›. [See **412**]

337 (34) ... Thomas Pearcye, husbandman, recently of Godshill, on the 1st September 1634 in a place near to Godshill Gate in the bailiwick of Godshill, made and newly inclosed a purpresture, and hedged a parcel of land containing three roods within the soil of the king ... ‹Fine 10s›. [See **409**]

338 (35) ... Thomas Percy, husbandman, recently of Godshill, on the 1st September 1634 in various places within the bailiwick of Godshill, cut and dug a thousand turves worth 2s, and the same he took and carried off ... ‹Fine ...›.

339 (36) ... William Jubber, husbandman, recently of Stuckton, on the 14th November 1633, in a certain place within the covert of Amberwood in the bailiwick of Godshill, cut and felled a load of heath *(bruer')* worth 12d ... ‹Fine 10s pardon etc›. [See **413**]

340 (37) ... Thomas Wolfe, husbandman, recently of Minstead, on the 8th September 1634 in a place called Longbrooke [SU2510] in Fritham bailiwick, cut, took, and carried away a cart load of heath *(erica)* and herbage *(silicis)* there growing ... ‹Fine 5s›. [See **410**].

341 (38) ... Erasmus Bradber, victualler, of Heeth [Hythe] on the 1st September 1634 in a place near to the Noads in the East bailiwick, cut and dug nine thousand turves worth 18s, and these he took and carried away ... ‹Fine £4 [cancelled] 10s by warrant›. [See **731**]

342 Which all is signed with their seals by the verderers, foresters, regarders, and all the other ministers of the forest following the form of the statute thus ordained and provided.
William Battin, Cuth Bacon, Ric Goddard, Will Beeston, Andrew Hobbs, Henry Gifford, William Twyne, John Smith, John Bannister, Richard Ingpen, Edward Scott, Walter Drue, Richard Strong', Ambrose Ringwood, Willm Gosse, Willm Coles, Tho Penruddock, John Chamberlayne, Robt Knapton, Thomas Browne, James Brokenshaw, Willm Rogers [made his mark].

C.99/49

m.1

343 ‹The New Forest in the county of Southampton› Forest Pleas held at Lyndhurst and adjourned on Wednesday 24th September 1634 before sir Richard Tichborne Bt., Robert Mason and Thomas Lee, armigers, deputies for the New Forest of the most noble Henry earl of Holland, chief justice and justice in eyre of all the forests, parks, chases, and warrens of the king this side of the river Trent, knight of the Order of the Garter and a privy counsellor, by virtue of the commission of the said Henry etc., by virtue of statute ordered and provided in a case of this kind, managing by the said sir Richard Tichborne Bt., Robert Mason and Thomas Lee, armigers, and others directed, given the 9th July 1631.

344	Keeper.	Thomas earl of Southampton, keeper and warden of the forest.
	Lieutenant.	Sir William Uvedale, lieutenant of the forest.
	Steward.	Robert Mason, armiger, steward of the forest.
	Bow Bearer.	John Kempe, armiger, bow bearer of the forest.
	Riding Forester.	Cuthbert Bacon, armiger, riding forester of the forest.
	Rangers.	Robert Knapton and Thomas Browne, gentlemen

345	Burley.	Philip earl of Pembroke and Montgomery, knight of the very noble Order of the Garter, lord of the king's chamber, and a privy counsellor, forester, is attending the perambulation.
	Battramsley.	Cuthbert Bacon, armiger, forester.
	Fritham.	Sir John Jephson, forester.
	Linwood.	Henry Hastings, armiger, forester.
	Godshill.	Sir Thomas Penruddocke, forester.
	Lyndhurst In bailiwick.	[left blank]
	East bailiwick.	Sir Richard Uvedale, forester.

	North bailiwick.	John Knight, armiger, forester.
	South bailiwick.	Michael le Jeune, gentleman, forester.
346	Verminer.	Henry Gifford, armiger, verminer of the forest.
	Verderers.	Richard Goddard, armiger, and William Beeston, armiger, verderers of the forest.
347	Regarders.	William Battyn, gentleman. Ambrose Ringwood, gentleman. William Gose, yeoman. Andrew Hobbs, yeoman. Michael Cawle, yeoman. Edward Skott, gentleman. They have appeared. John Smith, yeoman. William Coles, yeoman. John Bannister, yeoman. Thomas Hide, yeoman. William Twyne, gentleman. Richard Ingpen, gentleman.
348	Agisters.	James Brockenshawe, yeoman. William Rogers, yeoman. Richard Stote, yeoman.
	Riders	Richard Gastin Thomas Bullocke

349 Names of the under foresters.

	Burley.	William Grove, gentleman. Richard Woods. Henry Kember. John Barlin.
350	Battramsley.	Nicholas Cluer. Henry Butler. William Rossiter.

351 Fritham.	Thomas Venner. Thomas Clarke. Nicholas Lawes. Christopher Lawes. Richard Marsh.
352 Linwood	Thomas Lacye senior. William Lacye. Thomas Lacye. Lucas Larowse.
353 Godshill.	Francis Richardson. John Bremble. William Richardson.
354 In bailiwick.	John Cawle. Arthur Buckell.
355 East bailiwick.	Edward Bright. John Oldinge. Richard Dickman.
356 North bailiwick.	George Bright junior. Robert Butcher. Stephen Warwicke. John Burden.
357 South bailiwick	George Bright senior. Thomas Rossiter. Henry Trippocke.
358 Sheriff	Edward Hooper, armiger, sheriff of the county of Southampton.
Woodward.	Gabriel Lapp, armiger, woodward of all the forest.

m.1d

[Woodward of Minstead].	Michael Cawle senior, woodward of Minstead.

359 Names of the vills, and the reeve and four men of each vill. [Only the headings are listed. No names are entered].

Exbury and Lepe	Holbury and Langley	Buttsash and Hardley
Pilly and Warborne	Baddesley	Battramsley and Wootton
Brockenhurst and Brookley	Godshill and Linwood	Burley
Canterton and Fritham	Minstead	Lyndhurst
	Bartley Regis and London Minstead	

360 Names of the Freeholders of the New Forest.

Exbury and Lepe

John Hills
heir of Richard Cole
Edmund Cole
Richard Moone
Stephen Palmer
Richard Moone
Richard Akeridge
West Fashion, gentleman
Richard Cole
John Cole
Stephen March, gentleman
Sir Henry Compton Bt.
Daniel Whitehead
Gilbert Pope
Richard Deane
William Heyward
John Kempe, armiger
Richard Stronge
Richard Pittis, gentleman
Richard Deane

361	Buttsash	Sir John Crooke John Richard, gentleman Ann Osey widow
362	Hardley	Richard Pittis, gentleman Robert Swayne, gentleman John Sansome, gentleman George Baskett, gentleman Edmund Brice Joan Thorpe heir of John Barton Nicholas Pescod Henry Coomes John Wadmore John Brooke Edward Keelinge John Tipper John Harris
363	Pilley and Warborne	John Kempe, armiger Simon Miste Richard Knowles, gentleman William Goldwyer, gentleman Walter Drue John Rickman Joan Turner spinster James Plowghman George Carter Christopher Hills Thomas Boate Richard Elmes William Collins Edmund Reeves
364	Baddesley	Sir Henry Philpott Walter Drue Sir Henry Worsley Bt. Thomas South, armiger Richard Lyne George Bright senior William Kent

		John Dobbins Sir Henry Worsley Bt. Ambrose Marsh John Streete
365	Battramsley and Wootton	Sir Richard Tichborne Bt. Sir Francis Dowce Edward Skott, gentleman Henry Tulce, gentleman John Penruddocke, armiger William Goddard, gentleman Sir William Mewis William Edwards James Elmes William Etheridge Edward Skott junior, gentleman
366	Brockenhurst [and Brookley]	Robert Knapton, gentleman Ralph Willmott Richard Draper John Emberley Robert Crooke William Pitt William Tapp Nicholas Hollier Ralph Willmott Robert Uphill Thomas Norton
m.2		
		Ralph Gretnum William Tapp Arthur Luke, gentleman Ralph Gretnum Nicholas Hollier Thomas Purdue
367	Burley	William Battin, gentleman William Rogers John Nippered William Oviatt, gentleman Christopher Lyne

Joseph Coffyn
John Warne
Christopher Garrett
Henry Lyne senior, gentleman

368 Godshill and Linwood
Sir William Doddington
Richard Tucker
Thomas Bradshawe
John Aynell
William Gose
Philip Rooke
John Webb, armiger
Edmund Okeden, armiger
Edmund Weekes, gentleman

369 Canterton and Fritham
Sir Francis Dowce
Michael Cawle
Andrew Hobbs
Roger Reade
John Bannister
John Pinhorne
Thomas Davis
Stephen Browne John
Benjamin Edwards
William Easton *alias* Mew
Ann Knowell widow

370 London Minstead
Richard Goddard, armiger
Francis Rainger
John White
John Crowcher
John Roberts, gentleman

371 Bartley Regis
Sir John Mill Bt.
Sir George Wrosley
Richard Goddard, armiger
Edmund White
Charles Lovell, gentleman

372 Names of the Jurors for the lord king
Christopher Garrett of Burley

William Oviatt of the same
Henry Coomes of Langley
William White of Bartley Regis
John Stride of Minstead
Roger Reade of Fritham
Walter Drue of Pilley
William Purdue of Baddesley
Joseph Coffyn of Burley
Richard Tucker of Godshill
James Elcombe of Lyndhurst
Richard Stronge of Lepe
John Gose of Bramshaw
Daniel Whitehead of Exbury
Walter Pile of Lyndhurst

373 At the Swainmote held at Lyndhurst on Wednesday the 14th September 1631 it was presented by the foresters and other officers of the forest, and by twelve jurors, and proved by the verderers, that Hugh Gardner, husbandman, recently of Linwood, on the 27th March 1630 entered the New Forest and then and there within the demesne woods of the lord king in the bailiwick of Linwood cut down and lopped four cartloads of unlawful wood under the excuse of fuelwood, value twelve shillings, and these he took and carried away and did his will etc., and it was required what he could say for himself, and adjudged etc. Hugh now comes and has submitted himself to the grace of the court, and thereupon is fined ten shillings for his offence, and to pay the value of the said wood, namely twelve shillings, and he is sent to prison until the fine is paid.

374 At the Swainmote held on Monday the 14th September 1631[1] it was proved that Robert Coyte, blacksmith, recently of Brook, on the 24th January 1629 in a place near to Cowle Moore Hedge [Coalmeer] in the North bailiwick, cut and felled a beech of timber worth eight shillings. Robert now comes and is fined ten shillings and to pay the value of the beech. ‹Fine made›.

[1] probably in error for 1629

375 At the Swainmote held on Monday the 14th September 1629 it was proved that Thomas Bullocke, tailor, recently of Lyndhurst, on the 15th December 1628 in a place called Trusloes Wood [Truslers] in the In bailiwick, cut and felled an oak of timber worth twenty shillings. Thomas now comes and is fined three pounds and bound not to offend in future. ‹Fine made›.

376 At the Swainmote held on Thursday the 14th September 1626 it was proved that Walter Bright, husbandman, recently of Fordingbridge, on the 29th May 1626 in a place near to Elinge Thornes Hill [Island Thorns] in Godshill bailiwick, turned over, dug up, and cut ten thousand turves worth ten shillings. Walter now comes and is fined etc. [amount omitted]. ‹Fine made›.

377 At the Swainmote held by adjournment on Monday the 14th September 1629 it was proved that Peter Curtis, husbandman, recently of Freerne Courte [Fryern Court, Burgate], on the 25th May 1629 at Cockle Hill in Godshill bailiwick, turned over and dug up without permission four thousand turves worth four shillings. Peter now comes and is fined four shillings. ‹Fine made›.

378 At the Swainmote held by adjournment on Wednesday [14th September] 1631 it was proved that John Stent, husbandman, recently of Linwood, on the 26th March 1631 at Linwood in the bailiwick of Linwood, made a purpresture and newly built a dwelling house where no house was previously. John now comes and is fined twenty shillings for the offence, and the house rented at five shillings a year. ‹Fine made›.

379 ‹Recognizances›
‹1633› (1) Thomas Steevens, yeoman, of Ossemsley acknowledges to owe the king £40. On condition that Thomas Steevens will appear at the next court of the justices in eyre held for the New Forest to answer to them for as much as will be charged against him on behalf of the king, and he will not withdraw from the court without permission.

m.2d
380 ‹...› (2) Henry Drover, husbandman, ... £40. ..., yeoman, ... £20. ..., yeoman, ... £20. On condition that Henry Drover will appear ...

381 ‹1633› (3) Christopher Best, yeoman, of Linwood ... £40. On condition that Christopher Best will appear ...

382 ‹1632› (4) Henry Biston, tanner, of Blashford ... £100. Stephen

Rooke, yeoman, of Rockford ... £50. On condition that Henry Biston will appear ...

383 ‹1633› (5) Christopher Biddlecombe, yeoman, of Hightown ... £40. On condition that Christopher Biddlecombe will appear ...

384 ‹1633› (6) Richard Draper, yeoman, of Brockenhurst ... £40. John Emberley, yeoman, of the same ... £20. Thomas Purdue, yeoman, of the same ... £20. On condition that Richard Draper will appear ...

385 ‹1633› (7) Richard Warwick, gentleman, of Milton ... £40. On condition that Richard Warwick will appear ...

386 ‹1633› (8) Francis Oliver, husbandman, of Burley ... £40. On condition that Francis Oliver will appear ...

387 ‹1632› (9) Henry Ford, husbandman, of Royden ... £40. John Ghoste, yeoman, of Boldre ... £20. Richard Draper, yeoman, of Brockenhurst ... £20. On condition that Henry Ford will appear ...

388 ‹1633› (10) Christopher Lyne, yeoman, of Over Kingston ... £40. On condition that Christopher Lyne will appear ...

389 ‹1633› (11) Anthony Robbyns, husbandman, of Burley ... £40. Henry Robbyns, yeoman, of the same ... £20. On condition that Anthony Robbyns will appear ...

390 ‹1633› (12) Anthony Dimocke, yeoman, of Ellingham ... £40. On condition that Anthony Dimocke will appear ...

391 ‹1633› (13) William Rogers, yeoman, of Burley ... £40. On condition that William Rogers will appear ... ‹He has appeared and continues until the next [court]›

392 ‹1633› (14) Joseph Coffin, yeoman, of Burley ... £40. William Ovylett, gentleman, of Ringwood ... £20. On condition that Joseph Coffyn will appear ...

393 ‹1633› (15) Francis Barry, yeoman, of Hyde ... £40. On condition that Francis Barry will appear ...

394 ‹1632› (16) Robert Longe, yeoman, of Flexforde ... £40. Thomas Purdue, yeoman, of Brockenhurst ... £20. On condition that Robert Longe will appear ...

395 ‹1633› (17) Thomas Tee, yeoman, of Breamore ... £40. On condition that Thomas Tee will appear ...

396 ‹1633› (18) Walter Plumbly, yeoman, of Breamore ... £40. On condition that Walter Plumbly will appear ...

m.3

397 ‹1632› (19) John Barlin, yeoman, of Burley ... £40. John Bannister, yeoman, of Bramshaw ... £20. On condition that John Barlin will appear ...

398 ‹1633› (20) John Wilcox, tailor, of Lyndhurst ... £40. James Brockenshawe, yeoman, of the same ... £20. On condition that John Wilcox will appear ...

399 ‹1633› (21) William Warne, yeoman, of Ripley ... £40. On condition that William Warne will appear ...

400 ‹1633› (22) Tristram Fawlkner, husbandman, of Lyndhurst ... £40. John Hibbard, husbandman, of the same ... £20. On condition that Tristram Fawlkner will appear ...

401 ‹1632› (23) George Burrard, gentleman, of Lymington ... £40. John Stride, yeoman, of Minstead ... £20. On condition that George Burrard will appear ...

402 ‹1633› (24) Stephen Whiteare, yeoman, of Burley ... £40. Joseph Coffyn, yeoman, of the same ... £20. On condition that Stephen Whiteare will appear ...

403 ‹1634› (25) Richard Stote, yeoman, of Lyndhurst ... £40. John Stote, cooper, of the same ... £20. Thomas Bullocke, tailor, of the same ... £20. On condition that Richard Stote will appear ... [See **306**]

404 ‹1632› (26) Roger Webb, husbandman, of Exbury ... £40. Philip Pitt, husbandman, of the same ... £20. Thomas Odber, yeoman, of the same ... £20. On condition that Roger Webb will appear ...

405‹1632› (27) Philip Pitt, husbandman, of Exbury ... £40. Roger Webb, husbandman, of the same ... £20. Thomas Odber, yeoman, of the same ... £20. On condition that Philip Pitt will appear ...

406‹1634› (28) Charles Stallenge, gentleman, of Laverstock in the county of Wiltshire ... £100. Hugh Gore, yeoman, of Stoake Umber in the county of Somerset ... £50. John Blackhead, yeoman, of Laverstock ... £50. On condition that Charles Stallenge will appear ... [See **304**]

407 ‹1634› (29) Oliver Cowherd, yeoman, of Howmore in the parish of Breamore ... £40. Arthur Harris, yeoman, of the same ... £20. On condition that Oliver Cowherd will appear ... [See **308**]

408 ‹1634› (30) Robert Kember, labourer, of Fordingbridge ... £40. John Bremble, yeoman, of Hale ... £20. On condition that Robert Kember will appear ... [See **333**]

409 ‹1634› (31) Thomas Percye, husbandman, of Godshill ... £40. Arthur Harrison, yeoman, of Hale ... £20. On condition that Thomas Percye will appear ... [See **337**]

410 ‹1634› (32) Thomas Woolfe, labourer, of Minstead ... £40. Edward Wright, fusterer, of the same ... £20. Thomas Sanders, labourer, of Bartley Regis ... £20. On condition that Thomas Woolfe will appear ... [See **340**]

411 ‹1634› (33) Christopher Stride, charcoal burner, of Minstead ... £40. William Waterman, yeoman, of Lyndhurst ... £20. On condition that Christopher Stride will appear ... [See **334**]

412 ‹1634› (34) Simon Husse, labourer, of London Minstead ... £40. William Waterman, yeoman, of Lyndhurst ... £20. On condition that Simon Husse will appear ... [See **336**]

413 ‹1634› (35) William Jubber, husbandman, of Stuckton ... £40. Benjamin Sillye, carpenter, of Lyndhurst ... £20. Nicholas Reade, yeoman, of Godshill ... £20. On condition that William Jubber will appear ... [See **339**]

C.99/52

m.1

414 Swainmote held at Lyndhurst on the 9th [June] ... [before] the feast of St. John Baptist ... 1635, and thereafter to the 22nd June, and thereafter to the 22nd July ... [before] the foresters, verderers, regarders, agisters, ... of the forest.
[Heading badly damaged]

415	Keeper	Thomas earl of Southampton, keeper and warden of the forest, is attending the king
	Lieutenant	Sir William Uvedale, lieutenant of the forest, is attending the king
	Steward	Robert Mason, armiger, steward, has appeared by Hercules Turvile, gentleman, his deputy
	Bow Bearer	John Kempe, armiger, bow bearer of the forest, has appeared
	Riding Forester	Cuthbert Bacon, armiger, riding forester, has appeared
	Rangers	Robert Knapton and Thomas Browne, gentleman, have appeared but are presenting nothing

416	Burley	Philip earl of Pembroke and Montgomery, knight of the very noble Order of the Garter, lord of the king's chamber and a privy counsellor, forester, is perambulating attending the king
	Battramsley	Cuthbert Bacon, armiger, forester, has appeared
	Fritham	Sir John Jephson, forester, has not appeared because he is sick
	Linwood	Henry Hastinges, armiger, forester, has not appeared therefore in mercy 20s.
	Godshill	Sir Thomas Penruddocke, forester, has not appeared therefore in mercy 20s.
	Lyndhurst	[left blank]
	East bailiwick	Sir Richard Uvedale, forester, has appeared
	North bailiwick	John Knight, armiger, forester, has appeared

	South bailiwick	Michael Le Jeune, gentleman, forester, has appeared
417	Verminer	Henry Gifford, armiger, verminer of the forest, has appeared
	Verderers	Richard Goddard, armiger, and William Beeston, armiger, verderers of the forest, have appeared
418	Regarders	William Battyn, gentleman Ambrose Ringwood, gentleman William Gose, yeoman Andrew Hobbes, yeoman Andrew Yalman, gentleman Edward Skott, gentleman John Smith, yeoman William Coles, yeoman John Bannister, yeoman John Ellyot, gentleman William Twyne, gentleman Richard Ingpen, gentleman they have appeared
419	Agisters	James Brockenshaw, yeoman William Rogers, yeoman Richard Stote, yeoman they have appeared
	Riders	Thomas Purdue and Thomas Bullocke, have appeared

420 Names of the under foresters

	Burley	William Grove, gentleman, is attending the perambulation Richard Wood' is attending the perambulation Henry Kimber has appeared John Barlin is attending the perambulation
421	Battramsley	Nicholas Cluer they have appeared Henry Butler William Rossiter is attending the perambulation

422	Fritham	Thomas Vennar has appeared	
		Thomas Clarke Richard Marsh	are attending the perambulation
		Nicholas Lawes Christopher Lawes	they have appeared
423	Linwood	Thomas Lacy senior William Rooke	have appeared
		Lucas Larowse Michael Call	are attending the perambulation
424	Godshill	Francis Richardson John Bramble	have appeared
		William Richardson is attending the perambulation	
425	In bailiwick	John Call Arthur Buckle	have appeared
426	East bailiwick	Edward Bright John Oldinge Richard Dickman	have appeared
427	North bailiwick	Robert Hill Robert Butcher John Burden	have appeared
428	South bailiwick	George Bright senior Thomas Rossiter	have appeared
		Henry Trippocke is attending the perambulation	
429	Woodward of the forest	Gabriel Lapp, armiger, woodward of the whole forest, has appeared	
	Woodward of Minstead	Michael Call senior, woodward of Minstead has not appeared because he is sick	

430 Names of the vills, and the reeve and four men

Vill of	Richard Wood, reeve

	Exbury	William Hichcocke	
	and Lepe	John Tomson	sworn
		Hugh Palmer	
		William Dore	
431	Vill of	Nicholas Lambard, reeve	
	Holbury	Thomas Wheeler	
	and	Nathaniel Uvedale	sworn
	Langley	Thomas Cockes	
		Henry Hoddes	
432	Vill of	Nicholas Due, reeve	
	Buttsash	Edward Rookes	
	and	John Cole	sworn
	Hardley	James Tr...	
		William Collins	

m.1d

433	Vill of	Thomas Corbyn, reeve	
	Baddesley	John Dobbins	
		William Starke	sworn
		Ambrose Brigshon	
		William Nordle	
434	Vill of	Edward Watte, reeve	
	Holbury	Christopher Hills	
	and	Michael Ranstone	sworn
	Langley[1]	Ellis Stokes	
		Edmund Rowese	

[1] In error for Pilley and Warborne.

435	Vill of	William Samber, reeve	
	Battramsley	William Frueborn	
	and	Thomas Hall	sworn
	Wootton	Richard Gate	
		Thomas Fain	
436	Vill of	Edward Cooper, reeve	
	Brockenhurst	John Warricke	
	and	Thomas Bramble	sworn
	Brookley	Robert Uphill	
		John Meryfeild	

437	Vill of Godshill and Linwood	Andrew Downer, reeve Thomas Whitingstall John Scovell John Kennell Robert Rooke	sworn
438	Vill of Burley	John Tarry, reeve Thomas Randall Edward Burte Nicholas Marica Henry Etheridge	sworn
439	Vill of Canterton and Fritham	Stephen Brownejohn, reeve John Swift Robert Coyte William Bennett Joel Thringe	sworn
440	Vill of Minstead	William Heale, reeve George Nicholls Richard Gayne John Write senior John Gates	sworn
441	Vill of Lyndhurst	Thomas Bullock, reeve Robert Mortymer John Hebbert Henry Muslewhite Philip Stryde	sworn
442	Bartley Regis and London Minstead	John Bulbecke, reeve Thomas Lovell William Saunders Robert Orer John Moulton	sworn

443 Names of the Freeholders of the New Forest

Exbury and Lepe	John Hills has appeared Anica Cole spinster, under age Edmund Cole has appeared Richard Moone has appeared

Benjamin Akeridge has appeared
West Fashion, gentleman
Richard Cole has not appeared, therefore in mercy 6s 8d.
Stephen Marc', gentleman, has not appeared, therefore in mercy 10s.
Sir Henry Compton has not appeared, therefore in mercy 10s.
Daniel Whitehead has appeared
Gilbert Pope is excused because he is impotent
Richard Deane has appeared
William Hayward is excused because he is living in the Isle of Wight
John Kempe, armiger, has appeared
Richard Stronge has appeared
Richard Pittes, gentleman has appeared
Richard Deane has appeared

444 Buttsash

Sir John Crooke has not appeared because he lives outside the county
John Richards, gentleman, under age
Ann Osey widow

445 Hardley

Richard Pittis, gentleman, has appeared
Robert Swayne, gentleman
John Sansome, gentleman
George Baskett, gentleman
heir of Edmund Brice has appeared
Joan Thorpe spinster
heir of John Barton
Nicholas Pescod, gentleman, has appeared
Henry Coomes has appeared
John Wadmore has appeared
John Brookes has appeared
Edward Keelinge has not appeared
John Tapper has appeared
John Harris has appeared

446 Pilley and Warborne

John Kempe, armiger, has appeared
Richard Knowles, gentleman

Simon Mist has not appeared because apprenticed, therefore he is excused
William Goldwyer, gentleman, has [not] appeared, therefore in mercy 10s.
Walter Drue has appeared
John Rickman has appeared
Janet Turner spinster
James Plowghman has appeared
George Carter has appeared
Christopher Hills has appeared
Thomas Boate has appeared
Richard Elmes has not appeared, therefore in mercy 10s.
William Collins has appeared
Edmund Reeves has appeared

447 Baddesley

Henry Philpott, armiger, has not appeared, but is excused because he is sick
Walter Drue has appeared
Sir Henry Worsley Bt. is excused
Thomas Sowth, armiger, is excused because in business with the king
Richard Lyne, gentleman, has appeared
George Bright has appeared
William Kent has appeared
John Dobbins has not appeared, therefore in mercy 6s 8d.
Sir Henry Worsley Bt. is excused
Ambrose Marsh has appeared
John Streete has appeared

448 Battramsley and Wootton

Sir Francis Dowce is excused because in business with the king
Sir Richard Tichborne Bt. is excused because in business with the king
Edward Skott senior, gentleman, has appeared
Henry Tulce, gentleman, has not appeared therefore in mercy 10s.
Henry Goddard, gentleman, is under age
Sir William Mewis is excused because he is

living in the Isle of Wight
William Edwards is excused because he was not summoned
James Elmes has appeared
William Etheridge has appeared
Edward Skott junior has appeared

449 Brockenhurst and Brookley

Robert Knapton, gentleman, has appeared
Ralph Wilmott has appeared
Richard Draper has appeared
John Emberley is dead
Robert Crooke is dead
William Pitt is dead
William Tapp has appeared
Nicholas Hollyer has appeared
Ralph Wilmott has appeared
Robert Uphill has appeared
Thomas Norton has appeared
Ralph Gretnum has appeared
William Tapp has appeared
Arthur Luke, gentleman, is excused because he is ?outside …
Ralph Gretnum has appeared
Nicholas Hollyer has appeared
Thomas Purdue

m.2

450 Burley

William Battyn, gentleman, has appeared
William Rogers has appeared
John Nippered has appeared
William Ovyate, gentleman, has appeared
Christopher Lyne has appeared
Joseph Coffyn has appeared
John Warne has appeared
Christopher Garrett has appeared
Henry Lyne senior, gentleman, has appeared

451 Godshill and Linwood

Sir William Doddington is excused
Richard Tucker has appeared
Thomas Bradshawe has appeared
John Aynell is excused because he is impotent

William Gose has appeared
Philip Rooke has appeared
John Webb, armiger, is excused
Edmund Ogden, armiger, is excused
Edmund Weekes, gentleman, is excused
Sir John Bruen is excused
Thomas Rookeley has appeared
Henry Good has appeared
Henry Rooke has appeared

452 Canterton and Fritham
Sir Francis Dowce is excused
Michael Cawle is sick, therefore he is excused
Andrew Hobbs has appeared
Roger Reade has appeared
John Bannister has appeared
John Pinhorne is under age
Thomas Davis is under age
Stephen Browne John has appeared
Benjamin Edwards has appeared
John Wormestal' has appeared
William Easton *alias* Mew has appeared
Ann Knowell widow
[blank] Gawyn, armiger

453 London Minstead
Richard Goddard, armiger, has appeared
Francis Rainger has appeared
John Chater has appeared
John Crowcher has appeared
John Roberts, gentleman, has appeared

454 Lyndhurst
Sir White Beconsaw has appeared
Bartholomew Bulcley, gentleman, is under age
Henry Wiseman is outside the kingdom
Lawrence Hide, armiger, has appeared
James Elcombe has appeared
Walter Pyle has appeared
William Holloway has appeared
Robert Morris has appeared

455 Bartley Regis
Sir John Mill Bt. is excused
Richard Goddard, armiger, has appeared

Sir George Wrosley has appeared through Richard Ingpen, holder of the land
Edmund White, clerk, has appeared
Charles Lovell, gentleman, has appeared

456 Names of the Jurors for the lord king

John Searle, gentleman, of Holbury
John Andrews, yeoman, of Brockenhurst
William Privet, yeoman, of Buttsash
John Dason, yeoman, of Langley
Richard Deane, yeoman, of Exbury sworn
Thomas Hussey, yeoman, of Exbury
John Aldridge, yeoman, of Baddesley
John Streete, yeoman, of Baddesley
George Chater, yeoman, of Pilley
James Elmes, yeoman, of Battramsley

James Plowman, yeoman, of Pilley
Richard Knight, yeoman, of Brockenhurst
Morgan Haynes, gentleman, of London Minstead
Robert Stride, yeoman, of Bartley Regis
Richard Pococke, yeoman, of Lyndhurst
John Chater, yeoman, of Minstead sworn
Stephen Purchas, yeoman, of Burley
John Tapper, yeoman, of Buttsash
Edward Burgis, yeoman, of Burley

457 (1) It is presented by the foresters and other ministers of the forest and twelve jurors and proved by the verderers that Robert Treswell, gentleman, recently of Westminster in the County of Middlesex, and Andrew Treswell, gentleman, of the same, entered the forest of the lord king called the New Forest, and then and there since the last regard of the said forest, within the king's demesne woods within the said forest, cut and felled one thousand five hundred oaks and beeches worth £1000, and sold the same and did their will, to the great destruction of the woods of the lord king and harm of the forest and damage of the lord king, and against the laws and assizes of the forest. ‹Fine ... £2000›.

458 (2) ... Stephen Dancey, shipwright, recently of Ratcliffe in the

County of Middlesex, since the last regard within the demesne woods, cut and felled one thousand oaks of timber worth £2000 … ‹Fine £3000›.

459 (3) … Thomas Williams, shipwright, recently of Rochester in the County of Kent, on the 1st May 1631 within the demesne woods in the various bailiwicks of North, East, In, Battramsley, Burley, and Fritham, cut and felled two thousand oaks worth £4000 … ‹Fine £1000›.

460 (4) … Gabriel Lapp, armiger, woodward of the New Forest, recently of Durneforde in the County of Wiltshire, on the 7th June 1628 entered the forest of the lord king called the New Forest and then and there within the demesne woods of the lord king in the East bailiwick, cut and felled eighty six decayed *(decass')* oaks *anglice Stubbs* worth £26 15s 4d … ‹Fine £5›.

461 (5) … Gabriel Lapp … on the 1st May 1628 … in the bailiwick of Fritham, cut and felled fifty five decayed oaks *anglice dotard trees* worth £26 … ‹Fine £10›.

462 (6) … Gabriel Lapp … on the 1st May 1628 … in the North bailiwick, cut and felled fifty decayed oaks *anglice dotard trees* worth £25 … ‹Fine £5›.

463 (7) … Gabriel Lapp … on the 1st May 1628 … in the North, Fritham, and Burley bailiwicks, cut and felled fifty five decayed oaks *anglice dotard trees* worth £12 … ‹Fine £10›.

464 (8) … Gabriel Lapp … on the 1st May 1629 … in the bailiwicks of Godshill and Westlinwood, sold two hundred and fifteen decayed oaks *anglice stubbs and dotard trees* worth £111 … ‹Fine £20›.

465 (9) … Gabriel Lapp … on the 1st May 1629 … in South and In bailiwicks, cut and felled forty decayed oaks *anglice stubbs* worth £20 … ‹Fine £5›.

466 (10) … Gabriel Lapp … on the 1st May 1631 … in the bailiwicks of Fritham and Godshill, cut and felled fifty decayed oaks *anglice decayed trees* worth £30 … ‹Fine £5›.

m.2d

467 (11) ... Gabriel Lapp ... on the 1st May 1632 ... at Bartley Regis in the North bailiwick, cut and felled thirty five decayed oaks *anglice stubbs* worth £20 ... ‹Fine £5›.

468 (12) ... Gabriel Lapp .... on the 1st May 1632 ... in Battramsley bailiwick, cut and felled eight decayed oaks *anglice stubbs* worth £3 ... ‹Fine £5›.

469 (13) ... Gabriel Lapp ... on the 1st May 1632 ... near to Iware [Eyeworth] Lodge Rayles in Fritham bailiwick, cut and felled thirty five decayed oaks *anglice stubbs and dotard trees* worth £20 ... ‹Fine £5›.

470 (14) ... Gabriel Lapp ... on the 6th June 1632 ... in Burley bailiwick, cut and felled twenty decayed timber *(maeremii)* oaks worth £10 ... ‹Fine £5›.

471 (15) ... Gabriel Lapp ... on the 1st May 1632 ... near to Whitley Ridge Rayles in the South bailiwick, cut and felled thirty five decayed oaks *anglice stubbs* worth £18 ... ‹Fine £5›.

472 (16) ... Gabriel Lapp ... on the 4th June 1633 ... in the bailiwicks of Godshill and Linwood, sold one hundred and three decayed oaks *anglice stubbs and dotards* worth £56 10s 4d ... ‹Fine £5›.

473 (17) ... Gabriel Lapp ... on the 5th June 1633 ... in Linwood, Fritham, Godshill and South bailiwicks, cut, felled, and sold one hundred and thirty nine decayed oaks *anglice stubbs and dotard trees* worth £85 2s ... ‹Fine £5›.

474 (18) ... Gabriel Lapp ... on the 3rd June 1663 ... within In, East, and South bailiwicks, cut and felled one hundred and eighty three timber oaks worth £75 ... ‹Fine ...›.

475 (19) ... Gabriel Lapp ... on the 1st May 1635 ... in the bailiwick of Battramsley, cut and felled sixty decayed oaks *anglice decayed trees* worth £30 ... ‹Fine £5›.

476 (20) ... Thomas Leigh, armiger, recently of Testwood, on the

10th June 1635, near Cadnam path and Brockis Hill, and other places within the demesne woods in the North bailiwick, cut and felled eighty seven oaks and beeches containing one hundred loads worth £13 6s 8d, and these he took and carried off to Testwood … ‹Fine £40›.

477 (21) … Stephen March, gentleman, recently of Newport in the Isle of Wight, on the 1st March 1634, at Wootton Coppice in Battramsley bailiwick, cut and felled eight oaks *anglice pollard trees* worth 50s … ‹Fine £10›.

478 (22) … Charles Lovell, gentleman, recently of Bartley Regis, on the 8th June 1635, in a place called North Hay part of the fee of the said Charles within the North bailiwick, cut and felled thirty timber oaks *anglice tymber trees* worth £30, and sold the same … ‹Fine £10›.

479 (23) … Henry Gifford, armiger, recently of Burly Lodge, forester in the bailiwick of Burley, on the 1st May 1635 in various places in the said bailiwick, cut and lopped large branches of various oaks, beeches, and underwood on the pretence of browsewood *(cablicia)* worth £3, more to sell for his own use than for the necessary forage of the king's beasts … ‹Fine 5s›.

480 (24) … Cuthbert Bacon, armiger, recently of Rhinefield Lodge, forester in Battramsley bailiwick, on the 1st May 1635 in the said bailiwick, cut and lopped large branches of various oaks and beeches worth £3 under the pretence of browsewood, more to sell for his own use than for the necessary forage of the king's beasts … ‹Fine 5s›.

481 (25) … Henry Butler, yeoman, underforester recently of Wilverley Lodge in the bailiwick of Battramsley, on the 1st May 1635 in the said bailiwick, cut and lopped large branches of various trees of oak, holly and thorn … worth 20s … ‹Fine 2s›.

482 (26) … George Bright, yeoman, underforester of Whitley Ridge Lodge, on the 1st May 1635 in various places in the South bailiwick, cut and lopped large branches of various oaks and beeches worth 24s … ‹Fine 2s›.

483 (27) … Arthur Buckell, yeoman, recently of Pondhead, forester in the In bailiwick, on the 1st May 1635, in various places in the said bailiwick, cut and lopped large branches of oaks and beeches worth 10s ... ‹Fine 2s›.

484 (28) ... John Knight, armiger, recently of St. Denis, forester in the North bailiwick, the 1st January 1635 between Halpenny Hearne and Fritham Path in the said bailiwick, cut and lopped large branches of oaks and beeches worth £20 ... ‹Fine 20 nobles›.

485 (29) ... John Knight ... on the 19th June 1635 in various places in the North bailiwick, cut and lopped branches of oaks and beeches worth 40s under the pretence of browsewood, and it was converted into wood suitable for charcoal, and then and there similarly within the demesne woods in the North bailiwick, he cut and lopped various other branches of oaks and beeches worth 40s under the pretence of browsewood, and he took and carried away the same without the view of the regarders and did his will against the order of the court of the justice in eyre ... ‹Fine 10s›.

486 (30) ... John Knight ... on the 1st June 1635 in a place called Darke Hatt in the North bailiwick, cut and felled a beech worth 5s, and converted the same into wood suitable for charcoal ... ‹Fine 5s›.

487 (31) ... Robert Butcher, yeoman, underforester recently of Homy Hill Lodge in the North bailiwick, on the 1st May 1635 in the said bailiwick between Fritham Path and Homyhill, cut and lopped large branches of various oaks, beeches, and hollies worth 10s under the pretence of browsewood more to sell for his own use than for the necessary forage of the king's beasts ... ‹Fine 2s›.

m.3

488 (32) ... Arthur Oxford, gentleman, underforester recently of Bolderwood Lodge in the bailiwick of Fritham, on the 1st May 1635 in various places in the said bailiwick, cut and lopped large branches of oaks and beeches worth 20s ... ‹Fine 5s›.

489 (33) ... Edward Bright, yeoman, underforester recently of Dinny [Denny] Lodge in the East bailiwick, on the 1st May 1635 in various places within the East bailiwick, cut and lopped large branches of oaks and beeches and underwood worth 10s ... ‹Fine 2s›.

490 (34) ... Thomas Lacye, yeoman, recently of Linwood, and William Rooke, yeoman, of the same, on the 1st May 1635 in various places in Linwood bailiwick, cut, lopped, and felled vert, hollies, and thorns worth 10s under the pretence of browsewood, more to sell for their own use than for the necessary forage of the king's deer ... ‹Fine .. of them ... 2s›. [See **767**]

491 (35) ... Robert Oldinge, yeoman, recently of Berkly Betteshorne [Bartley Bisterne], on the 3rd June 1635 had incroached and intruded upon the king's demesne near to Pottersforde within the In and North bailiwicks, had cut and felled two oaks worth 20s, and took and carried them away to the disheritance of the king ... ‹Fine £5›.

492 (36) ... Richard Pococke, yeoman, recently of Lyndhurst; Robert Stryde, yeoman, of Bartley Regis; Thomas Browne, gentleman, of London Minstead; and John Barry, yeoman, of Fritham, tenants of the manor of Lyndhurst, on the 4th June 1635 within In, South, North, East, and other bailiwicks, took timber for building and repairing tenements or cottages, and similarly took branches *anglice frith* for making and repairing the hedges *(hayas)* upon their tenements at their liberty ... ‹Fine ... £5›. [See **784**]

493 (37) ... Giles Eyre senior, gentleman, recently of Brickworth in the county of Wiltshire, on the 6th April 1635 near Hore Wythy in the North bailiwick, cut and felled a timber oak, and thorns and *du. nos* then growing, worth 10s, and took and carried off the same ... ‹Fine 5s›. [See **780**]

494 (38) ... William Wilde, husbandman, recently of Brook, on the 12th January 1635 in a place called Broomehill [SU2614] in the North bailiwick, cut and felled an oak worth 6s 8d on the pretence of fuel wood ... ‹Fine 40s›.

495 (39) ... John Symons, labourer, recently of Bartley Regis, on the 10th March 1635 in a place called Lambs Corner [SU2912] in the North bailiwick, cut and felled a young beech worth 5s, and carried it away with a cart drawn by two horses worth £3, the property of a certain Richard Harris ... ‹Fine £10 and value etc.›.

496 (40) ... Henry Crocker, *alias* Carter, yeoman, recently of

Burley, on the 1st June 1635 near to Cannes within the bailiwick of Burley upon the fee of William Battin senior, gentleman, cut and felled three ash trees worth 10s ... ‹Fine £3›. [See **750**]

497 (41) ... Henry Crocker *alias* Carter on the 1st June 1635 near to Cannes upon the fee of William Battin, cut and felled three fertile *(frugifer')* oaks worth 9s ... ‹Fine 40s›. [See **750**]

498 (42) ... Hugh Attlane, yeoman, recently of Brookley, on the 1st March 1631 in Setthornes within the bailiwick of Battramsley, cut and felled an oak containing a cart load of timber worth 6s 8d, and carried it away with a cart drawn by two oxen and three horses worth £8 ... ‹Fine 40s and value etc.›.

499 (43) ... Hugh Attlane on the 1st October 1632 in Brinckton Wood [Brinken Wood] in Battramsley bailiwick, cut and felled an oak containing eight cartloads worth 20s, and carried it away with a cart drawn by two horses and two oxen worth £5 ... ‹Fine £5 and value etc.›.

500 (44) ... Thomas Furnar, husbandman, recently of Brockenhurst, on the 10th July 1635 at Copped Oake in Battramsley bailiwick, cut and lopped the green branches of an oak called Copped Oake worth 12s, and carried them away with his cart drawn by two horses and four oxen worth £8 ... ‹Fine 40s and value etc.›

501 (45) ... John Collett, husbandman, recently of Brockenhurst, on the 12th September 1634 in a place called Ramner [Ramnor] Greene within the South bailiwick, cut and lopped the branches of eight green oaks, on the pretence of fuelwood, containing four cartloads worth 10s, and carried them away with a cart drawn by a horse woth 20s ... ‹Fine £5 and value etc.›.

502 (46) ... John Collett *alias* Blacke, husbandman, recently of Brockenhurst, on the 9th November 1634 in a place called Barmore Wood [Balmer] in the South bailiwick, under the pretence of fuelwood cut and felled an oak worth 3s 4d, and with a cart drawn by a horse carried part of it away to the house of Joseph Collett at Brockenhurst ... ‹Fine £5 and value›.

503 (47) ... John Collett *alias* Blake on the 10th November 1634 in Holland Wood in the South bailiwick, cut and felled a green oak tree worth 2s ... ‹Fine £4›.

504 (48) ... John Purcas, charcoal burner, recently of Minstead, on the 27th March 1635 in a place called Ashers [Ashurst] within the East bailiwick, grubbed up *(eradicavit)* the roots of trees which he had felled worth 5s, contrary to the concession or dimission of the king ... ‹Fine 40s›. [See **770**]

505 (49) ... Sir John Cooper deceased, recently of Rockborne, on the 31st December 1633 in a close containing 12 acres called Whichbarry Meade in the bailiwick of Godshill, grubbed up and assarted two acres of coppice with various oaks growing there worth 40s, and now in the tenure of Lady Cooper the wife of John ... ‹Fine £20›.

506 (50) ... James Elmes, yeoman, recently of Battramsley, on the 1st May 1635 on his fee at Battramsley, grubbed up and assarted a close containing one hundred perches ... ‹Fine £5› [See **785**]

507 (51) ... William Whitehead, yeoman, recently of Battramsley, on the 1st June 1635, on the fee of Henry Goddard, gentleman, at Battramsley, grubbed up and assarted a covert containing one hundred and twenty perches ... ‹Fine £5›. [See **786**]

508 (52) ... Thomas Rossiter, yeoman, underforester recently of Ladye Crosse Lodge, on the 4th June 1635 within the rails about Ladye Crosse Lodge in the South bailiwick, grubbed up and assarted a parcel of heath containing by estimation half an acre, and he had brought back into cultivation *(in culturam redigevit)* and seeded with wheat, and enclosed with a high hedge so that the king's beasts were not able to jump at their liberty to and from the pasture ... ‹Fine 10s›.

m.3d

509 (53) ... Arthur Buckle, yeoman, underforester recently of Ashers [Ashurst] Lodge, on the 4th June 1632[1] within Ashers Lodge Rails in the East bailiwick, grubbed up and assarted a parcel of heath containing an estimated acre, and brought back into cultivation and seeded with oats and rye, and enclosed with a high hedge ... ‹Fine 5s›.

[1] possibly in error for 1635

510 (54) ... Francis Richardson, yeoman, underforester recently of Ashley Lodge, on the 4th June 1635 within Ashley Lodge Rails in the bailiwick of Godshill, grubbed up and assarted a parcel of heath containing an estimated acre, and brought back into cultivation and seeded with oats and rye, and enclosed with a high hedge ... ‹Fine 5s›.

511 (55) ... Edward Bright, yeoman, underforester recently of Dinny Lodge in the East bailiwick, on the 4th June 1635 within Dinny Lodge Rails, grubbed up and assarted an acre of heath, and brought back into cultivation and seeded with wheat, and enclosed with a high hedge ... ‹Fine 5s›.

512 (56) ... Cuthbert Bacon, armiger, forester recently of Rhinefield Lodge in Battramsley bailiwick, on the 4th June 1635 within the rails of Swesbury Lodge within the said bailiwick, grubbed up and assarted a parcel of heath containing an estimated four acres, and brought back into cultivation and seeded with wheat and rye, and enclosed with a high hedge ... ‹Fine 5s›.

513 (57) ... Robert Knapton, gentleman, recently of Brockenhurst, on the 15th June 1635 at Brockenhurst in the South bailiwick, grubbed up and assarted, within his fee, two closes of covert containing ten acres ... ‹Fine £20›.

514 (58) ... John Rodes, yeoman, recently of Brockenhurst, on the 15th June 1635 in the fee of Robert Knapton at Brockenhurst in the South bailiwick, grubbed up and assarted a close of covert containing four acres ... ‹Fine £12›. [See **756**]

515 (59) ... Christopher Davis, tanner, recently of Brockenhurst, on the 15th June 1635 in the fee of Robert Knapton, had grubbed up and assarted part of a coppice containing half an acre ... ‹Fine £5›. [See **757**]

516 (60) ... Hugh Attlane, yeoman, recently of Brookley, on the 1st November 1634 in Battramsley bailiwick, had grubbed up and assarted a parcel of Mox Coppice containing half an acre ... ‹Fine £3›. [See **728**]

517 (61) ... Richard Draper, yeoman, recently of Brockenhurst, on the 15th June 1635 within his fee at Brookley in the bailiwick of Battramsley, had grubbed up and assarted a close containing three acres ... ‹Fine £10›. [See **740**]

518 (62) ... Robert Knapton, gentleman, recently of Brockenhurst, on the 15th June 1635, at a place called Baltmore within his fee in the bailiwick of Battramsley, had grubbed up and assarted a parcel of covert containing one acre ... ‹Fine £6›.

519 (63) ... Nicholas Hollyer, yeoman, recently of Brookley, since the last regard of the forest, in his fee at Brookley in the bailiwick of Battramsley, had grubbed up and assarted a coppice containing half an acre ... ‹Fine £3›. [See **733**]

520 (64) ... John Morren, husbandman, recently of Brockenhurst, on the 15th June 1635 in the fee of Henry Goddard, gentleman, at Brockenhurst in the South bailiwick, had grubbed up and assarted a coppice containing half an acre ... ‹Fine £3›.

521 (65) ... Henry Crocker *alias* Carter, yeoman, recently of Burley, on the 1st June 1635, near a mount called Blacke Bush within the bailiwick of Burley in the fee of William Battyn senior, gentleman, had dug up and grubbed up two acres of gorse ... ‹Fine 40s›. [See **750**]

522 (66) ... Henry Crocker *alias* Carter, yeoman, recently of Burley, on the 10th June 1635, in an adjoining close near to Canens in the bailiwick of Burley, had dug and grubbed up three perches of large covert, and also he burned with fire *anglice hath burne beaked* an acre of land ... ‹Fine £4›. [See **750**]

523 (67) ... William Collins, husbandman, recently of Hardley, on the 9th June 1635 at Hardley in the East bailiwick in the fee of West Fashion, gentleman, had grubbed up and assarted fourteen perches of coppice ... ‹Fine 40s›. [See **752**]

524 (68) ... Henry Merceman, charcoal burner, recently of Exbury, on the 9th June 1635 in the fee of Gilbert Pope at Exbury in the East bailiwick, had grubbed up and assarted part of a coppice containing half an acre ... ‹Fine £3›. [See **776**]

525 (69) … William Battyn senior, gentleman, recently of Burley, on the 1st June 1635 in his fee at Burley, had enclosed with large ditches and high hedges ten acres of meadow and corn in separate closes … ‹Fine 40s and let them be thrown down›.

526 (70) … Stephen Whityer, yeoman, recently of Burley, on the 1st June 1635 at Burley, had enclosed with a large ditch and high hedge a pasture close containing two acres … ‹Fine 40s›. [See **753**]

527 (71) … John Randell, yeoman, recently of Burley, on the 1st June 1635 at Burley, had enclosed with a large ditch and high hedge, and had planted with oats, a close containing one and a half acres … ‹Fine 40s›. [See **742**]

528 (72) … Joseph Coffyn, yeoman, recently of Burley, on the 1st June 1635 at Burley, had enclosed with a large ditch and high hedge two closes of pasture and meadow containing four acres … ‹Fine 40s›. [See **771**]

529 (73) … Henry Etheridge, yeoman, recently of Burley, on the 1st June 1635 at Burley, had enclosed with a large ditch and high hedge a pasture close containing one acre … ‹Fine 40s›. [See **744**]

530 (74) … Henry Crocker *alias* Carter, yeoman, recently of Burley, on the 1st June 1635 in the fee of William Battyn at Burley, had enclosed with large ditches and high hedges twenty acres of pasture, corn, and meadow in separate closes … ‹Fine 20 nobles›. [See **750**]

531 (75) … Michael Saunders, yeoman, recently of Burley, on the 6th June 1635 in the fee of William Battyn at Bisterne Closes in the bailiwick of Burley, had enclosed with large ditches and hedges two closes containing eight acres … ‹Fine £3›. [See **743**]

m.4

532 (76) … William Elcombe, yeoman, recently of Lyndhurst, on the 12th June 1635, at Lyndhurst within the In bailiwick, had enclosed an acre of meadow with a high hedge … ‹Fine 40s› [See **773**]

533 (77) … William Elcombe on the 12th June 1635 at Lyndhurst in the In bailiwick had enclosed two acres of pasture with a high hedge … ‹Fine 40s›. [See **773**]

534 (78) ... Henry Randell, yeoman, recently of Lyndhurst, on the 12th June 1635 at Lyndhurst had enclosed two acres of meadow with a high hedge ... ‹Fine 40s›.

535 (79) ... Thomas Phillipps, yeoman, of Lyndhurst, on the 12th June 1635 at Lyndhurst, had inclosed with a high hedge two acres of meadow ... ‹Fine 40s›.

536 (80) ... Mellyor Emberly, widow, recently of Brockenhurst, on the 10th June 1635 in a place called Norlands Lane in the South bailiwick, had enclosed with a large ditch and a high hedge a close of meadow containing two and a half acres ... ‹Fine 40s›. [See **754**]

537 (81) ... Nicholas Hollyer, yeoman, recently of Brockenhurst, on the 10th June 1635 in Norlands Lane had enclosed with a large ditch and a high hedge a close of meadow containing two acres ... ‹Fine 40s›. [See **733**]

538 (82) ... William Tapp, yeoman, recently of Brockenhurst, on the 10th June 1635 in the Streete in the South bailiwick had enclosed with a large ditch and high hedge a close of meadow containing one and a half acres ... ‹Fine 40s›. [See **772**]

539 (83) ... John Rowland *alias* Burton, yeoman, recently of Brockenhurst on the 10th June 1635 in Norlands Lane had enclosed with a large ditch and a high hedge a close of pasture containing two acres ... ‹Fine 40s›. [See **741**]

540 (84) ... Edward Cooper, yeoman, recently of Brockenhurst, on the 20th June 1635 in Norlands Lane had enclosed with a large ditch and high hedge a meadow containing five acres ... ‹Fine £3›. [See **790**]

541 (85) ... John Burton and Nicholas Hollier, both yeomen recently of Brockenhurst, on the 21st June 1635 in Norlands Lane had enclosed with a large ditch and high hedge a close of meadow containing one and a half acres ... ‹Fine of each one 20s›. [See **733, 741**]

542 (86) ... Edward Cooper, yeoman, recently of Brockenhurst, on the 20th June 1635 in Norlands Lane had enclosed with a large ditch and high hedge a close of pasture containing three acres ... ‹Fine £3›. [See **790**]

543 (87) ... Thomas Norton, yeoman, recently of Brockenhurst, on the 10th June 1635 in Norlands Lane had enclosed with a large ditch and high hedge a close of meadow containing one acre ... ‹Fine 20s›. [See **759**]

544 (88) ... William Parsons, yeoman, recently of Brockenhurst, on the 10th June 1635 in Norlands Lane had enclosed with a large ditch and high hedge a close of pasture containing four acres ... ‹Fine £4›. [See **782**]

545 (89) ... Thomas Norton, yeoman, recently of Brockenhurst, on the 10th June 1635 at Brookley in Battramsley bailiwick had enclosed with a large ditch and high hedge a close of meadow containing half an acre ... ‹Fine 20s›. [See **759**]

546 (90) ... William Draper, yeoman, recently of Brockenhurst, on the 10th June 1635 at Brookley had enclosed with large ditches and high hedges two closes of meadow containing two acres ... ‹Fine 40s›. [See **758**]

547 (91) ... William Tapp, yeoman, recently of Brockenhurst, on the 10th June 1635 at Brookley had enclosed with a large ditch and high hedge a close of meadow containing one acre ... ‹Fine 20s›. [See **772**]

548 (92) ... Joan Norton, widow, recently of Brockenhurst, on the 10th June 1635 at Brookley had enclosed with a large ditch and high hedge a close of meadow containing two acres .... ‹Fine 40s›. [See **755**]

549 (93) ... Nicholas Hollyer, yeoman, recently of Brockenhurst, on the 10th June 1635 at Brookley had enclosed with a large ditch and high hedge a close of meadow containing five acres ... ‹Fine £5›. [See **733**]

550 (94) ... Thomas Burton, yeoman, recently of Brockenhurst, on the 10th June 1635 at Brookley had enclosed with a large ditch and high hedge a close of pasture containing two acres ... ‹Fine 40s›. [See **779**]

551 (95) ... Thomas Cooper, husbandman, recently of Brockenhurst, on the 10th June 1635 at Brookley had enclosed with a large ditch and high hedge a close of meadow containing half an acre ... ‹Fine 20s›. [See **761**]

552 (96) ... William Draper, yeoman, recently of Brookley, on the 10th June 1635 at Brookley had enclosed with a large ditch and high hedge a close of meadow containing two acres ... ‹Fine 40s›. [See **758**]

553 (97) ... Nicholas Hollyer, yeoman, recently of Brockenhurst, on the 10th June 1635 at Brookley had enclosed with a large ditch and high hedge a close of pasture containing two acres ... ‹Fine 40s›. [See **733**]

554 (98) ... Mellior Emberly, widow, recently of Brockenhurst, on the 15th June 1635 at Brookley had enclosed with a large ditch and high hedge three closes of pasture containing five acres ... ‹Fine £4›. [See **754**]

m.4d.

555 (99) ... Thomas Norton, yeoman, recently of Brockenhurst, on the 10th June 1635 at Brookley had enclosed with a large ditch and high hedge a close of meadow containing one acre ... ‹Fine 20s›. [See **759**]

556 (100) ... Ralph Gretnum, yeoman, recently of Brookley, on the 10th June 1635 at Brookley had enclosed with a large ditch and high hedge a close of meadow containing three acres ... ‹Fine £3›. [See **768**]

557 (101) ... John Halle, yeoman, recently of Brookley, on the 10th June 1635 at Brookley had enclosed with a large ditch and high hedge a close of meadow containing three acres ... ‹Fine £3›. [See **760**]

558 (102) ... Thomas Percy, husbandman, recently of Godshill, on the 1st June 1635 within the bailiwick of Godshill, had cut, dug, taken, and carried away one thousand turves worth three shillings and four pence ... ‹Fine 10s›.

559 (103) ... Nicholas Thomas, labourer, recently of Searchfield, on the 1st June 1635 upon a mount near Crownest [SU2416] in North bailiwick, cut and dug three thousand turves worth three shillings for various inhabitants of Downton ... ‹Fine 20s›.

560 (104) ... Nicholas Thomas on the 1st June 1635 within the North bailiwick had cut, dug, taken, carried away, and sold one thousand turves worth twelve pence to a certain William Loe of Downton ... ‹Fine 10s›.

561 (105) ... Robert Whittingstall, husbandman, recently of Godshill, is a common digger and seller of the turf of the king, and that Robert at various times between the 1st May and the 6th June 1635 in various places within the bailiwick of Godshill, had dug and cut ten thousand turves worth five shillings, and these he had taken and sold ... ‹Fine 40s›. [See **788**]

562 (106) ... John Whittingstall, husbandman, recently of Godshill, is a common malefactor, carrier, and seller of the king's turf, and that John at various times between 1st May and 6th June 1635 in various places within the bailiwick of Godshill had taken ten thousand turves worth five shillings, and these he had carried away with his cart drawn by three horses worth forty shillings, and these he had sold ... ‹Fine 40s and value ... etc.›. [See **789**]

563 (107) ... James Dunmeade, innkeeper, recently of Lymington, on the 9th June 1635 within the South bailiwick had cut and caused to be carried away to his house, four thousand turves ... ‹Fine 40s›.

564 (108) ... Thomas Urry, yeoman, recently of Lymington, within the South bailiwick from the 31st March to the 21st June 1635 had cut, taken, and carried away [turves] to various persons unknown ... ‹Fine 40s›.

565 (109) ... Richard Sheaffeild, yeoman, recently of Lymington, within the South bailiwick from the 31st March to the 21st June 1635 with two carts had taken and carried away [turves] to various persons unknown ... ‹Fine £4›.

566 (110) ... Henry Mallatt, labourer, recently of Pilly, is a common malefactor of turf, and within the South bailiwick from the

31st March to the 1st June 1635 had cut, dug, and sold [turves] to various persons unknown ... ‹Fine 40s›.

567 (111) ... Thomas Bulkely, yeoman, recently of Sway, within the South bailiwick from the 31st March to the 1st June 1635 had cut, dug, and sold [turves] to various persons unknown ... ‹Fine 40s›.

568 (112) ... John Thurstin, husbandman, recently of Royden, within the South bailiwick from the 31st March to the 1st June 1635 had cut, dug, and sold [turves] to various persons unknown ... ‹Fine 40s›. [See **764**]

569 (113) ... John Dore, yeoman, recently of Lymington, on the 30th May 1635 within the South bailiwick had caused to be cut six thousand turves, and these carried to his house in Lymington ... ‹Fine £6›.

570 (114) ... Richard Carter, husbandman, recently of Lymington, on the 30th May 1635 within the South bailiwick had caused to be cut four thousand turves, and these carried to his house in Lymington ... ‹Fine 40s›.

571 (115) ... John Young, husbandman, recently of Lymington, on the 30th May 1635 within the South bailiwick had caused to be cut five thousand turves, and these carried to his house in Lymington ... ‹Fine £5›. [See **735**]

572 (116) ... George Burrad, shipwright, recently of Lymington, on the 30th May 1635 within the South bailiwick had caused to be cut eight thousand turves and these carried to his house in Lymington ... ‹Fine £8›.

573 (117) ... Tristram Turgis, gentleman, recently of Redlynch in the county of Wiltshire, on the 30th March 1634 near Cley Pitts [SU2216] in the North bailiwick, had burned and destroyed fifteen acres of heathland ... ‹Fine £20›.

574 (118) ... In the night of the 1st July 1633 at Gotespendhill [Goatspen] in the bailiwick of Burley, a person unknown had burned one hundred acres of heath worth ten shillings, and the vills of

Burley and Wootton are closely adjacent to the said place ... ‹Fine of each one 40s›.

575 (119) ... Alice Wilmott, widow, recently of Brockenhurst on the 26th November 1634 in the bailiwick of Battramsley, had placed and kept ten unringed pigs destroying and feeding upon the herbage ... ‹Fine 40s›. [See **739**]

576 (120) ... Christopher Biddlecombe, yeoman, recently of Hightowne, on the 21st October 1634 within the bailiwick of Linwood, had placed and kept nine unringed pigs worth twenty six shillings and eightpence, feeding upon and destroying the herbage ... ‹Fine 40s›. [See **769**]

577 (121) ... Philip Rooke, yeoman, recently of Stuckton, on the 21st October 1634 within Linwood bailiwick had placed and kept ten unringed pigs worth thirty shillings, feeding upon and destroying the herbage ... ‹Fine 40s›. [See **737**]

m.5

578 (121) ... Thomas Lacye, junior, recently of Gorely, on the 21st October 1634 in the bailiwick of Linwood had placed and kept three unringed pigs worth fifteen shillings, feeding upon and destroying the herbage ... ‹Fine 10s›.

579 (122) ... Thomas Lacye senior, yeoman, underforester of Broomy Lodge, on the 21st October 1634 in the bailiwick of Linwood had placed and kept thirteen unringed pigs worth three pounds, feeding upon and destroying the herbage ... ‹Fine £3›. [See **767**]

580 (123) ... James Hardinge, miller, recently of Brockenhurst, on the 3rd June 1635 at Lyndhurst within the In bailiwick, had newly built a dwelling house, where previously no house was, on a parcel of land containing thirteen perches in the king's demesne, and that John Hardinge, the son of James, miller recently of Lyndhurst, now has and occupies the same ... ‹Fine £3›.

581 (124) ... William Peake, husbandman, recently of Lyndhurst, on the 4th June 1635 at Lyndhurst, had newly built a dwelling house where no house was previously ... ‹Fine £3›.

582 (125) ... John Rusbridge, blacksmith, recently of Lyndhurst, on the 3rd June 1635 at Lyndhurst occupied and held a dwelling house, built by George Hedger deceased, blacksmith, upon the king's demesne ... ‹Fine £3›.

583 (126) ... Christopher Heathcott, charcoal burner, recently of Lyndhurst, on the 10th June 1635 at Lyndhurst, occupied and held a dwelling house and garden containing four perches, built by John Fox, deceased, of Lyndhurst ... ‹Fine £3›.

584 (127) ... William Thaire, turner, recently of Lyndhurst, on the 10th June 1635 at Lyndhurst, occupied and held a dwelling house upon a parcel of the king's demesne containing forty perches, which house was built by William Hobbard deceased, husbandman of Lyndhurst ... ‹Fine £3›.

585 (128) ... Anthony Waterman, husbandman, recently of Lyndhurst, on the 10th June 1635 at Lyndhurst, occupied and held a dwelling house upon a parcel of the king's demesne containing five perches, which house was built by John Fox deceased, husbandman of Lyndhurst ... ‹Fine £3›.

586 (129) ... John Purse, husbandman, recently of Lyndhurst, on the 3rd June 1635 at Lyndhurst, had built a dwelling house where no house was previously, upon a parcel of the king's demesne containing four perches ... ‹Fine £3›.

587 (130) ... Mary Hedger, widow, recently of Lyndhurst, on the 10th June 1635 at Lyndhurst, occupied and held a dwelling house and an acre of land, which house was built by George Hedger deceased, blacksmith of Lyndhurst ... ‹Fine £3›.

588 (131) ... John Iver, husbandman, recently of Lyndhurst, on the 1st May 1634 at Lyndhurst had built a dwelling house, where no house was previously, upon a parcel of the king's demesne containing six perches ... ‹Fine £3›.

589 (132) ... Thomas Percy, husbandman, recently of Godshill, on the 1st June 1635 in a place near to Godshill Gate, had enclosed with a hedge and incroached upon a parcel of the king's demesne containing three perches ... ‹Fine 20s›.

590 (133) ... Hugh Wiseman, husbandman, recently of Wootton, on the 1st June 1635 at Wootton in Battramsley bailiwick, had enclosed with a hedge a parcel of the king's demesne, and upon the same had built a house or cottage ... ‹Fine £3›.

591 (134) ... John Thorne, husbandman, recently of Burley, on the 4th June 1635 at Burley upon the fee of William Battyn, gentleman, had built a cottage where no cottage was previously ... ‹Fine £3›.

592 (135) ... John Tarry, husbandman, recently of Burley, on the 4th June 1635 at Burley upon the fee of William Battyn senior, had built a cottage where no cottage was previously ... ‹Fine £3›.

593 (136) ... James Poole, husbandman, recently of Burley, on the 4th June 1635 at Burley upon the fee of William Battyn senior, had built a cottage where no cottage was previously ... ‹Fine £3›.

594 (137) ... Robert Cooke deceased, husbandman, recently of Burley, since the last regard at Burley upon the fee of William Rogers, had built a cottage where no cottage was previously, which cottage is now in the tenure of Stephen Hobbs, charcoal burner, of Burley ... ‹Fine £3›.

595 (138) ... Michael Saunders, husbandman, recently of Burley, on the 4th June 1635 at Burley upon the fee of William Battyn senior, had built a cottage where no cottage was previously ... ‹Fine £3›. [See **743**]

596 (139) ... John Sudale, husbandman, recently of South Baddesley, deceased, since the last regard at South Baddesley in the South bailiwick, had enclosed with a hedge a parcel of land containing four perches of the fee of Henry Philpott, armiger, and upon this had built a house or cottage where no house was previously, which house is in the tenure of William James ... ‹Fine £3›.

597 (140) ... Thomas Salter deceased, husbandman, recently of Battramsley, since the last regard of the forest had enclosed with a hedge a parcel of the king's demesne containing forty perches, and upon this had built a dwelling house where no house was previously, and now in the tenure of Roger Payne, husbandman, of Battramsley ... ‹Fine £5›. [See **775**]

598 (141) ... John Grantham deceased, husbandman, recently of South Baddesley, since the last regard of the forest had enclosed with a hedge a parcel of the king's demesne at South Baddesley containing eight perches, and upon this had built a house or cottage where no house was previously, which house is in the tenure of John Goff ... ‹Fine £3›.

599 (142) ... Henry Barlin, husbandman, recently of Wootton, on the 10th June 1635, at Wootton in the bailiwick of Battramsley, had enclosed with a hedge a parcel of the king's demesne land containing thirty perches, and upon this had built a house or cottage where no house was previously ... ‹Fine £3›.

600 (143) ... Edith Davis, widow, recently of Wootton, on the 10th June 1635 at Wootton, had enclosed with a hedge a parcel of the king's demesne containing one hundred perches worth two shillings ... ‹Fine £3›.

601 (144) ... Hugh Wiseman, husbandman, recently of Wootton, on the 10th June 1635 at Wootton, had enclosed with a hedge a parcel of the king's demesne containing twenty perches, and upon this had built a house or cottage where no house was previously ... ‹Fine £3›.

602 (145) ... Thomas Cutler, husbandman, recently of Battramsley, on the 10th June 1635 at Battramsley on the fee of sir Francis Dowce, had enclosed with a hedge a parcel of land, and upon this had built a house or cottage where no house was previously ... ‹Fine ...›.

m.5d

603 (146) ... Mary Dewe, recently of Brockenhurst, on the fee of Robert Knapton had built a house or cottage where no house was previously ... ‹Fine ...›. [The top of this membrane is damaged]

604 (147) ... Elizabeth Tymothy, spinster, of Brockenhurst, since the last regard of the forest had built a house or cottage where no house was previously, at Brockenhurst on the fee of Robert Knapton ... ‹Fine £3›.

605 (148) ... Thomas Baker, husbandman, recently of Brockenhurst, on the 11th June 1635 on the fee of Robert Knapton at Brockenhurst, had built a house or cottage where no house was previously ... ‹Fine £3›.

606 (149) ... Joan Rowland, widow, recently of Brockenhurst, since the last regard of the forest, on the fee of Robert Knapton at Brockenhurst, had enclosed with a hedge a parcel of land containing three perches, and upon this had built a house or cottage where no house was previously ... ‹Fine £3›.

607 (150) ... John Ivye, husbandman, recently of Brockenhurst, since the last regard of the forest, on the fee of Robert Knapton at Brockenhurst, had enclosed with a hedge a parcel of land containing two perches, and upon this had built a house or cottage where no house was previously ... ‹Fine £3›.

608 (151) ... Thomas Hobbs, husbandman, recently of London Minstead, on the 8th June 1635 at London Minstead within the North bailiwick, had enclosed with a hedge a parcel of the king's demesne land containing three perches, and upon this had built a house or cottage where no house was previously ... ‹Fine £3›.

609 (152) ... Richard Corbin, husbandman, recently of Minstead, on the 10th June 1635 upon the fee of sir Henry Compton at Minstead, had enclosed with a hedge a parcel of land containing four perches, and upon this had built a house or cottage where no house was previously ... ‹Fine £3›.

610 (153) ... John Pearce deceased, yeoman, recently of Minstead, since the last regard of the forest had enclosed with a hedge a parcel of land containing four acres on the fee of sir Henry Compton at Minstead, and upon this he had built a house or cottage where no house was previously, which house is now in the tenure of Robert Henbist ... ‹Fine £6›.

611 (154) ... Richard Hayes, tailor, recently of Minstead, on the 10th June 1635 on the fee of sir Henry Compton at Minstead, had built a house or cottage where no house was previously ... ‹Fine £3›.

612 (155) ... Nicholas Cobb, charcoal burner, recently of Minstead, on the 10th June 1635 on the fee of sir Henry Compton at

Minstead, had enclosed with a hedge a parcel of land containing twenty perches, and upon this had built a house or cottage where no house was previously ... ‹Fine £3›.

613 (156) ... Robert Whitehorne, husbandman, recently of Minstead, on the 10th June 1635 on the fee of sir Henry Compton at Minstead, had enclosed with a hedge a parcel of land containing half an acre, and upon this had built a house or cottage where no house was previously ... ‹Fine £3›.

614 (157) ... Alice Burgis, widow, recently of Minstead, on the 10th June 1635 on the fee of sir Henry Compton at Minstead, had enclosed with a hedge a parcel of land containing six perches, and upon this had built a house or cottage where no house was previously ... ‹Fine £3›.

615 (158) ... John Burden, yeoman, recently of Minstead, on the 10th June 1635 on the fee of sir Henry Compton at Minstead, had enclosed with a hedge a parcel of land containing forty perches, and upon this had built a house or cottage where no house was previously ... ‹Fine £3›.

616 (159) ... Edward Hobbs, charcoal burner, recently of Minstead, on the 10th June 1635 on the fee of sir Henry Compton at Minstead, had enclosed with a hedge a parcel of land containing ten perches, and upon this had built a house or cottage where no house was previously ... ‹Fine £3›.

617 (160) ... Joan Bromfeild, widow, recently of Minstead, on the 10th June 1635 on the fee of sir Henry Compton at Minstead, had enclosed with a hedge a parcel of land containing two perches ... ‹Fine 20s›.

618 (161) ... John Millis, shoemaker, recently of Minstead, on the 10th June 1635 on the fee of sir Henry Compton at Minstead, had enclosed with a hedge a parcel of land containing six perches, and upon this had built a house or cottage where no house was previously ... ‹Fine £3›.

619 (162) ... Thomas Rogers, tailor, of Minstead, on the 10th June 1635 on the fee of sir Henry Compton at Minstead, had enclosed with a hedge a parcel of land containing three perches, and upon this had built a house or cottage *anglice a fodder howse* where no house was previously ... ‹Fine £3›.

620 (163) ... John Pearce junior, the son of Richard Pearce, labourer, recently of Minstead, on the 10th June 1635 on the fee of sir Henry Compton at Minstead, had enclosed with a hedge a parcel of land containing eight perches, and upon this had built a house or cottage where no house was previously ... ‹Fine £3›.

621 (164) ... William Cobb, charcoal burner, recently of Minstead, on the 10th June 1635, on the fee of sir Henry Compton at Minstead [had built] a house or cottage where no house was previously ... ‹Fine £3›. [See **727, 766**]

622 (165) ... Madelin Michell, husbandman, recently of Minstead, on the 10th June 1635 upon the fee of sir Henry Compton at Minstead [had built] a house or cottage where no house was previously ... ‹Fine £3›.

623 (166) ... William Osman deceased, husbandman, recently of Canterton, had enclosed with a hedge a parcel of the king's demesne containing four perches, and upon this had built a house or cottage where no house was previously, which house is now held by Edward Bocoth ... ‹Fine £4›.

624 (167) ... John Wright, fusterer, recently of Minstead, on the 10th June 1635 on the fee of sir Henry Compton at Minstead, had enclosed with a hedge a parcel of land containing ten perches, and upon this had built a house or cottage where no house was previously ... ‹Fine £3›.

625 (168) ... Thomas Marshman, husbandman, recently of Minstead, on the 10th June 1635 on the fee of sir Henry Compton at Minstead, had enclosed with a hedge a parcel of land containing sixty perches, and upon this had built two houses, namely a barn and a carthouse, where no house was previously ... ‹Fine £3›.

m.6

626 (169) ... John Paynter, labourer, recently of London Minstead, on the 4th June 1635 on the fee of John Crowcher at London

Minstead, had built a house or cottage where no house was previously ... ‹Fine £3›.

627 (170) ... John Crowcher, yeoman, recently of London Minstead, on the 4th June 1635 had built on his fee a house or cottage where no house was previously ... ‹Fine £3›.

628 (171) ... Thomas Woolfe, labourer, recently of Minstead, on the 10th June 1935 at Minstead, had enclosed with a hedge a parcel of the king's demesne containing five perches, and upon this had built a house or cottage where no house was previously ... ‹Fine £3›.

629 (172) ... Richard Osman, labourer, recently of Minstead, on the 10th June 1635 at London Minstead, had enclosed with a hedge twenty perches of the king's demesne, and upon this built a dwelling house where no house was previously ... [Fine £3]. [See **729**]

630 (173) ... John Paynter, husbandman, recently of London Minstead, on the 8th June 1635 at London Minstead, had enclosed with a hedge a parcel of the king's demesne containing two perches ... ‹Fine 20s›.

631 (174) ... Stephen Warwick, yeoman, recently of Bartley Regis, on the 8th June 1635 on his fee at Bartley Regis, upon a parcel of land containing one and a half acres had built a house or cottage where no house was previously ... ‹Fine £3›.

632 (175) ... Andrew Bulkeley, tailor, recently of Brook, on the 20th October 1634 upon the demesne of the king in a place called Canterton Lane in the North bailiwick, had built a dwelling house where no dwelling house was previously ... ‹Fine £3›.

633 (176) ... Robert Knight deceased, miller, recently of Brook, had enclosed with pales a parcel of the king's demesne at Brook containing two perches, upon which Cosmus Reeves of Brook had built a house containing thirty feet, and the said Cosmus and Hugh Beckford have held the enclosed land since ... ‹Fine £5›.

634 (177) ... Rowland Damerham deceased, husbandman, recently of Pilley, since the last regard of the forest had enclosed with a hedge a parcel of the king's demesne at Pilley containing five perches, and upon it had built a house or cottage where no house was previously, which house is in the tenure of Elizabeth Damerham the wife of Rowland ... ‹Fine £3›.

635 (178) ... Richard Waterman, husbandman, recently of Pilley, since the last regard had enclosed with a hedge a parcel containing five perches of the king's demesne at Pilley, and upon it had built a house or cottage where no house was previously ... ‹Fine £3›. [See **763**]

636 (179) ... Weyman Carde, husbandman, recently of Pilley, since the last regard had enclosed with a hedge a parcel containing six perches of the king's demesne at Pilley, and upon which he had built a house or cottage where no house was previously ... ‹Fine £3›. [See **774**]

637 (180) ... Joel Salter deceased, husbandman, recently of Pilley, had enclosed with a hedge a parcel of six perches of the king's demesne at Pilley, and upon which he had built a house or cottage where no house was previously, which house is in the tenure of Joan Gosney, a widow, ... ‹Fine £3›.

638 (181) ... Thomas Jarvis, husbandman, recently of Pilley, since the last regard had enclosed with a hedge a parcel containing four perches of the king's demesne at Pilley, and upon which he had built a house or cottage where no house was previously ... ‹Fine £3›.

639 (182) ... John Marshall, husbandman, recently of Pilley, since the last regard had enclosed with a hedge a parcel containing six perches of the king's demesne at Pilley, and upon which he had built a house or cottage where no house was previously ... ‹Fine £3›.

640 (183) ... Ann Wavell, widow, recently of Pilley, on the 10th June 1632 upon the fee of John Wavell at Pilley, had built a house where no house was previously, which house is in the tenure of Ann Wavell ... ‹Fine £3›. [See **762**]

641 (184) ... William Goddard, gentleman, recently of Fordingbridge, since the last regard of the forest, upon a parcel of land within the fee of sir John Brune at Brunes Moor in the bailiwick of Godshill, had newly built a dwelling house where no house was previously ... ‹Fine £3›.

642 (185) ... Frances Ellyott, spinster, recently of Fritham, since the last regard had inclosed with a hedge twenty perches of the king's demesne at Fritham, and upon which she had newly built a dwelling house where no dwelling house was previously ... ‹Fine £3›.

643 (186) ... John Call, yeoman, recently of Ironshill Lodge, since the last regard had newly built a dwelling house where no dwelling house was previously upon a parcel of land within the fee of Andrew Hobbs at Fritham ... ‹Fine ...›.

644 (187) ... John Bennett, tanner, recently of Shaftesbury in the county of Dorset, since the last regard upon the fee of Andrew Hobbs at Fritham had newly built a tanhouse where no tanhouse was previously, and in the same house had exercised the mystery of a tanner ... ‹...›.

645 (188) ... William Silver, husbandman, recently of Holbury, on the 9th June 1635 in a place called Rollstone Grounds within the East bailiwick in the fee of Nicholas Pescod, gentleman, had built a dwelling house where no house was previously ... ‹...›. [See **751**]

646 (189) ... Nathan Uvedale, husbandman, recently of Holbury, on the 9th June 1635 in a place called Rollstone Grounds within the East bailiwick in the fee of Nicholas Pescod, had built a house where no house was previously ... ‹...›. [See **732**]

647 (190) ... John Chamberleyne, armiger, recently of Lyndhurst, on the ... June 1635 at Hardley had enclosed with a hedge a parcel of the king's demesne called Farmers Hill, which land is in the tenure of William Thorpe, yeoman, of ..., who on the said date had grubbed up seven trees *anglice pollard trees* worth ... and fourpence ... ‹...›.

648 (191) ... sir Henry Compton recently of Brambletye on the 9th June 1635 within his fee in the East bailiwick had newly built an almshouse ... ‹...›.

m.6d

649 (192) ... Margaret .aycroft[1] recently of Hardley ... [membrane damaged].

[1] ?Haycroft *alias* Heycrofte.

650 (193) ... Alice Tissard recently of Hardley on the ... June 1635 had built a house or cottage where no house had been previously within the king's demesne at Hardley within the East bailiwick ...

651 (194) ... Edward Amye junior, yeoman, and John Amye husbandman, on the 10th June ... at Linwood upon land containing thirty acres of pasture within the fee of Edmund Ogden armiger had built two houses or cottages where no house was previously ...

652 (195) ... Richard Veale, husbandman, on the 10th June 1635 in a place called Black Heath [SU1810] in the bailiwick of Linwood and upon a parcel of land containing four acres within the fee of Edmund Weekes gentleman, had built a house or cottage where no house was previously ...

653 (196) ... Stephen Whitear, yeoman, on the 1st June 1635 at Knap Greene in Burley bailiwick had enclosed with a hedge a parcel of the king's demesne containing fifteen feet, and there had placed eight hives *anglice beestalls* ... [See **753**]

654 (197) ... Joseph Coffin, yeoman, recently of Burley, on the 20th June 1635 at Sandhurst in Battramsley bailiwick had enclosed with a hedge a parcel of the king' demesne containing three perches, and there had placed ten hives ... [See **771**]

655 (198) ... Joseph Coffin on the 1st June 1635 at Peekes Lane in Burley bailiwick had enclosed with a hedge a parcel of the king's demesne containing one perch, and there he had placed seven hives ... [See **771**]

656 (199) ... Richard Woods, yeoman, recently of Burley, on the 1st June 1635 at Cley Hill in the bailiwick of Burley had enclosed with a hedge a parcel of the king's demesne containing half a perch, and there had placed three hives ...

657 (200) ... Henry Robbins, yeoman, recently of Burley, on the 1st June 1635 near to the Moots in Burley bailiwick had enclosed with a hedge a parcel of the king's demesne containing half a perch, and there had placed two hives ...

658 (201) ... Joseph Coffin, yeoman, recently of Burley, on the 1st

June 1635 at Yardly Bushes in Burley bailiwick had enclosed with a hedge two parcels of the king's demesne each containing one perch, and had placed three hives in one and one hive in the other ... [See **771**]

659 (202) ... John Warne, yeoman, recently of Lower Kingston, since the last regard of the forest, at Bratley Brook in Fritham bailiwick had made a purpresture and enclosed with a hedge one perch of the king's demesne, and upon it had placed twenty hives ... ‹Fine 5s›.

660 (203) ... Maurice Warne, yeoman, recently of Upper Kingston on the 1st June 1635 at Backly in Burley bailiwick had enclosed with a hedge a parcel of the king's demesne containing one perch, and there had placed eight hives ... ‹Fine 5s›.

661 (204) ... Alice Coish, widow, of Hightowne on the 1st June 1635 at the north end of Ridley in Burley bailiwick had enclosed with a hedge a parcel of the king's demesne containing half a perch, and there had placed three hives ... ‹Fine 5s›.

662 (205) ... Henry Etheridge, yeoman, recently of Burley, on the 1st June 1635 at Ridley Bushes in Burley bailiwick had enclosed with a hedge a parcel of the king's demesne containing twelve feet, and there had placed eight hives ... ‹Fine 5s›. [See **744**]

663 (206) ... John Warne, yeoman, recently of Upper Kingston on the 1st June 1635 at Anderwood in Burley bailiwick had enclosed with a hedge a parcel of the king's demesne containing one perch, and there had placed three hives ... ‹Fine 5s›.

664 (207) ... Maurice Warne, yeoman, recently of Upper Kingston on the 1st June 1635 at Blackenforde in Burley bailiwick had enclosed with a hedge a parcel of the king's demesne containing half a perch, and there had placed six hives ... ‹Fine 5s›.

665 (208) ... John Warne, yeoman, recently of Upper Kingston on the 1st June 1635 at Church Moore in Burley bailiwick had enclosed with a hedge a parcel of the king's demesne containing one perch, and there had placed three hives ... ‹Fine 5s›.

666 (209) ... John Warne on the 1st June 1635 at Anderwood in Burley bailiwick had enclosed with a hedge a parcel of the king's demesne containing fifteen feet, and there had placed seven hives ... ‹Fine 5s›.

667 (210) ... Richard Stormes, yeoman, recently of Netley, and Richard Hayes, yeoman, recently of Minstead, on the 3rd June 1635 at Woodcrast' in Fritham bailiwick had enclosed with a hedge a perch of the king's demesne, and there had placed four hives ... ‹Fine 5s›. [See **734**]

668 (211) ... Humphrey Collyer, gentleman, recently of Bisterne, and James Warne, yeoman, recently of Over Kingston, on the 3rd June 1635 at Bratly in Fritham bailiwick had enclosed with a hedge a perch and a half of the king's demesne, upon which they had placed fourteen hives ... ‹Fine 5s›.

669 (212) ... John Warne, yeoman, recently of Over Kingston on the 3rd June 1635 at Bratley Brook in Fritham bailiwick had enclosed with a hedge one perch of the king's demesne, upon which he had placed a hive ... ‹Fine 5s›.

m.7

670 (213) ... Richard Biddlecombe, yeoman, recently of Hightowne on the 22nd July 1635 at Thorne Bed in Burley bailiwick had enclosed with a hedge a parcel of the king's demesne containing half a perch, and placed there three hives ... ‹Fine 5s›.

671 (214) ... Thomas Barnes, yeoman, recently of Lower Kingston on the 3rd June 1635 at Bratley in Fritham bailiwick had enclosed with a hedge half a perch of the king's demesne, and upon which had placed two hives ... ‹Fine 5s›.

672 (215) ... Maurice Warne, yeoman, recently of Over Kingston on the 3rd June 1635 near Bolderwood Rails in Fritham bailiwick had enclosed with a hedge one perch of the king's demesne, and upon which he had placed nine hives ... ‹Fine 5s›.

673 (216) ... Thomas Lovell and John Andrews, yeomen, recently of Bartley on the 3rd June 1635 at Iland Water in Fritham bailiwick had enclosed with a hedge two and a half perches of the king's demesne, and upon which they had placed eight hives ... ‹Fine of each one 5s›. [See **787**]

674 (217) ... John Andrews and Thomas Lovell, yeomen, recently of Bartley Regis on the 3rd June 1635 at Ocknell Coppice in Fritham bailiwick had enclosed with a hedge three parcels of the king's demesne containing two perches, and upon these had placed eight hives ... ‹Fine of each one 5s›. [See **787**]

675 (218) ... Ambrose Austine, carpenter, recently of Goreley, and Giles Whinge, yeoman, of Gorely, on the 3rd June 1635 had made a purpresture in Godshill bailiwick, and had enclosed with a hedge a parcel of the king's demesne containing one perch, and upon this had placed a hive ... ‹Fine 5s›. [See **748**]

676 (219) ... Nicholas Norris, tanner, recently of Fordingbridge on the 3rd June 1635 in the bailiwick of Godshill had enclosed with a hedge three parcels of the king's demesne containing three perches and had placed there twelve hives ... ‹Fine 5s›.

677 (220) ... John Barry, yeoman, recently of Fritham on the 3rd June 1635 in Fritham bailiwick had enclosed with hedges seven parcels of the king's demesne containing seven perches, and had placed there fifty hives ... ‹Fine 5s› [See **784**]

678 (221) Thomas Mouland, husbandman, recently of Stucton, and John Veale, husbandman, recently of East Mill, on the 3rd June 1635 in Godshill bailiwick had enclosed with a hedge a parcel of the king's demesne containing one perch, and upon it had placed five hives ... ‹Fine of each 5s›. [See **778**]

679 (222) ... Richard Sex, yeoman, recently of Frogham on the 3rd June 1635 in Godshill bailiwick had enclosed with a hedge a parcel of the king's demesne containing half a perch, and had placed there three hives ... ‹Fine 5s›. [See **747**]

680 (223) ... Richard Stormes, yeoman, recently of Netley on the 10th June 1635 at Howbeach within the In bailiwick had enclosed with a hedge a parcel of the king's demesne containing one perch, and had placed there six hives ... ‹Fine 5s›. [See **734**]

681 (224) ... William Whitehead, husbandman, recently of Battramsley on the 1st June 1635 in certain places called Cocke Hill within Battramsley Lane End within the South bailiwick had enclosed with hedges a parcel of land containing four perches, and had placed there ten hives ... ‹Fine 5s›. [See **786**]

682 (225) ... Bartholomew Bulkeley, gentleman, recently of Sway on the 1st June 1635 in various places called Bulslade, Longeslade, and Setthornes in Battramsley bailiwick had enclosed with hedges three parcels of the king's demesne containing three and a half perches, and had placed there twenty seven hives ... ‹Fine 5s›. [See **765**]

683 (226) ... Thomas Moore, husbandman, recently of Hinton on the 10th June 1635 at Homesly in Burley bailiwick had enclosed a perch of the king's demesne, and upon the same had placed twenty hives ... ‹Fine 5s›.

684 (226) ... Edith Davis, widow, recently of Wootton on the 10th June 1635 at Panginge Shoot in Burley bailiwick had enclosed one perch of the king's demesne, and upon the same had placed twelve hives ... ‹Fine 5s›.

685 (227) ... Thomas Moore, yeoman, recently of Hinton on the 10th June 1635 at Haghole in Battramsley bailiwick had enclosed with a hedge a parcel of the king's demesne containing one perch, and placed there twenty one hives ... ‹Fine 5s›.

686 (228) ... William Lauder, yeoman, recently of Becklie on the 10th June 1635 at Haghole in Battramsley bailiwick had enclosed with a hedge a parcel of the king's demesne containing half a perch, and placed there three hives ... ‹Fine 5s›.

687 (229) ... John Kittier, yeoman, recently of Lymington on the 10th June 1635 at Wilverly Rayles in Battramsley bailiwick, [on] a parcel of the king's demesne land containing one perch, had placed ten hives ... ‹Fine 5s›.

688 (230) ... Ralph Gretnum, yeoman, recently of Brockenhurst on the 20th June 1635 at Blacke Knowle in Battramsley bailiwick upon a parcel of the king's demesne containing one perch, had placed five hives ... ‹Fine 5s› [See **768**]

689 (231) ... Bartholomew Bulcley, gentleman, recently of Sway on the 10th June 1635 near Hincheslea in Battramsley bailiwick, had enclosed with a hedge a parcel of the king's demesne containing one and a half perches, and placed there six hives ... ‹Fine 5s›. [See **765**]

m.7d

690 (232) ... Philip ?Veasy, husbandman, on the 10th June 1635 at ...iam in In bailiwick upon a parcel of the king's demesne containing one perch had placed ... hives ...

691 (233) ... Nicholas Lawes, yeoman, recently of Hale, since the last regard of the forest, at Godshill had enclosed with a hedge six perches of the king's demesne, and upon the same made an orchard *(pomarium)* and a place for bee hives *(alvear') anglice a bee garden* where no orchard or place for bee hives was previously ...

692 (234) ... Henry Lovell, yeoman, recently of Marchwood on the 9th June 1635 at South Hatts in East bailiwick had enclosed with a hedge a parcel of the king's demesne containing one perch and a half, and had placed there six hives ... ‹Fine 5s›.

693 (235) ... Henry Lovell on the 9th June 1635 at Matley in the East bailiwick had enclosed with a hedge a parcel of the king's demesne containing one perch, and had placed there seven hives ... ‹Fine 5s›.

694 (236) ... Richard Storme, yeoman, recently of Netley on the 9th June 1635 at Crookehill in the East bailiwick had enclosed with a hedge a parcel of the king's demesne containing one perch and a half, and had placed there five hives ... ‹Fine 5s›. [See **734**]

695 (237) ... Richard Storme on the 9th June 1635 at Matley in the East bailiwick had enclosed with a hedge a parcel of the king's demesne containing one perch, and had placed there eleven hives ... ‹Fine 5s›. [See **734**]

696 (238) ... Aphradocius Oviatt, yeoman, recently of Poulner on the 9th June 1635 at Rewend in Linwood bailiwick had enclosed with a hedge a parcel of the king's demesne containing three perches, and had placed there fourteen hives ... ‹Fine 5s›.

697 (239) ... Peter Alrudge, husbandman, recently of Rockford on the 9th June 1635 at Free Homes in Linwood bailiwick had enclosed with a hedge a parcel of the king's demesne containing three perches, and had placed there twelve hives ... ‹Fine 5s›.

698 (240) ... Whit Tarver, yeoman, recently of Blashford on the 9th June 1635 in a place called Amberslade near to Linwood Closes and Jordens Bridge in Linwood bailiwick, had enclosed with hedges two parcels of the king's demesne containing thirteen perches, and had placed there seventeen hives ... ‹Fine 5s›.

699 (241) ... Mary Warne, widow, recently of Nether Kingston on the 9th June 1635 at Backley in Linwood bailiwick had enclosed with hedges various parcels of the king's demesne containing four perches, and had placed there ten hives ... ‹Fine 5s›. [See **777**]

700 (242) ... Stephen Rooke, yeoman, recently of Rockford on the 9th June 1635 at Appledore Slade in Linwood bailiwick had enclosed with a hedge a parcel of the king's demesne containing one perch, and had placed there two hives ... ‹Fine 5s›.

701 (243) ... William Lacye and Anthony Beslin, yeomen, recently of North Gorley on the 9th June 1635 in places called Hartsley and Polde Oakes in the bailiwick of Linwood had enclosed with hedges two parcels of the king's demesne containing three perches, and there had placed thirteen hives ... ‹Fine of each 5s›. [See **749**]

702 (244) ... Richard Livelong, clothworker, recently of Fordingbridge on the 9th June 1635 at Hartsloe in Linwood bailiwick had enclosed with a hedge a parcel of the king's demesne containing one perch, and had placed there twelve hives ... ‹Fine 5s›. [See **746**]

703 (245) ... Ambrose Austine, yeoman, recently of Gorely on the 9th June 1635 at Bushie Lane in Linwood bailiwick had enclosed with a hedge a parcel of the king's demesne containing one perch and a half, and had placed there seven hives ... ‹Fine 5s›. [See **748**]

704 (246) ... Francis Barry senior, yeoman, recently of Hide on the 9th June 1635 at places called Sloden and Homyhatt in Linwood bailiwick had enclosed with hedges various parcels of the king's demesne containing four perches *anglice bee gardens*, and had placed there thirty hives *anglice bee stalls* ... ‹Fine 5s›. [See **745**]

705 (247) ... Richard Sex, yeoman, recently of Frogham on the 9th June 1635 at places called Rowhill and Ashie Lane in Linwood bailiwick, had enclosed with hedges two parcels of the king's demesne containing three perches, and had placed there nineteen hives ... ‹Fine 5s›. [See **747**]

706 (248) ... Nicholas Rickman, husbandman, recently of Upper Bisterne on the 10th June 1635 near to Thorny Hill in Burley bailiwick, had enclosed half a perch of the king's demesne, and upon the same had placed six hives ... ‹Fine 5s›.

707 (249) ... William Warne, yeoman, recently of Ripley on the 10th June 1635 at Homesly in Burley bailiwick had enclosed one perch of the king's demesne, and upon the same had placed sixteen hives ... ‹Fine 5s›.

708 (250) ... Thomas Smith and Hugh Attlane, yeomen, recently of Brockenhurst, on the 1st February 1633 were hunting at Brookley in Battramsley bailiwick with a dog *anglice a mongrell*, and they put to flight, chased, and harrassed to death a doe *(unam damam) anglice a bucke* ... ‹Fine of each one £20›. [See **728**]

m.8

709 (251) ... Thomas Smith and Hugh Attlane, yeomen, recently of Brockenhurst, in the night of the 28th February 1633 in a place called Trenly in the bailiwick of Battramsley, were hunting with a dog called a mongrel, and they worried to the death a doe *anglice a bucke* ... ‹Fine of each £20›. [See **728**]

710 (252) ... Hugh Attlane, yeoman, recently of Brockenhurst, on the 1st February 1633 at Brookley had custody of a dog called a mongrel, and he had ordered a certain Thomas Smith, at the time his servant, to enter the bailiwick of Battramsley with the dog, with the intention of hunting and chasing the deer *(damas)* within the peace of the forest. Which dog worried to death a doe *(unam damam) anglice a bucke* ... ‹Fine of each £20›. [See **728**]

711 (253) ... Hugh Attlane, yeoman, recently of Brockenhurst, on the 28th February 1633 in the night in a place called Trenley, was hunting with a dog called a mongrel, and had worried to death a buck, and he had taken and carried the body to his house ... ‹Fine £20›. [See **728**]

712 (254) ... Hugh Attlane is a common malefactor and destroyer of the venison of the New Forest, and an abetter of venison malefactors and destroyers throughout the New Forest, and accustomed to set and place snares in the hedges in Brookley in the bailiwick of Battramsley, and on the 31st October 1632 in a place called Darvalls in Battramsley bailiwick, in the hedges of the same enclosure placed various snares made of ropes, called halters, and with these he had taken and suspended two deer, one of which broke the rope or halter and fled, the other deer the said Hugh had cut and wounded about the neck with a knife, and thus he allowed it to get away ... ‹Fine £100›. [See **728**]

713 (255) ... George Thorpe, gentleman, recently of Crowe, with others unknown on the night of 10th February 1635 in a place called Bratley in Fritham bailiwick, were hunting with a greyhound, and they put to flight, chased, and harrassed to death a doe ... ‹Fine £20›.

714 (256) ... Richard Donce, gentleman, recently of Wallopp in the county of Southampton, Silvester Goter, clerk, recently of Whiteparish in the county of Wiltshire, and John Lynch, gentleman, recently of Whiteparish, on the 17th March 1635 in a place called Crowe Mast Bottome in the North bailiwick were hunting with two greyhounds, and they put to flight, chased, and harrassed to death a deer, and they took and carried away the body ... ‹all of them to pay a fine of £20. This fine is discharged by warrant of the chief justice in eyre›.

715 (257) ... John Andrews, yeoman, recently of Brooke, with two others unknown, on the 10th February 1635 near Burnt Fursen in the North bailiwick, were hunting with three greyhounds, and they put to flight, chased, and harrassed to death a brace of deer, and the bodies they took and carried away ... ‹Fine £100›.

716 (258) ... William Ingpen, gentleman, recently of Bartley Regis, on the 3rd May 1635 called M' Goddard Grownd in the North bailiwick was standing upon a tree with a gun loaded with powder and shot *anglice charged with hayle shott* with the intention of evildoing and killing the king's beasts ... ‹Fine £20›.

717 (259) ... Hugh Attlane, yeoman, recently of Blackmansly, on the 29th June 1635 at Blackmansley in Battramsley bailiwick, had and kept a pernicious dog, unexpeditated and a disturber of the king's beasts ... ‹Fine 40s›. [See **728**]

718 (260) ... Alexander Moore, yeoman, recently of Blackmansley on the 29th June 1635 at Blackmansley had and kept a pernicious dog, unexpeditated and a disturber of the king's beasts ... ‹Fine 40s›.

719 (261) ... John Ames, husbandman, recently of Brookley on the 29th June 1635 at Brookley in the bailiwick of Battramsley had and kept a pernicious dog, unexpeditated and a disturber of the king's beasts ... ‹Fine 40s›. [See **783**]

720 (262) ... William Tapp, yeoman, recently of Brockenhurst on the 29th June 1635 at Brockenhurst in Battramsley bailiwick had and kept two pernicious dogs, unexpeditated and disturbers of the king's beasts ... ‹Fine 40s›. [See **772**]

721 (263) ... Henry Hastings, armiger, recently of Woodland in the county of Dorset on the 29th June 1635 in the bailiwick of Battramsley had, placed, kept, and allowed to wander and depasture, two hundred sheep worth sixty six pounds thirteen shillings and four pence; grazing, trampling, consuming, and contaminating the herbage to the exclusion of the king's beasts ... ‹Fine £40›.

722 (264) ... John Forde, yeoman, recently of Royden on the 29th June 1635 in certain places called Banners Bushes and Setley within the king's demesne in Battramsley bailiwick, had, placed, kept, and allowed to wander and depasture forty sheep worth ten pounds, grazing, trampling, consuming, and contaminating the herbage to the exclusion of the king's beasts .... ‹Fine 40s›.

723 (265) ... William Tapp, yeoman, recently of Brockenhurst, on the 29th June 1635 in Battramsley bailiwick, had, placed, kept, and allowed to wander and depasture, six sheep worth thirty shillings, grazing, trampling, consuming, and contaminating the herbage to the exclusion of the king's beasts ... ‹Fine 10s›. [See **772**]

724 (266) ... John Nippered, yeoman, recently of Burley, on the 8th May 1635 within the king's demesne in Burley bailiwick, had, placed, and kept sixteen sheep worth four pounds, grazing, trampling, and contaminating the herbage to the exclusion of the king's beasts ... ‹Fine 40s›. [See **736**]

725 (267) ... John Young', husbandman, recently of Burley, on the 8th May 1635 within the king's demesne in Burley bailiwick, had, placed, and kept eight sheep worth [fifty] three shillings and four pence, grazing, trampling, and contaminating the herbage to the exclusion of the king's beasts ... ‹Fine 20s›. [See **735**]

726 (268) ... Christopher Davis, tanner, recently of Brockenhurst, on the 15th June 1635 at Brockenhurst within the South bailiwick occupied the discipline or mystery of a tanner, to the destruction of the king's beasts ... ‹Fine 20s›. [See **757**]

m.8d
‹Recognizances›

727 (1) William Cobbe ..., John Ventam ..., John Wellin ... On condition that William Cobbe will appear ... [See **621, 766**]

728 (2) Hugh Attlane, husbandman, of Brookley acknowledges to owe the king ..., William Perree of Minstead ..., Ralph Wilmott, yeoman, of Brockenhurst ... On condition that Hugh Attlane will appear at the next court of the justices in eyre held for the New Forest to answer to them for what will be charged against him on behalf of the king, and he will not withdraw from the court without permission. [See **516, 708–12, 717**]

729 (3) Richard Osman, husbandman, of Minstead acknowledges to owe the king £40. John Peirce son of Richard Peirce, husbandman, of the same place ... £20. John Hobbs, charcoal burner, of the same place ... £20. On condition that Richard Osman will appear ... [See **629**]

730 (4) Thomas Huett, husbandman, of Pawletts Moore ... £40. Thomas Trusloe, yeoman, of Bartley Regis ... £20. Henry Randal, husbandman, of Lyndhurst ... £20. On condition that Thomas Huett will appear ... [See **312**]

731 (5) Erasmus Bradber, butcher, of Heeth ... £40. William Lyne, gentleman, of the same place ... £20. Andrew Yalman, gentleman, of Buttsash ... £20. On condition that Erasmus Bradber will appear ... [See **341**]

732 (6) Nathaniel Uvedale, yeoman, of Holbury ... £40. Nicholas Lambard, yeoman, of the same ... £20. On condition that Nathaniel Uvedale will appear. [See **646**]

733 (7) Nicholas Hollier, yeoman, of Brockenhurst ... £40. Ralph Gretnum, yeoman, of Brockenhurst ... £20. On condition that Nicholas Hollier will appear ... [See **519, 537, 541, 549, 553**]

734 (8) Richard Storme, yeoman, of Netley ... £40. Robert Stride, yeoman, of Bartley Regis ... £20. Thomas Lovell, yeoman, of Bartley Regis ... £20. On condition that Richard Storme will appear ... [See **667, 680, 694–5**]

735 (9) John Younge, yeoman, of Burley ... £40. John Nippered, yeoman, of Burley ... £20. On condition that John Younge will appear ... [See **571, 725**]

736 (10) John Nippered, yeoman, of Burley ... £40. John Younge, yeoman, of Burley ... £20. On condition that John Nippered will appear ... [See **724**]

737 (11) Philip Rooke, yeoman, of Stuckton ... £40. Giles Rooke, yeoman, of Gorley ... £20. On condition that Philip Rooke will appear ... [See **577**]

738 (12) John Meryvale, yeoman, of Brockenhurst ... £40. William Ames, yeoman, of the same ... £20. On condition that John Meryvale will appear ...

739 (13) Alice Willmott, widow, of Brookley ... £40. James Elmes, yeoman, of Battramsley ... £20. On condition that Alice Willmott will appear ... [See **575**]

740 (14) Richard Draper, yeoman, of Brockenhurst ... £40. George Bright, yeoman, of the same ... £20. On condition that Richard Draper will appear ... [See **517**]

741 (15) John Burton, yeoman, of Brockenhurst ... £40. Richard Roffe, husbandman, of the same ... £20. On condition that John Burton will appear ... [See **539, 541**]

m.9

742 (16) John Randell, yeoman, of Burley ... £40. Henry Etheridge, husbandman, of the same ... £20. Michael Saunders, husbandman, of the same ... £20. On condition that John Randell will appear ... [See **527**]

743 (17) Michael Saunders, husbandman, of Burley ... £40. Henry Etheridge, husbandman, of the same ... £20. John Randell, husbandman, of the same ... £20. On condition that Michael Saunders will appear ... [See **531, 595**]

744 (18) Henry Etheridge, husbandman, of Burley ... £40. Michael Saunders, husbandman, of the same ... £20. John Randell, husbandman, of the same ... £20. On condition that Henry Etheridge will appear ... [See **529, 662**]

745 (19) Francis Barry senior, yeoman, of Hyde ... £40. Richard Livelonge, woollen weaver, of Fordingbridge ... £20. Richard Sex, yeoman, of Stuckton ... £20. On condition that Francis Barry will appear ... [See **704**]

746 (20) Richard Livelonge, woollen weaver, of Fordingbridge ... £40. Francis Barry senior, yeoman, of Hyde ... £20. Richard Sex, yeoman, of Stuckton ... £20. On condition that Richard Livelonge will appear ... [See **702**]

747 (21) Richard Sex, yeoman, of Stuckton ... £40. Richard Livelonge, woollen weaver, of Fordingbridge ... £20. Francis Barry senior, yeoman, of Hyde ... £20. On condition that Richard Sex will appear ... [See **679, 705**]

748 (22) Ambrose Austine, wheeler, of Gorley ... £40. William Lacye, husbandman, of the same ... £20. Richard Sex, yeoman, of Stuckton ... £20. On condition that Ambrose Austine will appear ... [See **675, 703**]

749 (23) William Lacye, husbandman, of Gorley ... £40. Ambrose Austine, wheeler, of the same ... £20. Richard Sex, yeoman, of Stuckton ... £20. On condition that William Lacye will appear ... [See **701**]

750 (24) Henry Crocker *alias* Carter, yeoman, of Burley ... £40. Michael Saunders, yeoman, of the same ... £20. Henry Etheridge, yeoman, of the same ... £20. On condition that Henry Crocker *alias* Carter will appear ... [See **496–7, 521–2, 530**]

751 (25) William Silver, husbandman, of Fawley ... £40. William Collins, husbandman, of Hardley ... £20. Walter Aman, husbandman, of Lepe ... £20. On condition that William Silver will appear ... [See **645**]

752 (26) William Collins, husbandman, of Hardley ... £40. William Silver, husbandman, of Fawley ... £20. Walter Aman, husbandman, of Lepe ... £20. On condition that William Collins will appear ... [See **523**]

753 (27) Stephen Whiteare, yeoman, of Burley ... £40. Michael Saunders, husbandman, of the same ... £20. Henry Etheridge, husbandman, of the same ... £20. On condition that Stephen Whiteare will appear ... [See **526, 653**]

754 (28) Meliora Emberly, widow, of Brockenhurst ... £40. Richard Huett, husbandman, of Eling ... £20. Robert Emberly, blacksmith, of Bramshaw ... £20. On condition that Meliora Emberly will appear ... [See **536, 554**]

755 (29) Joan Norton, widow, of Brookley ... £40. Thomas Purdue, yeoman, of Brockenhurst ... £20. On condition that Joan Norton will appear ... [See **548**]

m.9d

756 (30) John Rodes, ..., of Brockenhurst ... . of Lyndhurst ... On condition that John Rodes will appear ... [See **514**] [membrane damaged]

757 (31) Philip Davis,[1] tanner, of Brockenhurst ... £40. John Rodes, husbandman, of the same ... £20. Thomas Bullock, tailor, of

Lyndhurst ... £20. On condition that Philip Davis[1] will appear ... [See **515, 726**]

[1] possibly in error for Christopher Davis.

758 (32) William Draper, yeoman, of Brockenhurst ... £40. Thomas Norton, husbandman, of the same ... £20. John Moore, yeoman, of the same ... £20. On condition that William Draper will appear ... [See **546, 552**]

759 (33) Thomas Norton, husbandman, of Brockenhurst ... £40. William Draper, husbandman, of the same ... £20. John Moore, yeoman, of the same ... £20. On condition that Thomas Norton will appear ... [See **543, 545, 555**]

760 (34) John Hall, husbandman, of Brockenhurst ... £40. Thomas Cooper *alias* Rogers, husbandman, of the same ... £20. William Draper, husbandman, of the same ... £20. On condition that John Hall will appear ... [See **557**]

761 (35) Thomas Cooper *alias* Rogers, husbandman, of Brockenhurst ... £40. John Hall, husbandman, of the same ... £20. William Draper, husbandman, of the same ... £20. On condition that Thomas Cooper *alias* Rogers will appear ... [See **551**]

762 (36) Agnes Wavell,[1] widow, of Boldre ... £40. Richard Waterman, husbandman, of Pilley ... £20. John Thurstin, husbandman, of Brockenhurst ... £20. On condition that Agnes Wavell will appear ... [See **640**]

[1] Possibly in error for Anne Wavell.

763 (37) Richard Waterman, husbandman, of Pilley ... £40. John Thurstin, husbandman, of Brockenhurst ... £20. Agnes Wavell, widow, of Boldre ... £20. On condition that Richard Waterman will appear ... [See **635**]

764 (38) John Thurstin, husbandman, of Brockenhurst ... £40. Richard Waterman, husbandman, of Pilley ... £20. Agnes Wavell, widow, of Boldre ... £20. On condition that John Thurstin will appear ... [See **568**]

765 (39) Bartholomew Bulkley, gentleman, of Sway ... £40.

Richard Vesey, husbandman, of Lyndhurst ... £20. On condition that Bartholomew Bulkley will appear ... [See **682, 689**]

766 (40) William Cobb, charcoal burner, of Minstead ... £40. John Ventam, yeoman, of the same ... £20. John Wellin, butcher, of Lyndhurst ... £20. On condition that William Cobb will appear ... [?duplicate. See **621, 727**]

767 (41) Thomas Lacye senior, yeoman, of Broomy Lodge ... £40. Robert Emberly, yeoman, of Bramshaw ... £20. John Emberly, husbandman, of the same ... £20. On condition that Thomas Lacye will appear ... [See **490, 579**]

768 (42) Ralph Gretnum, yeoman, of Brookley ... £40. Richard Knight, yeoman, of Brockenhurst ... £20. On condition that Ralph Gretnum will appear ... [See **556, 688**]

m.10

769 (43) Christopher Biddlecombe, yeoman, of Hightown ... £40. John Young, yeoman, of Burley ... £20. On condition that Christopher Biddlecombe will appear ... [See **576**]

770 (44) John Purcas, charcoal burner, of London Minstead ... £40. John Crowcher, yeoman, of the same ... £20. Thomas Rogers, tailor, of Minstead ... £20. On condition that John Purcas will appear ... [See **504**]

771 (45) Joseph Coffyn, yeoman, of Burley ... £40. William Rogers, yeoman, of the same ... £20. On condition that Joseph Coffyn will appear ... [See **528, 654–5, 658**]

772 (46) William Tapp, yeoman, of Brockenhurst ... £40. Ralph Gretnam, yeoman, of Brockenhurst ... £20. On condition that William Tapp will appear ... [See **538, 547, 720, 723**]

773 (47) William Elcombe, yeoman, of Lyndhurst ... £40. John Vale, yeoman, of Wymson ... £20. On condition that William Elcombe will appear ... [See **532–3**]

774 (48) Weyman Carde, husbandman, of Pilley ... £40. James Elmes, husbandman, of Battramsley ... £20. On condition that Weyman Carde will appear ... [See **636**]

775 (49) Roger Payne, husbandman, of Battramsley ... £40. Ellis Stoakes, husbandman, of Pilley ... £20. On condition that Roger Payne will appear ... [See **597**]

776 (50) Henry Marshman, husbandman, of Exbury ... £40. Thomas Hussey, yeoman, of the same ... £20. Hugh Palmer, husbandman, of the same ... £20. On condition that Henry Marshman will appear ... [See **524**]

777 (51) Mary Warne, widow, of Nether Kingston ... £40. Henry Butler, gentleman, of Wilverley Lodge ... £20. On condition that Mary Warne will appear ... [See **699**]

778 (52) Thomas Mouland, husbandman, of Stuckton ... £40. John Kennell, husbandman, of Godshill ... £20. On condition that Thomas Mouland will appear [See **678**]

779 (53) Thomas Burton, husbandman, of Brockenhurst ... £40. Thomas Purdue, husbandman, of Brookley ... £20. On condition that Thomas Burton ... [See **550**]

780 (54) Giles Eyres senior, gentleman, of Brickworth in the county of Wiltshire ... £40. On condition that Giles Eyres senior will appear ... [See **493**]

781 (55) John Oldinge, yeoman, of Ashers [Ashurst] Lodge ... £40. On condition that Henry Lovell, groom, of Marchwood will appear ... [See **321**]

782 (56) William Parsons, gentleman, of Brockenhurst ... £40. Richard Knight, yeoman, of the same ... £20. On condition that William Parsons will appear ... [See **544**]

783 (57) John Aymes, husbandman, of Brockenhurst ... £40. Richard Rolfe, husbandman, of the same ... £20. On condition that John Aymes will appear ... [See **719**]

784 (58) John Barry, yeoman, of Fritham ... £40. Thomas Lovell, yeoman, of Bartley Regis ... £20. On condition that John Barry will appear ... [See **492, 677**]

m.10d

785 (59) James Elmes, husbandman, of Battramsley ... £40. William Whitehead, husbandman, of the same ... £20. On condition that James Elmes will appear ... [See **506**]

786 (60) William Whitehead, husbandman, of Battramsley ... £40. James Elmes, husbandman, of the same ... £20. On condition that William Whitehead will appear ... [See **507, 681**]

787 (61) Thomas Lovell, yeoman, of Bartley Regis ... £40. John Barry, yeoman, of Fritham ... £20. On condition that Thomas Lovell will appear ... [See **673–4**]

788 (62) Robert Whiteingstall, husbandman, of Godshill ... £40. John Witeingstall, husbandman, of the same ... £20. Philip Vesey, yeoman, of Lyndhurst ... £20. On condition that Robert Whiteingstall will appear ... [See **561**]

789 (63) John Whiteingstall, yeoman, of Godshill ... £40. Robert Whiteingstall, husbandman, of the same ... £20. Philip Vesey, yeoman, of Lyndhurst ... £20. On condition that John Whiteingstall will appear ... [See **562**]

790 (64) Edmund Cooper,[1] yeoman, of Brockenhurst ... £40. John Warwicke, yeoman, of the same ... £20. On condition that Edmund Cooper[1] will appear ... [See **540, 542**]

[1] possibly in error for Edward Cooper

791 Which all is signed with their seals by the foresters, verderers, regarders, and all other ministers of the forest following the form of the statute thus ordained and provided.

Thomas Penruddok
Cuthbert Bacon

Richard Goddard
William Beeston
William Rogers
[made his mark]

Richard Stote

Robert Knapton } Rangers
Thomas Browne }

Gabriel Lapp woodward

William Battin
Richard Ingpen
William Gose
Andrew Hobbs
William Coles
William Twyne

Ambrose Ringwood
Edward Scott
John Elyott
John Smith

E.32/174

m.1

792 ‹The New Forest in the county of Southampton›. Court and Pleas called the Swainmote, held at Lyndhurst on the 14th September, being fifteen days before Michaelmas, in the year 1660, before the foresters, verderers, regarders, agisters, and all other ministers of the forest, just as is written below

793	Keeper and Warden.	Thomas earl of Southampton has not appeared.
	Lieutenant.	[Blank]
	Steward	Richard Goddard esquire, steward of the forest, has appeared.
	Bow Bearer.	[Blank]
	Riding Forester.	Thomas Bacon esquire, riding forester, has appeared.
	Rangers.	Thomas Urry and Thomas Browne, gentlemen, have appeared.
794	Burley.	Robert Reade, gentleman, forester, has appeared.
	Battramsley.	Thomas Fitzjames esquire, forester, is excused.
	Fritham.	Arthur Oxford gentleman, forester, has appeared.
	Linwood.	John Bulkly esquire, forester, is excused.
	Godshill.	Sir John Penruddock, forester, is excused.
	In Bailiwick	George Rodney esquire, forester, is excused.
	East Bailiwick	Sir John Mill Bt., forester, has appeared.
	North Bailiwick	William Pawlett esquire, forester, has appeared.
	South Bailiwick.	Richard Norton esquire, forester, is excused.
795	Verminer.	Arthur Oxford, gentleman, has appeared.
	Verderers.	Thomas Knollis esquire and Thomas Mill esquire have appeared.

796 Regarders. Henry Godard, Bernard Knapton, John Cawle, Robert Olding, Thomas Lovell, Benjamin Edwards, Thomas Turner, James Barrow, John Drew, George Cole, Thomas Edwards, Richard Combes, all gentlemen, have appeared.

797 Agisters. Richard Draper and Thomas Ford have appeared. Riders. John Stote and Thomas Mershman are sworn in office.

798 Names of the under foresters.

Burley. Richard Woode has appeared, Henry Buckle is sick.

799 Battramsley. John Taplyn and Nicholas Barling have appeared. John Barling is attending the perambulation.

800 Fritham. Thomas Venner has appeared. John Buckett and John Mersman are attending the perambulation.

801 Linwood. John Lewen gentleman has appeared. Thomas Syms and John Davis are attending the perambulation.

802 Godshill. Edward Penruddock gentleman, George Harrison senior, George Harrison junior, John Sanders, have appeared.

803 In Bailiwick. Nicholas Bright has appeared. William Bright is attending the perambulation.

804 East Bailiwick. Edward Bright and Edward Buckle have appeared.

805 North Bailiwick. Walter Coleman is attending the perambulation. Hugh Piball has appeared.

806 South Bailiwick. William Rossiter and Clement Odway have appeared.

807 Woodward of the forest. Gabriel Lapp esquire has appeared. Woodward of Minstead. Robert Soff has appeared.

808 Names of the vills, and the reeve and four men of each vill.

Vill of Exbury and Lepe. Edward Stone reeve. James Tailor, Robert Draper, Arthur Gibbs, and William Bannister. Sworn and have appeared.

809 Vill of Holbury and Langley. William Hurmon is sick. Henry King, John Rider, William White, William Davis. Sworn and have appeared.

810 Vill of Buttsash and Hardley. Robert Bridger the reeve has not appeared. Therefore in mercy 2s 6d.

811 Vill of Pilley and Warborne. Edward Reeves the reeve. Richard Gasterd, Christopher Chaplyn, Arthur Watts, James Plowman. Sworn and have appeared.

812 Vill of Baddesley. Richard Cole reeve. William Haines, John Barnes, Kemberlin King, Christopher Scovell. Sworn and have appeared.

813 Vill of Battramsley and Wootton. John Ghost reeve. Thomas Lane, Richard Stote, William Fashatt, Henry Robbins. Sworn and have appeared.

814 Vill of Brockenhurst and Brookley. William Smith reeve. John Merrifield, William Farver, Richard Stoy, John Smith. Sworn and have appeared.

815 Vill of Godshill and Linwood. Thomas Randall, reeve, has not appeared. William Elfes, Thomas Persey, Francis Harris, Ambrose Bradshaw. Sworn and have appeared.

816 Vill of Burley. Michael Sanders reeve. Henry Etheridge, Thomas Randell, Alexander Purcas, Edward Burges. Sworn and have appeared.

817 Vill of Canterton and Fritham. John Compton reeve. Henry Edwards, Richard Bassett, Richard Iremonger, Edward Penton. Sworn and have appeared.

818 Vill of Minstead. Drew Penton, reeve, Richard Hayes, John House, Christopher Stride, John Purcas. Sworn and have appeared.

819 Vill of Lyndhurst. Simon Ashton reeve. John Hedges, William Wellen, Henry Batcheller, James Baker. Sworn and have appeared.

820 Vill of Bartley Regis and London Minstead. Thomas Newman, the reeve, has appeared. Thomas Wyatt.

821 Names of the Freeholders of the New Forest.

Exbury and Lepe. John Hills, Ann Cole [?by] Thomas Cole, Edward Cole, Richard Moone has appeared, John Osmond has appeared, Benjamin Ackridge, Nicholas Clement gentleman, Richard Cole appeared by ..., Stephen March gentleman has not appeared and in mercy 2s., Richard Compton esquire is excused, Benjamin Whithead claims land, Richard Cole is under age, the heir of Richard Deane, David Heyward — George Lesson claims the land, John Kempe esquire is dead — Henry Bromfeild junior, Richard Stronge has appeared and is excused, the heir of Richard Pittis gentleman, Richard West has not appeared.

822 Buttsash. John Crooke esquire, John Richards clerk, Humphrey Osey gentleman.

m.1d

823 Hardley. The heir of Richard Pittis gentleman — Thomas Edwards the tenant has appeared, the heir of Edward Baskett gentleman, the heir of Edmund Cole, the heir of Edmund Brice — Robert Shepheard claims the land, the heir of William Thorpe — Richard Abraham, the heir of John Barton gentleman, the heir of Nicholas Pescod, Henry Combes has appeared, John Wadmore is dead, the heir of John Brooke, Edward Keeling gentleman, John Stepto — William Crosse the tenant has appeared, William Crosse has appeared, Charles Lyne claims the land of John Yates.

824 Pilley and Warborne. Henry Bromfeild esquire has appeared, Richard Knowles gentleman — Eustace Man gentleman has appeared and claims the land, George Carter *alias* Crocker senior — John Carter claims the land, the heir of George Carter *alias* Crocker junior, John Grew[1] has appeared, John Rickman, Richard Arnold gentleman, James Ploughman, George Carter, Christopher Hills — Christopher Chapman[2] claims the land, Richard Boate, the heir of

John Elmes, the heir of William Collens — William Hale has appeared and claims the land, the heir of Edmund Reeves has appeared, Hugh Wheeler.

[1] *Recte* John Drew [2] *Recte* Christopher Chaplin

825 Baddesley. Henry Philpott esquire, John Drew, sir Henry Worsley Bt., Thomas South gentleman, Richard Line gentleman, Edward Bright, William Kent, the heir of John Dobbins, sir Henry Worsley Bt., William Colebrooke, John Streete, Richard Sampson gentleman.

826 Battramsley and Wootton. Sir Francis Dowce — Richard Ghost has appeared and claims the land, sir Richard Tichborne Bt., the heir of Edward Scott senior gentleman, the heir of Henry Tulse gentleman, Henry Goddard gentleman, sir John Meux Bt., John Edwards, James Elmes, William Amoore, Edward Scott junior.

827 Brockenhurst and Brookley. William Knapton gentleman has appeared, the heir of John Willmott, Richard Draper, John Attwood, Richard Row, Ann Pitt, John Topp, Elizabeth Hollier, the heir of John Willmott, William Castle, Thomas Norton, Thomas Gretnam, the heir of Thomas Purdew, the heir of Nicholas Hollier, Bernard Knapton gentleman, Thomas Gretnam, John Oliver.

828 Burley. William Batten gentleman, Thomas Tarver, John Nipreede — Thomas Chase — Francis Oliver, William Oviatt gentleman, the heir of Christopher Garrett, Christopher Lyne gentleman, Joseph Coffin, the heir of John Warne, the heir of Henry Lyne gentleman.

829 Godshill and Linwood. The heir of John Doddington esquire, Richard Goodridge, Henry Bradshaw, William Greete, William Gosse, Ogden Rooke, John Webb esquire, John Weekes gentleman, Edmund Okeden esquire, the heir of John Brewen esquire, John Stent, Henry Good, Henry Rooke, lady Cooper widow.

830 Canterton and Fritham. Sir Francis Dowce, John Call, Andrew Hobbs, Henry Roade, John Bannister, Benjamin Edwards has appeared and claims land, Matthew Bee gentleman, Stephen Brownjohn, Benjamin Edwards, John Holliday junior, William

Easton *alias* Mew, Ann Knollis widow, Thomas Gawin, John Emlyn.

831 London Minstead. Richard Goddard esquire, Francis Ranger, John Chater, John Crowcher, John Roberts.

832 Lyndhurst. John Lisle esquire, Bartholomew Bulkly gentleman, Anthony Wiseman, the heir of Lawrence Hide, James Elcombe, the heir of Walter Pile, William Gauntlet, John Morris, William Elcombe, Arthur Buckle, William Bright, Richard Elcombe.

833 Bartley Regis. Sir John Mill Bt., Richard Goddard esquire, the heir of Edmund White clerk, Robert Richbell gentleman, Thomas Lovell, Thomas Knapton gentleman.

834 Jurors for the lord king. Francis Courtney gentleman, Henry Edwarde, William Rookes, George Lesson, Tristram Ford, Thomas Fisher, John Carter, Henry Knight, Henry Combes, William Spelt, Joseph Brokenshaw, Richard Rowe, John Jordan. Sworn.

835 It is presented by the foresters and other ministers of the forest and the twelve jurors, and proved by the verderers, that George Hellier gentleman, recently underforester of the In Bailiwick, on the 13th February 1660 had entered the forest and in the demesne woods in various places within the said bailiwick had cut and lopped the branches of both oak and beech under colour of browsewood containing seventeen colefires, more for his own advantage than for the necessary forage of the king's beasts, of which was illegal a quantity worth £8 10s., to the destruction of the woods of the king and harm of the forest and damage of the king and against the laws and assize of the forest etc. ‹Not fined›.

836 That Robert Reade gentleman, recently forester of Burley bailiwick, on the 13th February 1660 in various places in the bailiwick had cut and lopped the branches of both oak and beech trees, containing twenty four colefires value £10 10s., under colour of browsewood. ‹Not fined›.

837 That William Pawlett esquire, recently forester of the North bailiwick, on the 13th February 1660 in various places in the bailiwick had cut and lopped thirty colefires of oak and beech branches worth £12. ‹Not fined›.

838 That Edward Talbott gentleman, recently underforester of Battramsley bailiwick, on the 13th February 1660, had cut and felled thirty six colefires of great branches of oak and beech trees worth £16. ‹Not fined›.

839 That Henry Browne gentleman, recently of Brockenhurst, on the 11th August 1660 in the South bailiwick had cut and felled a young timber oak worth 10s, which he had taken and carried away upon a cart drawn by three horses and two oxen worth £5. ‹£6 and value, and property £5 10s ...›.

840 That Arthur Oxford gentleman, forester of Fritham bailiwick, on the 13th February 1660 at a place called *Stonewood Pound* within the said bailiwick had cut and felled an oak containing five colefires worth 50s for cooper timber. ‹No fine›.

841 That Arthur Oxford on the 13th February 1660 in the said bailiwick of Fritham had cut and felled the branches of various trees containing fifty colefires worth £24 under colour of browsewood. ‹No fine›.

842 That Arthur Oxford on the 13th February 1660 at a place called Bratley in Fritham bailiwick had cut and felled an oak containing eight loads, and the branch of an oak containing a ton of timber, to the value of 50s. ‹No fine›.

843 That Thomas Ames, the servant of Henry Browne gentleman of Brockenhurst, on the 11th August 1660 in the South Bailiwick had cut and felled an oak of timber worth 10s, which he had taken and carried away on a cart drawn by three horses and two oxen value £5. ‹Fine £6, value of timber 10s, value of property £5›.

844 That Arthur Oxford on the 13th February 1660 at a place near *Haledales Hill* in Fritham bailiwick had cut and felled a beech tree containing one colefire of wood worth 10s. ‹No fine›.

m.2
845 Nicholas Rolph, yeoman of Beaulieu, because he has not

appeared before the verderers at this court by the recognizance he has undertaken. Penalty £20.

John Rolfe, yeoman of Beaulieu, one of the pledges of Nicholas Rolfe, because he did not have Nicholas before the verderers at this court by the recognizance he had undertaken. Penalty £10.

Alexander Cattell, husbandman of Beaulieu, one of the pledges of Nicholas Rolfe, because he did not have Nicholas before the verderers at this court by the recognizance he had undertaken. Penalty £10.

846 John Rolfe, yeoman of Beaulieu, because he has not appeared before the verderers at this court by the recognizance he has undertaken. Penalty £20.

Alexander Cattell, husbandman of Beaulieu, one of the pledges of the said John, because he did not have John before the verderers at this court by the recognizance he had undertaken. Penalty £10.

847 Alexander Cattell, husbandman of Beaulieu, because he has not appeared before the verderers at this court by the recognizance he has undertaken. Penalty £20.

Nicholas Rolfe, yeoman of Beaulieu, one of the pledges of the said Alexander, because he did not have Alexander before the verderers at this court by the recognizance he had undertaken. Penalty £10.

848 Which all and each thing is signed and sealed by the verderers, foresters, regarders, agisters, and all other ministers of the forest following the form of the statute.

849 ‹Recognizance› Henry Browne, gentleman of Brockenhurst, acknowledges to owe the king £20. On the condition that Henry Browne will appear at the next court of the justices in eyre held for the New Forest to answer to them for as much as will be charged against him on behalf of the king, and he will not withdraw from the court without permission.

850 [Signatures]. Tho. Knollys [verderer]. Hen. Goddard, Bernard Knapton, Robert Olding, Thomas Edwardes, Benjamin

Edwardes, James Barrow, Thomas Lovell, Richard Coombe, John Cawle, Thomas Turner, John Drew, George Coles [regarders]. Thomas Ford, Richard Draper agisters.

E.32/174

m.3

851 ‹The New Forest in the county of Southampton›. Court and Pleas of the New Forest, called the Swainmote, held at Lyndhurst on the 14th September, being fifteen days before Michaelmas, in the year 1661, before the foresters, verderers, regarders, agisters, and all other ministers of the forest, just as is written below

852 Keeper and Warden. Thomas earl of Southampton has not appeared.
Lieutenant. [Blank].
Steward. Richard Goddard esquire has appeared.
Bow Bearer. [Blank].
Riding Forester. Thomas Bacon esquire has appeared by Bernard Knapton gentleman, his deputy.
Rangers. Thomas Browne gentleman has appeared, Thomas Urry gentleman is sick.

853 Burley. Robert Reade gentleman, forester, has appeared.
Battramsley. Thomas Fitzjames esquire, forester, is sick.
Fritham. Arthur Oxford gentleman, forester, is excused by the court.
Linwood. John Bulkly esquire, forester, has appeared by John Lewen gentleman, underforester, and is thus excused.
Godshill. Sir John Penruddock, forester, has appeared.
In Bailiwick. George Rodney esquire, forester, has appeared.
East Bailiwick. Sir John Mill Bt., forester, has appeared.
North Bailiwick. William Pawlett esquire, forester, has appeared.
South Bailiwick. Richard Norton esquire, forester, is excused.

854 Verminer. Arthur Oxford gentleman is excused.
Verderers. Thomas Knollis esquire and Thomas Mill esquire have appeared.

855 Regarders. Bernard Knapton, Robert Olding, Thomas Lovell, James Barrow, Thomas Edwards, Richard Combes, Benjamin Edwards, William Henvist, Henry Edwards, William Fisher, William Lane, Edward Scott, all gentlemen, are sworn.

856 Agisters. Richard Draper has appeared, Thomas Ford is

excused.
Riders. John Stote and Thomas Mershman have appeared.

857 Names of the underforesters.

Burley. Richard Woods has appeared. John Palmer is sick.

858 Battramsley. John Taplin and Nicholas Barling have appeared.

859 Fritham. Arthur Oxford junior is sick, Thomas Venner has appeared, John Mershman is in perambulation.

860 Linwood. John Lewin gentleman has appeared. Thomas Syms and John Davis are in perambulation.

861 Godshill. Edward Penruddock gentleman and George Harrison junior have appeared. George Harrison senior and John Sanders are sick.

862 In Bailiwick. Nicholas Bright has appeared. William Bright is sick.

863 East Bailiwick. Edward Bright and Ralph Carter have appeared.

864 North Bailiwick. Robert Butcher and Moses Waldron have appeared. William Lansdale is in perambulation.

865 South Bailiwick. William Rossiter has appeared. Clement Odway is in perambulation.

866 Woodward of the forest. Gabriel Lapp esquire has appeared. Woodward of Minstead. Robert Soff has appeared.

867 Names of the vills, and the reeve and four men of each vill.

Vill of Exbury and Lepe. Edward Stone reeve. Henry Stephens, Henry Younges, Thomas Hobrooke, and Thomas Heyward are sworn.

868 Vill of Holbury and Langley. William Dipden reeve. John Pinhorne, Conwell Marlow, William Davis, and Richard Ventham are sworn.

869 Vill of Buttsash and Hardley. John Bradbe reeve. Thomas Edwards, Richard Combes, Thomas Steele, and Zacharius Steele are sworn.

870 Vill of Pilley and Warborne. Arthur Watts reeve. Richard Jones, Edward Gastard, Bartholomew Clements, and Martin Sanders are sworn.

871 Vill of Baddesley. Christopher Scovell reeve. Christopher Carde, John Tovey, Richard Ploughman, and Bartholomew Collens are sworn.

872 Vill of Battramsley and Wootton. John Toms reeve. Thomas Attwood, William Samber, Robert Amon, and Peter Penny are sworn.

873 Vill of Brockenhurst and Brookley. William Smith reeve. Richard Rewe, Thomas Earnly, William Lucas, and John Hall are sworn.

874 Vill of Godshill and Linwood. William Miller reeve. Nicholas Percy, Edward Amy, Edward Rogers, and William Sandeford are sworn.

875 Vill of Burley. John Younges reeve. Alexander Purcas, Edward Burges, Thomas Randell, and William Reekes are sworn.

876 Vill of Canterton and Fritham. Walter Coleman reeve. Richard Edwards, Matthew Warde, Henry Reade, and John Emblyn are sworn.

877 Vill of Minstead. Clement Morris reeve. Francis House, John House, Christopher Stride, and Robert Soff are sworn.

878 Vill of Lyndhurst. James Baker reeve. Simon Aston, Joseph Brokenshaw, John Gasken, and Richard Jones are sworn.

879 Vill of Bartley Regis and London Minstead. Thomas Mershman reeve. John Toms, Thomas Weaman, John Purcas, and James Purcas are sworn.

m.3d
880 Names of the Freeholders of the New Forest.

Exbury and Lepe. John Hills is sick, Thomas Coles has appeared, John Cole' has appeared, Richard Moone is dead, John Osmonde has appeared, Benjamin Ackridge has appeared, Nicholas Clement gentleman is excused as he is infirm, Richard Cole' is under age, Stephen March gentleman has not appeared and is therefore in mercy 2s 6d, Richard Compton esquire has appeared, Benjamin Whithead has not appeared and is in mercy 2s 6d, Richard Cole' has not appeared and is in mercy 2s 6d, the heir of Richard Deane has appeared, George Lesson is sick, Henry Bromfeild junior gentleman has appeared, Richard Strong has appeared by Nicholas Strong, the heir of Richard Pittis gentleman — Robert Hitchman the tenant has appeared, Richard West is excused.

881 Buttsash. John Crooke esquire is excused, John Richards clerk is excused, Humphrey Osey gentleman is excused.

882 Hardley. The heir of Richard Pittis gentleman is excused by the court, the heir of Edward Baskett gentleman — Richard Crosse junior claims the land and does not appear therefore in mercy 2s 6d, the heir of Edmund Cole is under age, Robert Shepheard has appeared, Richard Abraham has not appeared and is in mercy 2s 6d, the heir of John Barton gentleman — John Cornish claims the land and is under age, the heir of Nicholas Pescod — Adam de Cardonell claims the land and is sick, Henry Combes has appeared, John Wadmore is dead — John Stepto claims the land, John Brooke has appeared, Edward Keeling gentleman — Richard Auly claims the land but has not appeared and is in mercy 2s 6d, William Crosse has not appeared and is in mercy 2s 6d, Charles Lyne has appeared.

883 Pilley and Warborne. Henry Bromfeild esquire has appeared, Eustace Man gentleman -- John Drew the tenant has appeared, John Carter has appeared, John Drew has appeared, John Rickman is under age, Richard Arnold — John Drew the tenant has appeared, James Ploughman has appeared, John Carter has appeared, Christopher Chaplin is excused, Thomas Boate is under age — John Drew his guardian has appeared, the heir of John Elmes — Timothy Longe claims the land and has appeared, William Hale is under age — Robert Amon his guardian has appeared, the heir of Edmund Reeves — William Rasbridge claims the land and has appeared, Hugh Wheeler — Edward Gastrell the tenant has appeared.

884 Baddesley. Henry Philpott esquire is excused by the court, John Drew has appeared, sir Henry Worsley Bt. is excused by the court, John Marsh has not appeared and is in mercy 2s 6d, Richard Line gentleman — Tristram Ford claims the land and has appeared, Edward Bright has appeared, William Kent has not appeared and is in mercy 2s 6d, the heir of John Dobbins — Thomas Fisher claims the land and has appeared, sir Henry Worsley Bt. is excused, William Colebrooke — Thomas Fisher the tenant has appeared, John Streete — William Heynes claims the land and has appeared, Richard Sampson gentleman has not appeared and is in mercy 2s 6d.

885 Battramsley and Wootton. Richard Ghost has appeared, sir Henry Tichborne Bt. is sick, Edward Scott senior gentleman has appeared, the heir of Henry Tulse gentleman is sick, Henry Goddard gentleman is excused by the court, sir William Meux Bt. has not appeared and is in mercy 2s 6d, John Edwards is sick, James Elmes — Robert Amon claims the land and has appeared, William Amoore — Peter Penny claims the land and has appeared, Edward Scott junior has appeared.

886 Brockenhurst and Brookley. William Knapton gentleman has appeared, Nicholas Willmott is sick, Richard Draper has appeared, John Atwood has not appeared and is in mercy 2s 6d, Richard Rowe has appeared, John Topp — John Taplyn the tenant has appeared, Richard Willmott is sick, William Castle — Henry Williams claims the land and has appeared, John Norton has not appeared and is in mercy 2s 6d, Thomas Gretnam is under age, William Purdue — Joan Purdue the tenant is excused, the heir of Nicholas Hollier is excused, Bernard Knapton gentleman has appeared, Thomas Gretnam is under age, John Oliver has not appeared but is excused by the court.

887 Burley. William Batten gentleman is excused by the court, Thomas Tarver is dead, William Oviatt gentleman — Alexander

Purcas the tenant has appeared, Christopher Garrett has appeared, Christopher Lyne gentleman has appeared, Joseph Coffin has appeared, the heir of John Warne is excused, the heir of Henry Lyne gentleman — Christopher Garrett claims the land and has appeared.

888 Canterton and Fritham. Sir Francis Dowce is dead — Jonathan Rivett gentleman claims the land and is excused, John Cawle is dead — Edward Acton claims the land and has appeared, Andrew Hobbs is dead — the widow Elliott claims the land and is excused, Henry Roade has appeared, John Bannister — Richard Archard claims the land and has appeared, Benjamin Edwards has appeared, Matthew Bee gentleman — Richard Edwards the tenant has appeared, Stephen Brownejohn has appeared, Benjamin Edwards has appeared, John Holliday junior — Richard Archer claims the land and has appeared, William Easton *alias* Mew — John Compton the tenant has not appeared and is in mercy 2s 6d, Ann Knollis widow — George Venner gentleman claims the land and is excused, Thomas Gawny — Edmund Perkins gentleman claims the land and is excused, John Emlyn has appeared.

889 Godshill and Linwood. The heir of John Doddington esquire is excused, Richard Goodridge has not appeared and is in mercy 2s 6d, Ambrose Bradshaw has appeared, William Greete is excused, William Gosse — William Miller claims the land and has appeared, Ogden Rooke has appeared, John Webb esquire — Richard Philpot the tenant has appeared, John Weekes gentleman is under age, Edmund Okeden esquire — Edward Amy the tenant has appeared, the heir of John Brewen esquire — William Miller the tenant has appeared, John Stent is excused as infirm, Henry Good has not appeared and is in mercy 2s 6d, Henry Rooke has appeared, the widow Cooper is excused.

890 London Minstead. Richard Goddard esquire — Thomas Browne claims the land and has appeared, Francis Ranger is dead, John Chater has appeared, Robert Crowcher has appeared, John Roberts is dead.

891 Lyndhurst. Bartholomew Bulkly gentleman has not appeared and is in mercy 2s 6d, Anthony Wiseman — William Pocock the tenant has appeared, the heir of Lawrence Hide — Thomas Graunte claims the land and has appeared, James Elcombe has appeared, the heir of Walter Pile — Edward Bright claims the land and has appeared, William Gauntlett has appeared, John Morris has appeared, William Elcombe is dead, Arthur Buckle is sick, William Bright is sick, Richard Elcombe — John Hodges the tenant has appeared.

892 Bartley Regis. Sir John Mill Bt. has appeared, Richard Goddard esquire has appeared, the heir of Edmund White clerk — Edward Hamon claims the land and has appeared, Robert Richbell gentleman is excused, Thomas Lovell has appeared, Thomas Knapton gentleman has appeared.

893 Jurors for the lord king. Christopher Garrett gentleman, Edward Scott gentleman, Richard Jones, William Pocock, William Haynes, Ogden Rooke, John Merrifield, James Ploughman, Henry Reade, John Emlyn, Thomas Fisher, Christopher Scovell, Thomas Attlane; Alexander Purcas, Rowland Deane, Edward Hamond. Sworn.

894 (1) It is presented by the foresters and other ministers of the forest and the twelve jurors, and proved by the verderers, that Hugh Lyne husbandman, recently of Ringwood, in the 13th year of king Charles II [1661] in various places in the bailiwick of Linwood without permission had turned over and dug 1000 turves to the consumption and devastation of the pasture and exile of the beasts of the forest, to the damage of the king and against the laws and assize of the forest etc. ‹40s›.

895 (2) That Roger Russell yeoman, recently of Winsor, in the year 1661 in the North bailiwick had taken a load of wood worth 5s which he found there, and had carried it away for his own use to the harm of the forest and damage of the king. ‹20s›.

896 (3) That John Etheridge yeoman, recently of Highwood, on the 18th November 1660 in the bailiwick of Linwood had cut and lopped the branches of various trees worth £3 under colour of firewood, and had carried them away. ‹£30›.

897 (4) That William Cogell yeoman, recently of Burton, in 1661 in various places in the bailiwick of Burley, without permission had turned over and dug [blank] turves, and had taken and carried them away. ‹40s›

898 (5) That Edward Amy yeoman, recently of Linwood, in the bailiwick of Linwood had cut and felled two trees containing three loads of wood worth 20s, and these he had carried away.

899 (6) That Richard Rooke yeoman, recently of Linwood, in the bailiwick of Linwood had cut and felled an oak containing three loads of wood worth 10s, and these he had carried away.

900 (7) That Henry Rooke yeoman, recently of Linwood, in the bailiwick of Linwood had cut and felled an oak containing three loads of wood worth 20s, and these he had carried away.

901 (8) That John Wort yeoman, recently of Woodside, in 1661 in Beaulieu Heath in the South Bailiwick had dug 5000 turves, and with a cart drawn by four horses worth £6 had carried them out of the forest to the house of Francis Guidott gentleman in New Lymington. ‹£10 and the value of the chattels›.

m.4

902 (9) That Thomas Mislin husbandman, recently of Pilley, in 1661 within the South Bailiwick had turned over and dug 9000 turves without permission for several persons, who had carried them away. ‹£18›.

903 (10) That Alice Harding widow, recently of Sway, in 1661 in Beaulieu Heath in the South Bailiwick had taken [blank] thousand turves, and with a cart drawn by four horses worth £4 had carried them out of the forest to the house of John Blake in Lymington. ‹40s and value›.

904 (11) That Thomas Tarrant yeoman, recently of Milford, in 1661 in Beaulieu Heath had taken 1000 turves, and with a cart drawn by four horses worth £5 had carried them out of the forest to the house of Thomas Glevin gentleman in Lymington. ‹40s and value›.

905 (12) That James Baker yeoman, recently of Lyndhurst, in the In Bailiwick under colour of roots *(radicium)* allowed by the king, called *moores*, had cut and lopped the branches of oaks and also had dug up the roots of green oaks growing, worth 2s 4d, and the same had cut into firewood *(ligni carbonibus)* called *colewood*.

906 (13) That John Spencer yeoman, recently of Lyndhurst, in the In Bailiwick under colour of roots allowed by the king, had cut and lopped the branches of oaks and also had dug up the roots of various growing green oaks worth 2s, and the same had cut into firewood.

907 (14) That George Fox yeoman, recently of Hale, in the year 1660–1 in a place called Deadman in Godshill Bailiwick had taken and carried away four loads of hollies and thorn worth 10s.

908 (15) That William Rossiter, underforester of the South Bailiwick, in 1661 in various places within the bailiwick under colour of browsewood *(cablicie anglice browsewood)* had cut and lopped great branches of various oaks containing fifteen colefires worth £7. ‹£100 and the value›.

909 (16) That Clement Odway, underforester of the South Bailiwick, in 1661 under colour of browsewood had cut and lopped the great branches of various oaks containing seventeen colefires worth £9. ‹His heir £9›.

910 (17) That Thomas Venner, underforester of the bailiwick of Fritham, in 1661 under colour of browsewood had cut and lopped the great branches of various oaks containing fifteen colefires worth £7. ‹£7 upon the heir›.

911 (18) That Arthur Oxford gentleman, recently forester of Fritham Bailiwick, in 1661 under colour of browsewood had cut and lopped the great branches of various oaks containing 59 colefires worth £25. ‹As above›.

912 (19) That John Lewin gentleman, recently forester of Linwood Bailiwick, in 1661 under colour of browsewood had cut and lopped great branches of various oaks containing seventeen colefires worth £8. ‹£100›.

913 (20) That George Rodney esquire, forester of the In Bailiwick, in 1661 under colour of browsewood had cut and lopped great branches of various oaks containing twenty two colefires worth £10. ‹£100›.

914 (21) That Robert Reade gentleman, recently forester of the bailiwick of Burley, in 1661 under colour of browsewood had cut and lopped the great branches of various oaks containing fifty six colefires worth £25. ‹£100›.

915 (22) That William Pawlett, recently forester of the North Bailiwick, in 1661 under colour of browsewood had cut and lopped the great branches of various oaks containing twenty three colefires worth £10. ‹£100›.

916 (23) That Edward Bright underforester, recently of the East Bailiwick, in 1661 under colour of browsewood had cut and lopped the great branches of various oaks containing twelve colefires worth £5. ‹£100›.

917 (24) That Edward Talbott, recently forester of Battramsley Bailiwick, in 1661 under colour of browsewood had cut and lopped the great branches of various oaks containing sixty two colefires worth £25. ‹£100›.

918 (25) That Robert Andrewes yeoman, recently of Cadnam, on the 16th September 1660 at a place near Ocknell in Fritham Bailiwick was hunting, and with a gun loaded with powder and lead had shot and killed a buck. ‹£25›.

919 (26) That Henry Buckle, recently underforester of Holmsley in the bailiwick of Burley, in 1661 at Holmsley had cut and lopped, or had caused to be cut and lopped, a great quantity of holly, and this he had converted into colewood worth 3s of which he had sold a parcel to James Dewy and six colefires to William Dale of Purewell, and this he had carried to them, and had disposed of the remainder. ‹Not fined›.

920 (27) That James Parkins gentleman, recently of Brook, on the 20th April 1661 at Allum Green in the bailiwick of Battramsley was hunting with a greyhound, and had chased and disturbed the king's beasts. ‹£5›.

921 (28) That James Perkins on the 7th May 1661 at Allum Green was hunting with a greyhound. ‹£5›.

922 (29) That Thomas Pickfatt gentleman, recently of Burley, on the 13th February 1661 near Blackensford in the bailiwick of Burley was hunting with dogs, and he had chased and driven to death a deer, and had taken and carried away the flesh. ‹£25›.

m.4d

923 (30) That Robert Thorne yeoman, recently of Beaulieu, on the 13th May 1661 at Abbotstanding in the South Bailiwick was carrying a gun with the intention of harming and killing the king's beasts. ‹20s›.

924 (31) That Nicholas Rolfe yeoman, recently of Beaulieu, on the 13th May 1661 at Abbotstanding was carrying a gun with the intention of harming and killing the king's beasts. ‹20s›.

925 (32) That Alexander Cattle yeoman, recently of Beaulieu, on the 13th May 1661 at Abbotstanding was carrying a gun with the intention of harming and killing the king's beasts. ‹20s›.

926 (33) That Mary Moore widow of Brockenhurst in 1661 at a place near Hincheslea in Battramsley Bailiwick had taken 5000 turves, and in a cart drawn by four horses worth £4 had carried them out of the forest to the house of Andrew Hurst in Lymington. ‹20s›.

927 Which all and each thing is signed and sealed by the verderers, foresters, regarders, agisters, and all other ministers of the forest following the form of the statute.

928 [Signatures]. Thomas Knollys [verderer]. Bernard Knapton, Edward Scott, Thomas Edwardes, William Henvest, Benjamin Edwards [made his mark], Thomas Lovell, Richard Coombs, James Barrow, Robert Olding, William Fisher, William Lane, Henry Edwards [regarders]. Thomas Ford [made his mark], Richard Draper agisters.

E.32/174

m.5

929 ‹**The New Forest in the county of Southampton**›. **Court and Pleas called the Swainmote held at Lyndhurst on the 14th September, being fifteen days before Michaelmas, in the year 1662, before the foresters, verderers, regarders, agisters, and all other ministers of the forest, just as is written below**

930 Keeper and Warden. Thomas earl of Southampton, keeper and lord warden.
Lieutenant. [Blank]
Steward. Richard Goddard esquire has appeared.
Bow Bearer. Henry Bromfield junior esquire has appeared.
Riding Forester. Thomas Bacon esquire has not appeared.
Rangers. Thomas Urry gentleman has not appeared and is in mercy 5s. Robert Reade gentleman has appeared.

931 Burley. John Neale esquire, forester, has appeared.
Battramsley. Thomas Fitzjames esquire, forester, in the service of the king.
Fritham. Arthur Oxford gentleman, forester.
Linwood. John Bulkly esquire, forester, is dead.
Godshill. Sir John Penruddock, forester, has appeared.
In Bailiwick. George Rodney esquire, forester.
East Bailiwick. Sir John Mill Bt., forester.
North Bailiwick. William Pawlett esquire, forester.
South Bailiwick. Richard Norton esquire, forester, has not appeared.

932 Verderers. Thomas Knollis esquire is sick, Thomas Mill esquire has appeared.
Verminer. Arthur Oxford gentleman.

933 Regarders. Bernard Knapton, Thomas Lovell, James Barrow, Thomas Edwards, Richard Combes, Benjamin Edwards, William Henvist, Edward Scott, William Batten, William Miller, Thomas Fisher, Richard Edwards, all gentleman, and all have appeared and are sworn.

934 Agisters. Richard Draper and Thomas Forde have appeared.

Riders. John Stote has appeared, Thomas Mershman is sick.

935 Names of the underforesters.

Burley. George Bright has appeared, John Woods is in perambulation, John Palmer is sick.

936 Battramsley. John Taplyn is in perambulation, Nicholas Barling has appeared.

937 Fritham. Arthur Oxford junior and Thomas Venner have appeared, John Mershman is sick.

938 Linwood. John Lewin gentleman is excused, John Davis is in perambulation.

939 Godshill. Edward Penruddock gentleman and George Harrison senior are in perambulation, George Harrison junior and John Sanders have appeared.

940 In Bailiwick. Isaac Knight is in perambulation, William Bright has appeared.

941 East Bailiwick. Edward Bright, Ralph Carter has appeared.

942 North Bailiwick. Robert Butcher, Moses Waldron, and William Lansdale have appeared.

943 South Bailiwick. Edward Tutt gentleman, William Rossiter, and Clement Odway have appeared.

944 Woodward of the forest. Gabriel Lapp esquire.
Woodward of Minstead. Robert Soff has appeared.

945 Names of the vills, and the reeve and four men of each vill.

Vill of Exbury and Lepe. Thomas Heyward the reeve has appeared. Francis Lesson, John Osmond, William Michil, and Thomas Salter are sworn.

946 Vill of Buttsash and Hardley. William Osey reeve has appeared. William Harvey, William Crowcher, and Thomas Ecton are sworn. Thomas Tarrant has not appeared and is in mercy 2s 6d.

947 Vill of Holbury and Langley. Roger Barfoot reeve has appeared. John Rider and William Davis have not appeared and are excused. Conwell Malew and Ambrose Bound are sworn.

948 Vill of Pilly and Warborne. Bartholomew Clements reeve has appeared. Arthur Watts, Timothy Longe, Martin Sanders, and Thomas Mifflin are sworn.

m.5d

949 Vill of Baddesley. William Haines the reeve has appeared. James Ploughman, Richard Ploughman, William Henning, and Kemberlaine King are sworn.

950 Vill of Battramsley and Wootton. Robert Fry the reeve has appeared. Thomas Lane, Richard Stote, and Thomas Leach are sworn. John Smith has not appeared and is in mercy 2s 6d.

951 Vill of Brockenhurst and Brookley. Thomas Browne the reeve has appeared. Samuel Michill, Henry Williams, John Urry, and Nicholas Willmott are sworn.

952 Vill of Godshill and Linwood. Thomas Pearce the reeve has appeared. Thomas Toomer, John Warwick, William Ford, and John Hide are sworn.

953 Vill of Burley. John Tarry the reeve has appeared. William Rooke, William Reekes, Anthony Fish, and Robert Hollier are sworn.

954 Vill of Canterton and Fritham. John Barling the reeve has appeared. Matthew Warde, Edward Yeoman, Nicholas Hatch, and John Deale are sworn.

955 Vill of Minstead. Richard Hurst the reeve has not appeared and is in mercy 2s 6d. Christopher Stride, James Phillipps, Clement Morris, and Phillip Stride are sworn.

956 Vill of Lyndhurst. Thomas Pearce the reeve has appeared. Edward Welsh has not appeared and is in mercy 2s 6d. Nicholas Phillipps, Benjamin Edwards, and Henry Batcheller are sworn.

957 Vill of Bartley Regis and London Minstead. John Toms the reeve has appeared. William Olding, Robert Over junior, Phillip Page, and Thomas Newman are sworn.

958 Names of the Freeholders of the New Forest.

Exbury and Lepe. John Hilks has not appeared, Thomas Coles is dead, John Coles has appeared, the heirs of Richard Moone — Hugh Moone claims the land and has appeared, John Osmond has appeared, Benjamin Ackridge has not appeared — the tenant has appeared, Nicholas Clement gentleman is sick, Richard Coles — Henry Younges the tenant has appeared, Stephen March gentleman is sick, Richard Compton esquire has appeared, Richard Cole — Rowland Deane the tenant has appeared, the heir of Richard Deane — William Cole claims the land, George Lesson is dead, Henry Bromfield junior gentleman has appeared, Richard Stronge has appeared, the heir of John Pittis gentleman, Richard West — Henry Younges the tenant has appeared.

959 Buttsash. John Crooke esquire, Humphrey Osey gentleman is excused.

960 Hardley. The heir of John Pittis gentleman, Richard Crosse junior — Edward Harvy claims the land, the heir of Edmund Cole, Robert Shepheard has appeared, Richard Abraham has not appeared. John Cornish has appeared, Adam de Cardonnel — Richard Combes the tenant has appeared, John Stepto — William Crosse the tenant has appeared, John Brooke has appeared, Richard Auly has not appeared and is in mercy 2s 6d, John Stepto, William Crosse has appeared, Charles Lyne has appeared, Thomas Edwards has appeared, Richard Combes has appeared.

961 Pilley and Warborne. Henry Bromfield esquire has appeared, Eustace Man gentleman — John Drew the tenant has appeared, John Carter has appeared, John Drew has appeared, John Rickman, Richard Arnold — John Drew the tenant has appeared, James Ploughman has appeared, John Carter has appeared, Christopher

Chaplyn has appeared, Thomas Boate — Arthur Watts the tenant has appeared, Timothy Long has appeared, William Hale minor, William Rasbridge has appeared, Hugh Wheeler has not appeared and is in mercy 2s 6d.

962 Baddesley. Henry Philpott esquire, John Drew has appeared, sir Henry Worsley Bt., John March — Christopher Scovell the tenant has appeared, Tristram Ford is dead, Edward Bright has appeared, William Kent has not appeared and is in mercy 2s 6d, Thomas Fisher has appeared, sir Henry Worsley Bt., William Colebrooke — Thomas Fisher the tenant has appeared, William Haines has appeared, Richard Sampson gentleman — John Cole the tenant has appeared.

963 Battramsley and Wootton. Richard Ghost has appeared, sir Henry Tichborne Bt. has not appeared, Edward Scott senior gentleman has appeared, the heir of Henry Tulse gentleman has not appeared and is in mercy 2s 6d, Henry Goddard gentleman is excused, sir Wiliam Meux Bt. — Ellis Holliway the tenant has appeared, John Edwards has appeared, Robert Amon — Richard King claims the land, Peter Penny has not appeared and is in mercy 2s 6d, Edward Scott junior has appeared, William Burrard is sick, Thomas Robarts gentleman — Thomas Atlane the tenant has appeared.

964 Brockenhurst and Brookley. William Knapton gentleman, John Willmott has not appeared and is in mercy 2s 6d, Richard Draper has appeared, John Atwood has not appeared and is in mercy 2s 6d, Richard Rowe has appeared, John Topp, Henry Williams has appeared, John Norton has not appeared and is in mercy 2s 6d, Thomas Gretnam is under age, William Purdue has not appeared, the heir of Nicholas Hollier, Bernard Knapton gentleman has appeared, Thomas Gretnam has not appeared, John Oliver has not appeared and is in mercy 2s 6d, Richard King has appeared.

965 Burley. William Batten gentleman has appeared, the heir of Thomas Tarver, William Oviatt gentleman, Christopher Garrett has not appeared, Christopher Lyne gentleman has not appeared, Joseph Coffin has appeared, the heir of John Warne.

966 Godshill and Linwood. The heir of John Doddington esquire

— lord Robert Brooke claims the land, Richard Goodridge has appeared, Ambrose Bradshaw has appeared, William Miller has appeared, Ogden Rooke has appeared, John Webb esquire has not appeared and is in mercy 2s 6d, John Weekes gentleman has not appeared and is in mercy 2s 6d, Edmund Okeden has appeared, the heir of John Brewen esquire — William Miller the tenant has appeared, John Stent is excused, Henry Good has appeared, Henry Rooke has appeared, lady Cooper widow.

967 Canterton and Fritham. Jonathan Rivett gentleman has not appeared and is in mercy 2s 6d, Edward Acton — John Aldridge the tenant has appeared, widow Elliot — Richard Bassett the tenant has appeared, Henry Reade is sick, Richard Archer, Benjamin Edwards has appeared, Matthew Bee gentleman has appeared by Richard Edwards the tenant, Stephen Brownjohn — Samuel Mattocks the tenant has appeared, Benjamin Edwards has appeared, Richard Archer, William Easton *alias* Mew is dead, George Venner gentleman — Richard Edwards the tenant has appeared, Edmund Perkins gentleman has appeared, John Emlyn has appeared.

968 London Minstead. Thomas Browne, the heir of Francis Ranger, John Chater has appeared, Robert Crowcher has not appeared, the heir of John Roberts.

969 Lyndhurst. Bartholomew Bulkly gentleman — William Waterman the tenant has appeared, Anthony Wiseman — William Pocock the tenant has appeared, Thomas Graunte — William Oxford the tenant has appeared, James Elcombe has appeared, Edward Bright has appeared, William Gauntlet has appeared, John Morris has appeared, the heir of William Elcombe — Thomas Pearce claims the land, Arthur Buckle has appeared, William Bright has appeared, Roger Elcombe — John Hedges the tenant.

970 Bartley Regis. sir John Mill Bt. has appeared, Richard Goddard esquire has appeared, Edward Hammond — Philip Page, Robert Richbell is excused, Thomas Lovell has appeared, Thomas Knapton gentleman has appeared.

971 Jurors for the lord king. Ogden Rooke, Henry Rooke, William Pocock, Christopher Scovell, Henry Etheridge, John Carter senior,

William Cole, Rowland Deane, Ambrose Brodshaw, Charles Lyne, Christopher Lyne, John Pinhorne, Henry Younges, and James Ploughman are sworn.

m.6

972 (1) It is presented by the foresters and other ministers of the forest and twelve jurors, and proved by the verderers, that Arthur Oxford gentleman, recently forester of Fritham Bailiwick, in the 13th year of the reign [January 1661 — January 1662] within the said bailiwick at White Moor had cut up a moorefall beech for his own use to the destruction of the woods and the damage of the king, and against the laws and assize of the forest.

973 (2) That Arthur Oxford in the year 1661–2 in the bailiwick of Fritham had grubbed up a stubb that was 14ft. high, and he had cut it up for his own use.

974 (3) That Mary Sexey widow, recently of Stuckton, in 1662 in various places in Godshill Bailiwick had dug and carried away a load of turves without permission.

975 (4) That Henry Rooke husbandman, recently of Brook, in the year 1661–2 at Danes Hill in the North Bailiwick had found a timber oak which had been felled by a person unknown, which he had taken for his own use. ‹13s 4d›.

976 (5) That Clement Hobbs yeoman, recently of Canterton, on the 16th January 1662 in a place called Blackwool in the North Bailiwick, had cut the branch of an oak worth 3s. ‹30s›.

977 (6) That Emanuel Coyte yeoman of Brook on the 3rd December 1661 at Brook Path in the North Bailiwick had cut and felled an oak worth 20s. ‹£10 and the value›.

978 (7) That William Loukes husbandman, recently of Norley, on the 28th February 1662 at Norley in the South Bailiwick had made a purpresture and had enclosed and hedged about half an acre of land adjoining a house or cottage where no house previously was. ‹6s 8d and seized. Fine paid›.

979 (8) That Edward Buckle yeoman, recently of Lyndhurst, on the 10th February 1662 at Kings Hat in the South Bailiwick had cut and lopped various green branches and bushes, and had carried these away. ‹6s 8d›.

980 (9) That Moses Waldron recently underforester of the North Bailiwick in 1661–2 had caused two oaks which had been assigned for fuelwood *(pro focalia)* to be converted into coalwood *(lignum carbonibus aptum)*.

981 (10) That John King yeoman, recently of Cadnam, in 1662 had hunted in the North Bailiwick with a gun loaded with powder and lead, and had shot at a buck with the intention of killing. ‹40s›.

982 Which all and each thing is signed and sealed by the verderers, foresters, regarders, agisters, and all other ministers of the forest following the form of the statute.

983 [Signatures]. Thomas Knollys [verderer]. William Batten, James Barrow, John Drew, Richard Edwards, Thomas Lovell, Benjamin Edwards, Bernard Knapton, Thomas Edwards, Richard Combes, William Henvist, William Miller, Thomas Fisher [regarders].

m.7

984 ‹The New Forest in the County of Southampton›. Court and Pleas called the Swainmote held at Lyndhurst on the 14th September 1663 before the foresters, verderers, regarders, agisters, and all other ministers of the forest, just as is written below

985 Keeper and Warden. Thomas earl of Southampton has appeared.
Steward. Richard Goddard esquire has appeared.
Bow Bearer. Henry Bromfield junior esquire has appeared.
Riding Forester. Thomas Bacon esquire has appeared.
Rangers. Thomas Urry and Robert Reade, gentleman, have appeared.

986 Burley. John Neale esquire, forester, is sick.
Battramsley. Thomas Fitzjames esquire, forester, has appeared.
Fritham. Arthur Oxford gentleman, forester, has appeared.
Linwood. Anthony lord Ashly, forester, has appeared.
Godshill. Sir John Penruddock, forester, has appeared.
In Bailiwick. George Rodney esquire, forester, has appeared.
East Bailiwick. Sir John Mill Bt., forester, has appeared.
North Bailiwick. William Pawlett esquire, forester, has appeared.
South Bailiwick. Richard Norton esquire, forester, has appeared.

987 Verderers. Thomas Knollis esquire and Thomas Mill esquire.
Verminer. Arthur Oxford has appeared.

988 Regarders. Christopher Garrard, Thomas Lovell, James Barrow, Thomas Edwards, Richard Combes, Benjamin Edwards, William Henvist, Edward Scott, William Batten, William Miller, Thomas Fisher, Richard Draper, all gentleman, have appeared. Sworn for this occasion only.

989 Agisters. Richard Draper and Thomas Forde.
Rider. John Stote.

990 Names of the underforesters.

Burley. George Bright, John Woods, and John Palmer have appeared.

991 Battramsley. John Taplin and Nicholas Barling have appeared.

992 Fritham. Arthur Oxford junior gentleman, Thomas Venner, and John Mershman have appeared.

993 Linwood. John Lewin gentleman and John Davis.

994 Godshill. Edward Penruddock gentleman has appeared. George Harrison senior, George Harrison junior, and John Sanders.

995 In Bailiwick. Isaac Wright.

996 East Bailiwick. Edward Bright and Ralph Carter.

997 North Bailiwick. Robert Butcher, Moses Waldron, and William Lansdale.

998 South Bailiwick. Edward Tutt gentleman, William Rossiter, and Clement Odway.

999 Woodward of the forest. Gabriel Lapp esquire.
Woodward of Minstead. Robert Soff.

1000 Names of the vills, and the reeve and four men of each vill.

Vill of Exbury and Lepe. Thomas Heyward reeve has appeared. Edward Stote, Bartholomew Wright, and Francis Stowell have appeared and are sworn. William Banister has not appeared and is in mercy 2s 6d.

1001 Vill of Holbury and Langley. Richard Foster reeve. Robert Ruther, James Waleford, Nicholas Bernard, and Edward Cutler are sworn.

1002 Vill of Buttsash and Hardley. William Crowcher reeve. James Osey, William Heyward, Zacharius Steele, and Andrew Harvy are sworn.

1003 Vill of Pilley and Warborne. Martin Sanders reeve. Peter Goslin, Arthur Watts, Bartholomew Clement, and Christopher Chaplin are sworn.

1004 Vill of Baddesley. Bartholomew Collins. Richard Ploughman, John Pope, John Barnes, and Richard Moore are sworn.

1005 Vill of Battramsley and Wootton. John Toms reeve. John Smith, William Samber, Richard Ghost, and Robert Amon are sworn.

1006 Vill of Brockenhurst and Brookley. William Ames reeve. William Farver, Richard Stoy, Edward Rowland, and John Pilliean are sworn.

1007 Vill of Godshill and Linwood. Thomas Randoll reeve. Ogden Rooke, William Miller, Ambrose Brodshaw, and Henry Rooke are sworn.

1008 Vill of Burley. John Tarrey reeve. Alexander Purcas, Thomas Randall, James Randall, and Edward Pitt are sworn.

1009 Vill of Canterton. John Barling reeve. Thomas Stantor, John Deale senior, Henry Reade, and Richard Iremonger are sworn.

1010 Vill of Minstead. Drew Penton reeve. William Cull, George House, Richard Godden, and John Peane are sworn.

1011 Vill of Lyndhurst. John Rasbridge reeve. Joseph Brokenshaw, Nicholas Phillips, James Harding, and John Batcheller are sworn.

1012 Vill of Bartley Regis and London Minstead. John Toms reeve. Thomas Knapton, Walter Rogers, William Stride, and Thomas Jeanes are sworn.

m.7d
1013 Names of the Freeholders of the New Forest.

Exbury and Lepe. John Hills has not appeared and is in mercy 2s,

Thomas Coles, John Coles, Hugh Moone, John Osmond, Benjamin Ackridge, Nicholas Clement gentleman, Richard Coles, the heirs of Stephen March, Richard Compton esquire, Benjamin Whithead, Richard Cole, William Cole, the heirs of George Lesson, Henry Bromfeild, Richard Stronge, the heir of John Pittis gentleman, and Richard West.

1014 Buttsash. John Crooke esquire, and Humphrey Osey gentleman.

1015 Hardley. The heir of John Pittis gentleman, Edward Harvy, the heir of Edmund Cole, Robert Shepheard, Richard Abraham, John Cornish, Adam de Cardonnel, John Stepto, John Brooke, Richard Auly, John Stepto, William Crosse, Charles Line, Thomas Edwards, and Richard Combes.

1016 Pilley and Warborne. Henry Bromfield ... [Due to a scribal error this is followed by entries for Baddesley].

1017 [Baddesley]. ... John Drew, sir Henry Worsley Bt., John March is dead, William Walton, Edward Bright, William Kent, Thomas Fisher, sir Henry Worsley Bt., William Colebrooke, William Haines, and Richard Sampson.

1018 Battramsley and Wootton. Richard Ghost, sir Henry Tichborne Bt., Edward Scott senior gentleman, the heir of Henry Tulse gentleman, Henry Goddard gentleman, sir William Meux Bt., John Edwards, Robert Amon, Peter Penny, Edward Scott junior, William Burrard, and Thomas Roberts.

1019 Brockenhurst and Brookley. William Knapton gentleman, John Willmott, Richard Draper, John Atwood, Richard Rowe, John Topp, Henry Williams, John Norton, Thomas Gretnam, William Purdue, the heir of Nicholas Hollier, Bernard Knapton gentleman, John Oliver, and Richard King.

1020 Burley. William Batten gentleman, the heir of Thomas Tarver, William Oveatt gentleman, Christopher Garrett, Christopher Lyne, Joseph Coffin, and the heir of John Warne.

1021 Godshill and Linwood. Lord Robert Brooke, Richard Goodridge, Ambrose Brodshaw, William Miller, Ogden Rooke, John Webb esquire, John Weekes gentleman, Edmund Okeden, the heir of John Brewen esquire, John Stent, Henry Good, Henry Rooke, and lady Cooper widow.

1022 Canterton and Fritham. Jonathan Rivett gentleman, Edward Acton, the widow Elliott, Henry Reade, Richard Archer, Benjamin Edwards, Matthew Bee gentleman, Stephen Brownjohn, Benjamin Edwards, Richard Archer, William Easton *alias* Mew, George Venner gentleman, Edmund Perkins gentleman, and John Emlyn.

1023 London Minstead. Thomas Browne, the heir of Francis Ranger, John Chater, Robert Crowcher, and the heir of John Roberts.

1024 Lyndhurst. Bartholomew Bulkly gentleman, Anthony Wiseman, Thomas Graunte, James Elcombe, Edward Bright, William Gauntlett, John Morris, Thomas Pearce, Anthony Buckle, William Bright, and George Rodney gentleman.

1025 Bartley Regis. Sir John Mill Bt., Richard Goddard esquire, Edward Hammond, Robert Richbell esquire, Thomas Lovell, and Thomas Knatpon.

1026 Jurors for the lord king. Ogden Rooke, John Rider, William Olding, John Haskin, Robert Shepheard, John Aldridge, Richard Bassatt, James Ploughman, John Carter, William Spelt, Peter Penny, and Thomas Toomer are sworn.

1027 (1) It is presented by the foresters and other ministers of the forest and the twelve jurors, and proved by the verderers, that Edward Amy husbandman, recently of Linwood, on the 12th January 1663 in a place called [blank] in the bailiwick of Linwood had cut and felled covert to the value of [blank] to the destruction of the heath and covert of the forest.

1028 (2) That Henry Cozier yeoman, recently of Linwood, on the 12th January 1663 at High Corner in the bailiwick of West Linwood had cut and felled various holly trees containing [blank] loads worth [blank] and these he had taken and carried away. ‹20s›.

1029 (3) That Richard Stoy yeoman, recently of Brockenhurst, on the 17th August 1663 at Setley had placed and permitted his ten sheep to wander and depasture in and upon the herbage growing in the forest, depasturing and laying waste to the surcharge of the forest. ‹6s 8d›.

1030 (4) That William Michell yeoman, recently of Brockenhurst, on the 17th August 1663 at Setley had placed and permitted his three sheep to wander and depasture. ‹3s 4d›.

1031 (5) That Henry Goddard gentleman, recently of Brook, on the 17th August 1663 at Setley had placed and permitted his twenty sheep to wander and depasture ‹6s 8d fine paid›.

1032 (6) That Richard Smith yeoman, recently of Brockenhurst, on the 17th August 1663 at Setley had placed and permitted his eight sheep to wander and depasture. ‹paid 6s 8d›.

1033 (7) That William Penney yeoman, recently of Brockenhurst, on the 17th August 1663 at Setley had placed and permitted his seven sheep to wander and depasture. ‹6s 8d›.

m.8

1034 (8) That Thomas Browne yeoman, recently of Brockenhurst on the 17th August 1663 at Setley had placed and permitted his two sheep to wander and depasture.

1035 (9) That Bernard Knapton gentleman, recently of Brockenhurst, on the 17th August 1663 at Setley had placed and permitted

1036 (10) That Lewknor Mill gentleman, recently of Brockenhurst, on the 17th August 1663 at Setley had placed and permitted his six sheep to wander and depasture. ‹3s 4d fine paid›.

1037 (11) That Arthur Watts yeoman, recently of Pilley, on the 21st August 1663 at Pilley Heath had placed and permitted his eight sheep to wander and depasture. ‹5s fine paid›.

1038 (12) That Edward Reeves yeoman, recently of Pilley, on the 21st August 1663 at Pilley Heath had placed and permitted his twelve sheep to wander and depasture. ‹6s 8d›.

1039 (13) That Roger Hollier yeoman, recently of Royden, on the 21st August 1663 at Pilley Heath had placed and permitted his two hundred sheep to wander and depasture. ‹£5›.

1040 (14) That Christopher Carde yeoman, recently of South Baddesley, on the 21st August 1663 at Pilley Heath had placed and permitted his eight sheep to wander and depasture ‹3s 4d›.

1041 (15) That John Drew yeoman, recently of Pilley, on the 21st August 1663 at Pilley Heath had placed and permitted his thirty sheep to wander and depasture ‹6s 8d fine paid›.

1042 (16) That Richard Smith yeoman, recently of Brockenhurst, on the [21st] day of August 1663 at Pilley Heath had placed and permitted his five sheep to wander and depasture. ‹3s 4d paid›.

1043 (17) That Richard Sanders yeoman, recently of [blank], on the 23rd July 1663 in and adjacent to the bounds of Burley Bailiwick had hunted with greyhounds and had put to flight, chased, and disturbed the king's beasts within the peace of the forest. ‹£5›.

1044 (18) That George Hastings gentleman, recently of [blank], on the 23rd July 1663 in and adjacent to the bounds of Burley Bailiwick had hunted with greyhounds. ‹50s fine paid›.

1045 (19) That Ralph Hastings gentleman, recently of [blank], on the 23rd July 1663 in and adjacent to the bounds of Burley Bailiwick had hunted with greyhounds. ‹50s fine paid›.

1046 (20) That [blank] Gatherill husbandman, recently of [blank], on the 23rd July 1663 within Burley Bailiwick had hunted with a gun loaded with lead and powder and had shot at a buck with intent to kill.

m.8d

1047 (21) That John Sanders yeoman, recently of [blank], on the 23rd July 1663 in and adjacent to the bounds of Burley Bailiwick had hunted with greyhounds. ‹50s›.

1048 (22) That Henry Hastings, George Hastings, and Ralph Hastings gentlemen of [blank] and John Sanders yeoman of [blank] on the 3rd August 1663 in Burley Bailiwick had hunted with greyhounds and had put to flight, chased, and had driven to death a sorel, and they had taken and carried away the flesh.

1049 (23) That Arthur Oxford gentleman, forester of the bailiwick of Fritham, on the [blank] day of April 1663 had cut and felled the branches of various trees containing 67 colefires under the colour of browsewood, of which as much was unlawful browsewood as is truly worth £33 10s.

1050 (24) That George Bright, underforester of the bailiwick of Burley, on the [blank] day of April 1663 had cut and felled the branches of various trees containing 48 colefires under colour of browsewood, worth £24. ‹£120›.

1051 (25) That Thomas Fitzjames esquire, forester of the bailiwick of Battramsley, on the [blank] day of April 1663 had cut and felled the great branches of various trees containing 36 colefires worth £19 under colour of browsewood. ‹all his fines remitted to £20›.

1052 (26) That William Pawlett esquire, forester of the North Bailiwick, on the [blank] day of April 1663 had cut and felled the branches of various trees containing 56 colefires worth £28. ‹fine remitted›.

1053 Which all and each thing is signed and sealed by the verderers, foresters, regarders, agisters, and all other ministers of the forest following the form of the statute.

1054 [Signatures]. Thomas Knollys verderer. James Barrow, Thomas Lovell, Christopher Garrard, Richard Combes, Thomas Edwards, Benjamin Edwards, William Henvist, Edward Scott, William Batten, William Miller, Thomas Fisher, Richard Draper.

E.32/174

m.9

1055 ‹The New Forest in the County of Southampton›. Court and Pleas called the Swainmote, held at Lyndhurst on the 14th September 1664 before the foresters, verderers, regarders, agisters, and all other ministers of the forest, just as is written below

1056 Keeper and Warden. Thomas earl of Southampton.
Lieutenant. [Blank].
Steward. Richard Goddard esquire.
Bow Bearer. Henry Bromfield junior esquire.
Riding Forester. Thomas Bacon esquire.
Rangers. Thomas Urry and Robert Reade gentleman.

1057 Burley. John Neale esquire, forester.
Battramsley. Thomas Fitzjames esquire, forester.
Fritham. Arthur Oxford gentleman, forester.
Linwood. Lord Anthony Ashly, forester.
Godshill. Sir John Penruddock, forester.
In Bailiwick. George Rodney esquire, forester.
East Bailiwick. Sir John Mill Bt., forester.
North Bailiwick. William Pawlett esquire, forester.
South Bailiwick. Richard Norton esquire, forester.

1058 Verderers. Thomas Knollis esquire and Thomas Mill esquire.
Verminer. Arthur Oxford gentleman.

1059 Regarders. James Barrow, Thomas Lovell, Benjamin Edwards, Thomas Edwards, Thomas Fisher, William Miller, William Batten, Richard Combes, Edward Hamond, Christopher Lyne, William Pocock, William Olding. Sworn for this occasion only.

1060 Agisters. Richard Rowe and William Bright.

1061 Names of the underforesters.

Burley. George Bright, John Palmer, and John Woods have appeared.

1062 Battramsley. John Taplyn and Nicholas Barling have appeared.

1063 Fritham. Arthur Oxford and Thomas Venner have appeared.

1064 Linwood. John Lewin gentleman and Thomas Fry have appeared.

1065 Godshill. Edward Penruddock and John Sanders have appeared.

1066 In Bailiwick. Thomas Graunte and Henry Buckle.

1067 East Bailiwick. Edward Bright and Ralph Carter.

1068 North Bailiwick. Robert Butcher and Moses Waldron.

1069 South Bailiwick. John Sparrow and William Rossiter.

1070 Woodward of the forest. William Horne esquire.
Woodward of Minstead. Robert Soph.

1071 Names of the vills, and the reeve and four men of each vill.

Vill of Exbury and Lepe. James Tayler reeve has appeared. William Michell, Thomas Tee, Bartholomew White, and Thomas Salte are sworn.

1072 Vill of Holbury and Langley. Edward Cutler reeve. James Wakeford, Robert Luther, William Dipden, and Robert Smith are sworn.

1073 Vill of Buttsash and Hardley. Thomas Steele reeve. Zacharius Steele, John Harvy, Nicholas Hancock, and William Heyward are sworn.

1074 Vill of Pilley and Warborne. Ambrose Watts reeve. William Rusbridge, Christopher Chaplin, Thomas Mislin, and John Carter are sworn.

1075 Vill of Baddesley. Thomas Burgis reeve. James Brafoot,

Richard Ploughman, Henry Pocock, and Thomas Cozens are sworn.

1076 Vill of Battramsley and Wootton. Peter Penny reeve. Henry Robbins and Richard Stote are sworn. Richard Ghost has not appeared and is in mercy 2s 6d.

1077 Vill of Brockenhurst and Brookley. Thomas Browne reeve. Richard Knapton, Edward Batten, Thomas Willmott, and Henry Baker are sworn.

1078 Vill of Godshill and Linwood. Thomas Randall reeve. Thomas Yelfes, William Smeeford, Edward Amy, and Nicholas [blank] are sworn.

m.9d

1079 Vill of Burley. John Younge reeve. John Wiseman, John Tarrie, Batten Selfe, and Henry Graunte are sworn.

1080 Vill of Canterton and Fritham. John Barling reeve. Edward Yeoman, Henry Reade, John Deale, and Thomas Locke are sworn.

1081 Vill of Minstead. Robert Soff reeve, John Pieres senior, John Burden, Drew Penton, and Charles Heyward are sworn.

1082 Vill of Lyndhurst. Thomas Pearce reeve. Richard Gaskin, John Morris, John Batcheller, and James Baker are sworn.

1083 Vill of Bartley Regis and London Minstead. John Carter reeve. Thomas Knapton, William Rogers, William Olding, and Robert Hiscock are sworn.

1084 Names of the Freeholders of the New Forest.

Exbury and Lepe. John Hill, Thomas Coles, John Coles, Hugh Moone, John Osmond is dead — William Cowdry, Benjamin Ackeridge, Nicholas Clement gentleman — James Tayler, Richard Cole, the heirs of Stephen March, Richard Compton esquire, Benjamin Whithead, Richard Cole — Henry Younge tenant, William Cole, the heirs of George Lesson, Henry Bromfield junior gentleman, Richard Stronge, the heir of John Pittis gentleman, Richard West is dead — Henry Younge tenant.

1085 Buttsash. John Crooke esquire and Humphrey Osey gentleman.

1086 Hardley. The heir of John Pittis gentleman — Thomas Edwards tenant, Edward Harvy, the heir of Edmund Cole, Robert Shepheard, Richard Abraham — William Heyward tenant, John Cornish, Adam de Cardonnel — Richard Combes tenant, John Stepto, John Brooke, Richard Auly, John Stepto, William Crosse, Charles Line, Thomas Edwards, Richard Combes.

1087 Pilley and Warborne. Henry Bromfeild esquire, Eustace Man gentleman — John Drew tenant, John Carter, John Drew, John Rickman, Richard Arnold — John Drew tenant, James Ploughman, John Carter, Christopher Chaplyn, Thomas Boate, Timothy Longe, William Hale, William Rasbridge, Hugh Wheeler.

1088 Baddesley. Henry Philpott esquire, John Drew, sir Henry Worsley Bt. — Henry Philpott esquire tenant, the heir of John March — Christopher Scovell tenant, William Walton — John Pope tenant, Edward Bright, William Kent — Henry Pocock tenant, Thomas Fisher, sir Henry Worsly Bt., William Colebrooke — Thomas Fisher tenant, William Haines, Richard Sampson gentleman.

1089 Battramsley and Wootton. Richard Ghost, sir Henry Tichborne Bt. — William Spelt tenant, Edward Scott senior gentleman, the heir of Henry Tulse gentleman, Henry Goddard gentleman, sir William Meux — Ellis Holliway tenant, John Edwards, Robert Amon, Peter Penny, Edward Scott junior, William Burrard, Thomas Roberts gentleman — Thomas Atlane tenant.

1090 Brockenhurst and Brookley. William Knapton gentleman, John Willmott is dead — Margaret Smith, Richard Draper, John Atwood, Richard Rowe, William Knapton gentleman, Henry Williams, John Norton is dead — Thomas Burton, Thomas Gretman, William Purdue, the heir of Nicholas Hollier, Bernard Knapton gentleman, John Oliver, Richard King.

1091 Burley. William Batten gentleman, the heir of Thomas Turner,[1] William Oveatt gentleman, Christopher Garrett, Christopher Lyne, Joseph Coffin, John Warne.

[1] *recte* Tarver.

1092 Godshill and Linwood. Lord Robert Brooke, Richard Goodridge, Ambrose Bradshaw, William Miller, Ogden Rooke, John Webb esquire — Richard Philpott tenant, John Weekes gentleman, Edmund Obden — John Hide tenant, the heir of John Brewen, John Stent, Henry Good, Henry Rooke, lady Cooper widow.

1093 Canterton and Fritham. Jonathan Rivett gentleman, Edward Acton, widow Elliott, Henry Reade, Richard Archer, Benjamin Edwards, Matthew Bee gentleman, Stephen Brownjohn, Benjamin Edwards, Richard Edwards, William Easton *alias* Meux, George Venner gentleman — Richard Edwards tenant, Edmund Perkins gentleman — Francis Perkins tenant, John Emblyn.

1094 London Minstead. Thomas Browne — William Olding tenant, the heir of Francis Ranger, John Chater, Robert Crowcher, the heir of John Roberts.

1095 Lyndhurst. Bartholomew Bulkly gentleman, Anthony Wiseman — William Pocock tenant, Thomas Graunte, James Elcombe, Edward Bright, William Gauntlett, John Morris, Thomas Pearce, Arthur Buckle, William Bright, George Rodney gentleman.

1096 Bartley Regis. Sir John Mill Bt., Richard Goddard esquire, Edward Hammond, Robert Richbell, Thomas Lovell gentleman, Thomas Knapton gentleman.

1097 Jurors for the lord king. Ogden Rooke, William Stride, Richard Bassat, Matthew Warde, Thomas Atlane, William Spelt, Henry Combs, Henry King, Robert Shepheard, Charles Lyne, Arthur Watts, John Mortimer, John Pope, John Barnes, George Coles, William Rooke. Sworn.

m.10

[The following presentments, **1098–1115**, omit the usual phrase 'and proved by the verderers' *(et convictus per viridarios)*, instead blank spaces have been left. Also, although signed, the usual subscription that 'all and each thing is signed and sealed by the verderers etc.' has been omitted although a space has been left for its insertion].

1098 (1) It is presented by the foresters and other ministers of the forest and the twelve jurors [blank] that Ralph Carter, underforester of the East Bailiwick, on the 21st June 1664 had cut and felled the branches of various trees containing ten colefires under colour of browsewood, of which as much was unlawful browsewood as is worth £5, more for his own advantage than for the necessary forage of the king's beasts.

1099 (2) That William Rossiter, underforester of the South Bailiwick, on the 21st June 1664 had cut and felled the branches of various trees containing nineteen colefires worth £18 10s.

1100 (3) That John Sanders, underforester of Godshill Bailiwick, on the 21st June 1664 had cut and felled the branches of various trees containing four colefires worth 40s.

1101 (4) That John Sparrow, underforester of the South Bailiwick, on the 21st June 1664 had cut and felled the branches of various trees containing nineteen colefires worth £8 10s.

1102 (5) That Edward Bright, underforester of East Bailiwick, on the 21st June 1664 had cut and felled the branches of various trees containing twenty five colefires worth £12 10s.

1103 (6) That Thomas Venner, underforester of Fritham Bailiwick, on the 21st June 1664 had cut and felled the branches of various trees containing twenty colefires worth £10.

1104 (7) That John Taplyn, underforester of Battramsley Bailiwick, on the 21st June 1664 had cut and felled the branches of various trees containing eleven colefires worth £5 10s.

1105 (8) That John Palmar, underforester of Burley, on the 21st June 1664 had cut and felled the branches of various trees containing four colefires worth 40s.

1106 (9) That John Lewin gentleman, underforester of Linwood Bailiwick, on the 21st June 1664 had cut and felled the branches of various trees containing thirty one colefires worth £15 10s.

1107 (10) That Thomas Fitzjames esquire, forester of Battramsley Bailiwick, on the 5th January 1664[1] had cut and felled the branches of various trees containing two colefires worth 20s.

[1] This is given as year 16, the same as for the preceding and subsequent entries. Presumably, as the regnal year ended on the 29th January, this is in error for year 15.

1108 (11) That Arthur Oxford gentleman, forester of Fritham Bailiwick, on the 21st June 1664 had cut and felled the branches of various trees containing seventy four colefires worth £37.

1109 (12) That George Bright, underforester of Burley Bailiwick, on the 21st June 1664 had cut and felled branches containing thirty eight colefires worth £19.

1110 (13) That William Pawlett esquire, forester of the North Bailiwick, on the 21st June 1664 had cut and felled branches containing fifty two colefires worth £26.

1111 (14) That Thomas Fitzjames of Battramsley Bailiwick on the 21st June 1664 had cut and felled branches containing fifty three colefires worth £26 10s.

m.10d

1112 (15) That Arthur Oxford gentleman, forester of Fritham Bailiwick, on the 5th January 1664[1] under colour of roots sold to him by the king, had dug up and destroyed various roots and the green stumps of growing trees, not sold to him and containing five colefires worth 5s.

[1] Year 16 written in error.

1113 (16) That George Rodney, forester of the In Bailiwick, on the 5th January 1664[1] under colour of roots sold by the king, had dug up and destroyed various roots and stumps containing seven colefires worth £3 10s.

[1] Year 16 written in error.

1114 (17) That William Pawlett, forester of the North Bailiwick, on the 5th January 1664[1] had dug up and destroyed various roots and stumps containing two colefires worth 20s.

[1] Year 16 written in error.

1115 (18) That George Bright, underforester of Burley Bailiwick, on the 5th January 1664[1] had cut and lopped under colour of browsewood, containing twelve colefires worth £6.

[1] Year 16 written in error.

1116 [Signatures]. Thomas Knollys verderer. James Barrow, Thomas Lovell, Benjamin Edwards, Thomas Edwards, Thomas Fisher, William Millar, William Batten, Richard Combes, Edward Hamond, William Pocock, William Olding, Christopher Lyne [regarders].

E.32/174

m.11

1117 ‹New Forest in the county of Southampton›. Court and Pleas called the Swainmote held at Lyndhurst on the 14th September 1665 before the foresters, verderers, regarders, agisters, and all other ministers of the forest, just as is written below

1118 Keeper and Warden. Thomas earl of Southampton.
Lieutenant. [Blank].
Steward. Richard Goddard esquire has appeared.
Bow Bearer. Henry Bromfeild junior has appeared.
Riding Forester. Thomas Bacon esquire is excused.
Rangers. Thomas Urry gentleman is excused, Robert Reade gentleman has appeared.

1119 Burley. John Neale esquire forester.
Battramsley. Thomas Fitzjames esquire, forester.
Fritham. Arthur Oxford gentleman, forester, has appeared.
Linwood. Sir Adam Browne Bt., forester.
In Bailiwick. George Rodney esquire, forester.
Godshill. Sir John Penruddick, forester.
East Bailiwick. Sir John Mill Bt., forester.
North Bailiwick. William Pawlett esquire, forester.
South Bailiwick. Richard Norton esquire, forester.

1120 Verderers. Thomas Knollis esquire and Philip Leigh esquire have appeared.
Verminer. Arthur Oxford gentleman has appeared.

1121 Regarders. James Barrow, Thomas Lovell, Thomas Edwards, Thomas Fisher, William Batten, James Osey, Richard Combes, Edward Hamond, William Pocock, William Olding, Ogden Rooke, and Nicholas Lambert. Sworn for this occasion only.

1122 Agisters. Richard Rowe and William Pocock have appeared. William Bright and William Stride.
Riders. John Stote and James Bayly have appeared.

1123 Names of the underforesters.

Burley. George Bright has appeared, John Woods.

1124 Battramsley. John Taplin has appeared, Nicholas Barling.

1125 Fritham. Arthur Oxford junior and Thomas Venner have appeared.

1126 Linwood. Hugh Pyball and Henry Rooke have appeared.

1127 In Bailiwick. William Signe has appeared.

1128 Godshill. Edward Penruddock gentleman, John Sanders, and George Harrison have appeared.

1129 East Bailiwick. Edward Bright and Ralph Carter have appeared.

1130 North Bailiwick. Moses Waldron and William Lansdale have appeared.

1131 South Bailiwick. John Sparrow and William Rossiter have appeared.

1132 Woodward of the forest. William Horne has appeared. Woodward of Minstead. Robert Soff has appeared.

1133 Names of the vills, and the reeve and four men of each vill.

Vill of Exbury and Lepe. Francis Lesson reeve. Arthur Gibbs, Robert Frier, David Wiseman, and Robert Draper.

1134 Vill of Holbury and Langley. Nicholas Barnard reeve. Samuel Machoe, Robert Arnes, and Richard Gates.

1135 Vill of Buttsash and Hardley. Robert Shepheard reeve. William Knight, William Hayward, Robert Cowdrey, and Nicholas Hancock.

1136 Vill of Pilley and Warborne. Arthur Watts, William Rasbridge, John Carter, and John Rickman.

1137 Vill of South Baddesley. Christopher Scoveli, Kemberlin King, Richard Plowman, and Richard Moore.

1138 Vill of Battramsley and Wootton. Thomas Hapgood, James Warwick, Richard Ghost, and John Chase.

1139 Vill of Brockenhurst and Brookley. John Tarver, Thomas Burton senior, Edward Rowland, William Furne, and Robert Crooke.

1140 Vill of Godshill and Linwood. [No names entered].

1141 Vill of Burley. Thomas Randell, William Miste, and Thomas Cruse.

1142 Vill of Canterton and Fritham. John Deale senior, Richard Bassett, Thomas Lock, and Richard Iremonger.

1143 Vill of Minstead. Clement Morris, Charles Hayward, John Bound, and John Burden.

m.11d
1144 Vill of Lyndhurst. John Goffe, John Knight, George Hedger, Edward Stride, and Richard Prickhand.

1145 Vill of Bartley Regis and London Minstead. [No names entered].

1146 Names of the Freeholders of the New Forest.

Exbury and Lepe. John Hills, Thomas Cole, John Coles, Hugh Moone, William Cowdrey, Benjamin Ackeridge, Nicholas Clement gentleman, Richard Cole, the heir of Stephen March, Richard Compton esquire, Benjamin Whithead, Richard Cole, William Cole, the heir of George Lesson, Henry Bromfeild junior, Richard Stronge, the heir of John Pittis gentleman, Richard West.

1147 Buttsash. John Crooke esquire, James Osey gentleman.

1148 Hardley. The heir of John Pittis gentleman, Edward Harvy, the heir of Edmund Cole, Robert Shepheard, Richard Abraham,

John Cornish, Adam de Cardonell gentleman, John Stepto, John Brooke, Richard Amy, John Stepto, William Crosse, Charles Lyne, Thomas Edwards, Richard Combes.

1149 Pilley and Warborne. Henry Bromfeild esquire, Eustace Man gentleman, John Carter, John Drew, John Rickman, Richard Arnold, James Plowman, John Carter, Christopher Caplyn, Thomas Boate, Timothy Long, William Hale, William Rasbridge, Hugh Wheeler.

1150 Baddesley. Henry Phillpott esquire, John Drew, sir Henry Worsley Bt., the heir of John March, William Walton, Edward Bright, William Read', Thomas Fisher, sir Henry Worsley Bt., William Colebrooke, William Haines, Richard Sampson gentleman.

1151 Battramsley and Wootton. Richard Ghost, sir Henry Titchborne Bt., Edward Scott gentleman, the heir of Henry Tulse gentleman, Henry Goddard gentleman, sir William Meux Bt., John Edwards, Robert Amon, Peter Penny, Edward Scott, William Burrard, Thomas Roberts gentleman.

1152 Brockenhurst and Brookley. William Knapton gentleman, Margaret Smith, Richard Draper, John Atwood, Richard Rowe, William Knapton gentleman, Henry Williams, Thomas Burton, Thomas Gretnam, William Purdue, the heir of Nicholas Hollier, Bernard Knapton gentleman, John Oliver, Richard King.

1153 Burley. William Batten gentleman, the heir of Thomas Tarver, William Bampton, Christopher Garrett gentleman, Christopher Lyne, Joseph Coffin, John Warne.

1154 Godshill and Linwood. Lord Robert Brooke, Richard Goodridge, Ambrose Bradshawe, William Miller, Ogden Rooke, John Webb, John Weeks gentleman, Edmund Ockden, the heir of John Brewen, John Stent, Henry Good, Henry Rooke, lady Cooper widow.

1155 Canterton and Fritham. Jonathan Rivett gentleman, Edward Acten, the widow Elliott, Henry Reade, Richard Archer, Benjamin Edwards, Matthew Bee gentleman, Stephen Brownjohn, Benjamin

1156 London Minstead. Thomas Browne, the heir of Francis Ranger, John Chater, Robert Crowcher, the heir of John Roberts.

1157 Lyndhurst. Bartholomew Bulkly gentleman, Anthony Wiseman, Thomas Grante, James Elcombe, Edward Bright, William Gauntlett, John Morris, Thomas Pearce, Arthur Buckle, William Bright, George Rodney gentleman.

1158 Bartley Regis. Sir John Mill Bt., Richard Goddard esquire, Edward Hammond, Robert Richbell gentleman, Thomas Lovell gentleman, Thomas Knapton gentleman.

m.12

1159 Jurors for the lord king. James Plowman, William Rogers junior, John Moone, Matthew Wilson, William Spelt, Henry Combes, Richard Foster, Gabriel Butler, John Harvey, Joseph Coffin, John Emblyn, John Pope, and John Barnes are sworn.

1160 It is presented by the foresters and other ministers of the forest and the twelve jurors, and proved by the verderers, that Henry Hastings and George Hastings, gentlemen recently of Hinton, on the 3rd August 1664 between East Close and Chamberlains Corner had two greyhounds to the terror and destruction of the king's beasts.

1161 That George Rodney, recently forester of the In Bailiwick, on the 10th July 1665 near to Faire Cropp under colour of browsewood had taken and sold a moorfall beech *(unum eradicatum fagum)* worth 12s ‹24s. All his fines remitted to £10›.

1162 That William Waterman yeoman, recently of Lyndhurst, on the 10th July 1665 near to Allum Green had cut and felled a green beech worth £4, without assignation by woodward or regarder, and he had taken and carried away the top. ‹£40›.

1163 That George Rodney esquire, recently forester of the In Bailiwick, on the 10th July 1665 in two places called Coxlease and Park Ground had cut, felled, and lopped branches of various trees containing fourteen colefires worth £7. ‹£50 remitted as above›.

1164 That Nicholas Clement gentleman, recently of Marchwood, on the 10th July 1665 at Kings Coppice in the East Bailiwick had cut and felled, or had caused to be cut, fifty four loads of timber worth £32 4s. ‹The heir to pay £32 10s.›.

1165 That Nicholas Clement on the 10th July 1665 at *Pitch Ditch* in the East Bailiwick had cut and felled, or had caused to be cut, eleven young oaks containing four and a half loads worth £2 10s. ‹As above, value £2 10s›.

1166 That Thomas Wyatt yeoman, recently of Milton, on the 10th July 1665 at a place called [blank] had made a purpresture, and had enclosed with hedges a parcel of land containing by estimation one acre ‹13s 4d. Seize›.

1167 That [blank] Wyatt widow, recently of Milton, on the 10th July 1665 had made a purpresture and had enclosed with hedges a parcel of land containing ninety perches, and upon it had built a house or cottage and a fodder house where no house was before. ‹The presenters fined 3s 4d each›.

1168 That Nicholas Durrant yeoman, recently of [blank], on the 15th November 1664 in a place called Bulslade had built a house or cottage where no house was before. ‹20s. Seize›.

1169 That William Hoocker yeoman of Redbridge on the 5th June 1665 in the North Bailiwick had cut and felled four timber oaks worth £5 5s, and he had taken and carried them away after they were assigned for the use of the king by the regarders and the woodward. ‹£40 and the value›.

1170 That John Aldridge yeoman, recently of Fritham, on the 10th June 1665 within the bailiwick of Fritham had taken a parcel of wood worth [blank], assigned to him for fuel wood, and in a cart drawn by four horses worth [blank] had carried it towards Salisbury with the intention of selling it there.

1171 William Hooker yeoman, recently of Redbridge, acknowledges to owe the king £20. [On condition] that William Hoocker will appear at the next court of the justices in eyre held for the New Forest to answer to them for as much as will be charged against him on behalf of the king, and he will not withdraw from the court without permission.

1172 Which all and each thing is signed and sealed by the verderers, foresters, regarders, agisters, and all other ministers of the forest following the form of the statute.

1173 [Signatures]. Thomas Knollys, Philip Leigh [verderers]. James Barrow, Thomas Lovell, Thomas Edwards, Thomas Fisher, William Batten, James Osey, Richard Combe, William Pococke, William Olding, Ogden Rooke, Nicholas Lambert, Edward Hammon [regarders].

E.32/174

m.13

1174 ‹New Forest in the county of Southampton›. Court and Pleas called the Swainmote held at Lyndhurst on the 14th September 1666 before the foresters, verderers, regarders, agisters, and all other ministers of the forest as here appear underwritten

1175 Keeper and Warden. Thomas earl of Southampton.
Steward. [Blank].
Bow Bearer. Henry Bromfeild junior esquire.
Riding Forester. Thomas Bacon esquire.
Rangers. Thomas Urry and Robert Read have appeared.

1176 Burley. John Neale esquire, forester, has appeared.
Battramsley. Thomas Fitzjames esquire, forester, has appeared.
Fritham. Arthur Oxford gentleman, forester, has appeared.
Linwood. Sir Adam Browne Bt., forester, has appeared.
Godshill. Sir John Penruddock, forester, has appeared.
In Bailiwick. George Rodney esquire, forester, has appeared.
East Bailiwick. Sir John Mill Bt., forester, has appeared.
North Bailiwick. William Pawlett esquire, forester, has appeared.
South Bailiwick. Richard Norton esquire, forester, has appeared.

1177 Verderers. Thomas Knollis esquire and Philip Leigh esquire.
Verminer. Arthur Oxford gentleman.

1178 Regarders. James Barrow gentleman, Thomas Lovell gentleman, Thomas Edwards, Thomas Fisher, William Batten gentleman, James Osey gentleman, Richard Combes, Edward Hamond, William Pocok, Ogden Rooke, Nicholas Lambert, Richard Edwards. Sworn.

1179 Agisters. Richard Rowe, William Bright, William Pocock, and William Stride have appeared.
Riders. John Stote and James Bayly have appeared.

1180 Names of the underforesters.

Burley. George Bright has appeared, John Woods.

1181 Battramsley. John Taplin has appeared, Nicholas Barling.

1182 Fritham. Arthur Oxford junior has appeared, Thomas Venner.

1183 Linwood. Henry Rooke has appeared.

1184 East Bailiwick. Edward Bright and Ralph Carter have appeared.

1185 Godshill. Edward Penruddock gentleman, John Saunders, and George Harrison have appeared.

1186 In Bailiwick. William Signe is sick.

1187 North Bailiwick. Moses Waldron and William Lansdale.

1188 South Bailiwick. John Sparrowe, William Rossiter has appeared.

1189 Woodward of the forest. William Horne esquire has appeared.
Woodward of Minstead. Robert Sophe has appeared.

1190 Names of the vills, and the reeve and four men of each vill.

Vill of Exbury and Lepe. John Hayward reeve. James Taylor, Luke Mashe, William Banister, and John Willmott.

1191 Vill of Holbury and Langley. [No names entered].

1192 Vill of Buttsash and Hardley. Robert Shepheard reeve. Christopher Trueman, William Gray, Hugh Nashe, and Moses Hobbart.

1193 Vill of Pilley and Warborne. Edward Gastard reeve. Christopher Chaplin, Christopher Lewis, William Rasbridge, and John Carter.

1194 Vill of Battramsley and Wootton. Henry Robins reeve. Robert Frye, John Toms, John Smith, and John Chase.

1195 Vill of Baddesley. Richard Plowman, John Pope, John Barnes, John Jourdaine, and William Hall.

1196 Vill of Brockenhurst and Brookley. William Smith reeve. John Pillean, John Smith, Edward Rowland, and William Warne.

1197 Vill of Godshill and Linwood. John Gibbs reeve. Richard Pearcy, Nicholas Stotchier, Henry Coshier, and William Sandever.

m.13d

1198 Vill of Burley. John Youngs reeve. William Rooke, John Younges junior, John Randoll, and Batten Selfe.

1199 Vill of Canterton and Fritham. Not appeared, therefore in mercy 2s 6d.

1200 Vill of Minstead. John Mershman reeve. Charles Hayward, John Perry, John Borden, and William Stride.

1201 Vill of Lyndhurst. John Rasbridge reeve. Richard Gaskin, John Morris, James Wilcox, and George Hedger.

1202 Vill of Bartley Regis and London Minstead. Thomas Ingspen gentleman reeve. Thomas Knapton gentleman, George Rogers, Thomas Cowdry, and John Purcas.

1203 Names of the Freeholders of the New Forest.

Exbury and Lepe. John Willmott, Matthew Wilson, John Flight, John Moone, William Cowdry, Benjamin Ackeridge, Nicholas Clement, Richard Cole, the heir of Stephen March, Richard Compton esquire, Benjamin Whithead, Richard Cole, William Cole, the heir of George Lesson, Henry Bromfeild junior gentleman, Nicholas Stronge, the heir of John Pittis gentleman, Nicholas West.

1204 Buttsash. John Crooke esquire, and James Osey gentleman.

1205 Hardley. The heir of John Pittis gentleman, William Bound, the heir of Edmund Cole, Robert Shepheard, Moses Hebbart, John Cornish, Adam de Cardonnell gentleman, John Stepto gentleman, John Brooke, Richard Auley, John Steptoe, William Crosse, Charles Lyne, Thomas Edwards, Richard Combes.

1206 Pilley and Warborne. Henry Bromfeild junior esquire, William Slaun' gentleman, John Carter, John Drew, John Rickman, Richard Arnold, James Ploughman, John Carter, Christopher Chaplin, Thomas Boate, Timothy Longe, William Hale, William Rasbridge, Arthur Watts.

1207 Baddesley. Henry Philpott esquire, John Drew, sir Henry Worsley Bt., the heir of John March, William Walton, Thomas Fisher, sir Henry Worsley Bt., William Colebrooke, William Haines, Richard Sampson gentleman.

1208 Battramsley and Wootton. Richard Ghost, Henry Titchborne, Edward Scott senior gentleman, the heir of Henry Tulse gentleman, Henry Goddard gentleman, sir William Meux Bt., John Edwards, John Chase, Peter Penny, Edward Scott junior, William Burrard, Thomas Roberts gentleman.

1209 Brockenhurst and Brookley. William Knapton gentleman, Margaret Smith, Richard Draper, John Atwood, Richard Rowe, William Knapton, Henry Williams, Thomas Burton, Thomas Gretman, William Purdue, the heir of Nicholas Hellier, Bernard Knapton gentleman, John Oliver, Richard King.

1210 Burley. William Batten gentleman, the heir of Thomas Tarver, William Bampton, Christopher Garrett gentleman, Joseph Coffin, John Warne.

1211 Godshill and Linwood. Lord Robert Brooke, Richard Goodridge, Ambrose Bradshawe, William Miller, Ogden Rooke, John Webb esquire, John Weeks gentleman, Edmund Okden, the heir of John Brewen, John Stent, Henry Good, Henry Rooke, lady Cooper widow.

1212 Canterton and Fritham. [Due to a scribal error the names of the freeholders of London Minstead have been inserted here].

1213 [London Minstead]. Thomas Browne, the heir of Francis Ranger, John Chater, Thomas Cowdry, the heir of John Robberts.

1214 Bartley Regis. Sir John Mill Bt., Richard Goddard esquire, Edward Hammond, Robert Richbell gentleman, Thomas Lovell gentleman, Thomas Knapton gentleman.

1215 Lyndhurst. William Waterman, Anthony Wiseman, Thomas Grante, James Elcombe, Edward Bright, William Gautlett, John Morris, Thomas Pearce, John Buckle, William Bright, George Rodney gentleman.

1216 Jurors for the lord king. John Drew, James Elcombe, Henry Bright, Joseph Coffin, Arthur Watts, William Morris, Clement Rogers, Christopher Scovell, Thomas Steele, Thomas Toomer, Robert Frye, Richard Draper, John Jordan, William Olding. Sworn.

1217 It is presented by the foresters and other ministers of the forest and the twelve jurors, and proved by the verderers, that Nicholas Clement gentleman, recently of Marchwood, and William Knapton gentleman of Royden on the 8th March 1666 had entered the forest at Kings Coppice in the East bailiwick, and they had cut the branches of various timber trees by estimation containing [blank] and worth [blank].

1218 Which all and each thing is signed and sealed by the verderers, foresters, regarders, agisters, and all other ministers of the forest following the form of the statute.

1219 [Signatures]. Thomas Knollys, Philip Leigh [verderers]. Thomas Fisher, William Batten, James Osey, Richard Combs, Edward Hamon, William Pococke, Ogden Rooke, Nicholas Lambert, James Barrow, Thomas Lovell, Richard Edwards, Thomas Edwards [regarders].

E.32/174

m.14

1220 ‹New Forest in the county of Southampton›. Court and Pleas called the Swainmote held at Lyndhurst on the 9th November 1666, and adjourned to the 20th November at Lyndhurst, before the foresters, verderers, regarders, agisters, and all other ministers of the forest as here appear underwritten

1221 Keeper and Warden. Thomas earl of Southampton has appeared.
Lieutenant. [Blank].
Steward [Blank].
Bow Bearer. Henry Bromfeild junior esquire has appeared.
Riding Forester. Thomas Bacon esquire has appeared.
Rangers. Thomas Urry gentleman and Robert Read gentleman have appeared.

1222 Burley. John Neale esquire, forester, has not appeared. Therefore in mercy 5s.
Battramsley. Thomas Fitzjames esquire, forester, has not appeared. Therefore in mercy 5s.
Fritham. Arthur Oxford gentleman, forester, has appeared.
Linwood. Sir Adam Browne Bt., forester, has appeared.
Godshill. Sir John Penruddock, forester, has appeared.
In Bailiwick. George Rodney esquire, forester, has appeared.
East Bailiwick. Sir John Mill Bt., forester, has appeared.
North Bailiwick. William Pawlett esquire, forester, has appeared.
South Bailiwick. Richard Norton esquire, forester, has appeared.

1223 Verderers. Thomas Knollis esquire and Philip Leigh esquire have appeared.
Verminer. Arthur Oxford gentleman has appeared.

1224 Regarders. James Barrow, Thomas Lovell, Thomas Edwards, Thomas Fisher, William Batten, James Osey, William Fisher, Richard Combes, Edward Hamond, William Pocock, Nicholas Lambert, Richard Edwards. Sworn.

1225 Agisters. Richard Rowe, William Bright, William Pocock, William Stride.

Riders. John Stote, James Bayly.

1226 Names of the underforesters.

Burley. George Bright, John Woods.

1227 Battramsley. John Taplin and Nicholas Barling.

1228 Fritham. Arthur Oxford junior and Thomas Venner.

1229 Linwood. Thomas Frye.

1230 Godshill. Edward Penruddock gentleman, John Saunders, George Harrison.

1231 In Bailiwick. William Signe.

1232 East Bailiwick. Edward Bright and Ralph Carter.

1233 North Bailiwick. Moses Waldron and William Landsdale.

1234 South Bailiwick. John Sparrowe and William Rossiter.

1235 Woodward of the forest. William Horne esquire.
Woodward of Minstead. Robert Sophe.

1236 Names of the vills, and the reeve and four men of each vill.

Vill of Exbury and Lepe. Henry Sich reeve. Henry Stephans, Arthur Gibbs, David Mills, and Andrew Kernell.

1237 Vill of Holbury and Langley. [No names entered].

1238 Vill of Buttsash and Hardley. John Brooks reeve. William Haywood, John Rawlings, John Harvey, and Richard Gater.

1239 Vill of Pilley and Warborne. Arthur Watts reeve. Timothy Long, John Carter, Christopher Lewis, and John Lake.

1240 Vill of Battramsley and Wootton. John Toms reeve. Robert Frye, John Chace, Thomas Hapgood, Peter Penny.

1241 Vill of Baddesley. Thomas Hall reeve. Kemberlin King, Bartholomew Collins, Thomas Cozens, and Richard Moore.

1242 Vill of Brockenhurst and Brookley. William Smith, Richard Stoy, John Hall, John Moore, and Thomas Ames.

1243 Vill of Godshill and Linwood. Thomas Randell, Edward Rogers, William Elfes, and John Scovell.

1244 Vill of Burley. John Tyller reeve. John Tarry, Nicholas America, Hugh Tiller, and John Randoll.

1245 Vill of Canterton and Fritham. Richard Andrews reeve. John Deale, John Dove, William Cull, and Nicholas Hatch.

1246 Vill of Minstead. John Perries reeve. John Purcas, John Burden, John Henvist, and Joseph Stride.

1247 Vill of Lyndhurst. John Rasbridge reeve. William Carpenter, Thomas Pearce, Thomas Paul, and John Gascombe.

m.14d
1248 Vill of Bartley Regis and London Minstead. William Rogers junior, Thomas Knapton gentleman, Thomas Newman, George Barlin, and John Purcas.

1249 Names of the Freeholders of the New Forest.

Exbury and Lepe. John Willmott, Matthew Wilson, John Flight, John Moone, William Cowdry, Benjamin Ackeridge, Nicholas Clement gentleman, Richard Cole, the heir of Stephen March, Richard Compton esquire, Benjamin Whithead, Richard Cole, William Cole, the heir of George Lesson, Henry Bromfeild junior gentleman, Nicholas Stronge, the heir of John Pittis, Richard West.

1250 Buttsash. John Crooke esquire and James Osey gentleman.

1251 Hardley. The heir of John Pittis gentleman, William Bond, the heir of Edmund Cole, Robert Shepheard, Moses Hebbart, Adam de Cardonell, John Steptoe gentleman, John Brooke, Richard Auley, John Steptoe, William Crosse, Charles Lyne, Thomas Edwards, Richard Combes.

1252 Pilley and Warborne. Henry Bromfeild esquire, William Slaun', John Carter, John Drew, John Rickman, Richard Arnold, James Ploughman, John Carter, Christopher Chaplin, Richard King gentleman, Timothy Long, William Hale, William Rasbridge, Arthur Watts, Thomas Mislin.

1253 Baddesley. Henry Philpott esquire, John Drew, sir Henry Worsley Bt., the heir of John March, William Walton, Thomas Fisher, sir Henry Warsley Bt., William Colebrooke, William Haines, Richard Sampson.

1254 Battramsley and Wootton. Richard Ghost, sir Henry Titchborne Bt., Edward Scott senior gentleman, the heir of Henry Tulce gentleman, Henry Goddard gentleman, sir William Meux Bt. is sick, John Edwards, John Chase, Peter Penny, William Scott junior, William Burrard, Thomas Roberts is sick.

1255 Brockenhurst and Brookley. William Knapton gentleman, Margaret Smith, Richard Draper, John Atwood, Richard Rowe, Henry Williams, Thomas Burton, Thomas Gretnam, William Purdue, the heir of Nicholas Hollier, Bernard Knapton gentleman, John Olliver, Richard King.

1256 Burley. William Batten gentleman, John Warne, the heir of Thomas Tarver, William Bampton, Christopher Gerrard, Christopher Lyne, Joseph Coffin.

1257 Godshill and Linwood. Lord Robert Brooks, Robert[1] Goodridge, Ambrose Bradshawe, William Miller, Ogden Rooke, John Webb esquire, John Weeks gentleman, Edmund Okden, the heir of John Brewen, John Stent, Henry Good, Henry Rooke, lady Cooper widow.

[1] *recte* Richard.

1258 Canterton and Fritham. John[1] Rivett gentleman, Edward Acton, the widow Elliott, Henry Reade, Richard Archer junior, the heir of Benjamin Edwards, Richard Edwards, Stephen Brownjohn, Benjamin Edwards, Richard Archer, William Easton *alias* Meux, George Venner gentleman, Edmund Perkins gentleman, John Emblyn.

[1] *recte* Jonathan.

1259 London Minstead. Thomas Browne gentleman, the heir of Francis Ranger, John Chater, Thomas Cowdrey, the heir of John Roberts.

1260 Bartley Regis. Sir John Mill Bt., Richard Goddard esquire, Edward Hammond, Robert Richbell gentleman, Thomas Lovell, Thomas Knapton gentleman.

1261 Lyndhurst. Bartholomew Bulkly gentleman, Anthony Wiseman, Thomas Grante, James Elcombe, Edward Bright, John Hodges, John Morris, Thomas Pearce, John Buckle, William Bright, George Rodney esquire.

1262 Jurors for the lord king. John Drew, James Elcombe, Joseph Brokenshaw, Joseph Coffin, James Randoll, Edward Yeoman, William Penton, George House, Clement Morris, William Rooke, Henry Rooke, John Spelt, Arthur Watts, William Furner, Albany Knapton gentleman, Christopher Scovell, Gabriel Butler, Charles Lyne.

m.15

1263 It is presented by the foresters and other ministers of the forest and the twelve jurors, and proved by the verderers, that William Pawlett, recently forester of the North Bailiwick, on the 10th July 1666 had cut and lopped the branches of oak and beech trees under colour of browsewood, containing thirty five colefires, more for his own advantage than for the necessary forage of the king's beasts, of which about five colefires worth 50s were unlawful. ‹£50. Remitted›.

1264 That Sir Adam Browne Bt., recently forester of Linwood Bailiwick, on the 10th July 1666 had cut and lopped the branches of oak and beech trees containing seventeen colefires, of which about ten worth £5 were unlawful. ‹£50. Remitted to £10›.

1265 That Thomas Fitzjames esquire, recently forester of Battramsley Bailiwick, on the 10th July 1666 had cut and lopped the branches of oak and beech trees containing forty four colefires, of which about eight or nine worth £4 were unlawful. ‹£40. Remitted as before›.

1266 That John Neale, recently forester of Burley Bailiwick, on the 10th July 1666 had cut and lopped the branches of oak and beech trees containing thirty nine colefires of which about eight colefires worth £8 were unlawful. ‹£50. All fines for him and George Bright remitted to £100. Paid›.

1267 That William Rossiter, recently forester of the South Bailiwick, on the 10th July 1666 had cut and lopped the branches of oak and beech trees containing twenty seven colefires of which about eight worth £4 were unlawful. ‹£40. All his fines remitted to £50. Paid›.

1268 That Arthur Oxford, recently forester of Fritham Bailiwick, on the 10th July 1666 had cut and lopped the branches of oak and beech trees containing sixty nine colefires of which about ten worth £5 were unlawful. ‹Writ against his heir›.

1269 That Thomas Venner, recently underforester of Fritham Bailiwick, on the 10th July 1666 had cut and lopped the branches of oak and beech trees containing seventeen colefires of which two worth 20s were unlawful. ‹As above›.

1270 That Ralph Carter, recently underforester of the East Bailiwick, on the 10th July 1666 had cut and lopped the branches of oak and beech trees containing twelve colefires of which three worth 30s were unlawful. ‹£15›.

1271 That George Rodney esquire, recently forester of the In Bailiwick, on the 10th July 1666 had cut and lopped the branches of oak and beech trees containing seventeen colefires of which five worth 50s were unlawful. ‹£20. Remitted as before›.

1272 That Nicholas Barling, recently underforester of Battramsley Bailiwick, on the 10th July 1666 had cut and lopped the branches of oak and beech trees containing seven colefires of which one or two worth 20s were unlawful. ‹Writ against his heir›.

1273 That John Sparrowe, recently underforester of the South Bailiwick, on the 10th July 1666 had cut and lopped the branches of oak and beech trees containing twenty one colefires of which five or six worth 50s were unlawful. ‹Writ as above›.

1274 Which all and each thing is signed and sealed by the verderers, foresters, regarders, and other ministers of the forest following the form of the statute.

1275 [Signatures]. Thomas Knollys, Philip Leigh [verderers]. James Barrow, Thomas Lovell, Richard Edward, Thomas Edwards, Thomas Fisher, William Batten, James Osey, William Fisher, Richard Combs, Edward Hamon, William Pococke, Nicholas Lambert [regarders].

E.32/174

m.16

1276 ‹New Forest in the county of Southampton›. Court and Pleas called the Swainmote held at Lyndhurst on the 14th September 1667 before the foresters, verderers, regarders, agisters, and all other ministers of the forest as here appear underwritten

1277 Keeper and Warden. [Blank].
Lieutenant. [Blank].
Steward. [Blank].
Bow Bearer. Henry Bromfeild esquire.
Riding Forester. Thomas Bacon esquire has appeared.
Rangers. Thomas Urry gentleman and Robert Read gentleman have appeared.

1278 Burley. John Neale esquire, forester, has appeared.
Battramsley. Thomas Fitzjames esquire, forester, has appeared.
Fritham. Arthur Oxford gentleman, forester, has appeared.
Linwood. Sir Adam Browne Bt., forester, has appeared.
Godshill. Sir John Penruddock, forester, is sick.
In Bailiwick. George Rodney esquire, forester, has appeared.
East Bailiwick. Sir John Mill Bt., forester, has appeared.
North Bailiwick. William Pawlett esquire, forester, has appeared.
South Bailiwick. Richard Norton esquire, forester, has appeared.

1279 Verderers. Thomas Knollis esquire and Philip Leigh esquire have appeared.
Verminer. Arthur Oxford gentleman has appeared.

1280 Regarders. William Batten gentleman, James Barrow, Thomas Lovell, Thomas Edwards, Thomas Fisher, William Fisher, Richard Combes, Edward Hamond, William Pocock, Nicholas Lambert, Richard Edwards, Ogden Rook. Sworn and have appeared.

1281 Agisters. Richard Rowe, William Bright, William Pocock, and William Stride have appeared.
Riders. John Stote and James Bayly have appeared.

1282 Names of the underforesters.

Burley. George Bright has appeared. John Woods has not appeared.

1283 Battramsley. John Taplin has appeared. Nicholas Barling has not appeared.

1284 Fritham. Arthur Oxford has appeared. Thomas Venner is sick.

1285 Linwood. Thomas Frye has appeared.

1286 East Bailiwick. Edward Bright and Ralph Carter have appeared.

1287 Godshill. Edward Penruddock gentleman, John Saunders, and George Harrison have appeared.

1288 In Bailiwick. John Davies has appeared.

1289 North Bailiwick. Moses Waldron is sick. William Lansdale has not appeared.

1290 South Bailiwick. John Sparrow and William Rossiter have appeared.

1291 Woodward [of the forest]. William Horne esquire has appeared.

Woodward of Minstead. Robert Sophe has appeared.

1292 Names of the vills, and the reeve and four men of each vill.

Vill of Exbury and Lepe. Henry Shich reeve. Henry Stephens, Arthur Gibbs, David Mills, and Andrew Lovell.

1293 Vill of Holbury and Langley. [No names entered].

1294 Vill of Buttsash and Hardley. John Brooke reeve. William Hayward, John Rawlings, John Harvey, and Richard Gater.

1295 Vill of Pilley and Warborne. Arthur Watts reeve. Timothy

Long, John Carter, Christopher Lewis, and John Lake.

1296 Vill of Battramsley and Wootton. John Toms reeve. Robert Frye, John Chace, Thomas Hapgood, and Peter Penny.

1297 Vill of Baddesley. Thomas Hall reeve. Kemberlin King, Bartholomew Collins, Thomas Cozens, and Richard Moore.

1298 Vill of Brockenhurst and Brookley. William Smith reeve. Richard Stoy, John Hall, John Moore, and Thomas Ames.

1299 Vill of Godshill and Linwood. Thomas Randoll reeve. Edward Rogers, William Elfes, and John Scovell.

1300 Vill of Burley. John Tiller reeve. John Tarrey, Nicholas America, Hugh Tiller, and John Randoll.

1301 Vill of Canterton and Fritham. Richard Andrews reeve. John Deale, John Dove, William Cull, and Nicholas Hatch.

1302 Vill of Minstead. John Perrier reeve. John Purcas, John Burden, John Henvist, and Joseph Stride.

1303 Vill of Lyndhurst. John Rasbridge reeve. William Carpenter, Thomas Pearce, Thomas Paull, and John Gascombe.

m.16d

1304 Vill of Bartley Regis and London Minstead. William Rogers junior reeve. Thomas Knapton gentleman, Thomas Newman, George Barlin, John Purcas.

1305 Names of the Freeholders of the New Forest.

Exbury and Lepe. John Willmott, Matthew Wilson, John Flight, John Moone, William Cowdry, Benjamin Ackeridge, Nicholas Clement gentleman, Richard Cole, the heir of Stephen March, Richard Compton esquire, Benjamin Whithead, Richard Cole, William Cole, the heir of George Lesson, Henry Bromfeild junior gentleman, Nicholas Stronge, the heir of John Pittis, Richard West.

1306 Buttsash. John Crooke esquire and James Osey gentleman.

1307 Hardley. The heir of John Pittis gentleman, William Bond, the heir of Edmund Cole, Robert Shepheard, Moses Hebbart, Adam de Cardonell, John Steptoe gentleman, John Brooke, Richard Auley, John Steptoe, William Crosse, Charles Lyne, Thomas Edwards, Richard Combes.

1308 Pilley and Warborne. Henry Bromfeild esquire, William Slaun, John Carter, John Drew, Christopher Lewis, Nicholas Gunit, James Plowman, John Carter, Christopher Chaplin, Richard King gentleman, Timothy Long, Henry Johnson gentleman, William Rasbridge, Arthur Watts, Thomas Mislin.

1309 Baddesley. Henry Bromfeild esquire, John Drew, sir Henry Worsley Bt., the heir of John March, William Walton, Thomas Fisher, sir Henry Worsley Bt., William Colebrooke, William Haynes, Richard Sampson.

1310 Battramsley and Wootton. Richard Ghost, sir Henry Titchborne Bt., Edward Scott senior gentleman, the heir of Henry Tulse gentleman, Henry Goddard gentleman, sir William Meux Bt., John Edwards, John Chase, Peter Penny, William Scott junior, William Burrard, Thomas Roberts.

1311 Brockenhurst and Brookley. William Knapton gentleman, Margaret Smith, Richard Draper, John Atwood, Richard Rowe, Henry Williams, Thomas Burton, Thomas Gretnam, William Purdue, the heir of Nicholas Hollier, Bernard Knapton gentleman, John Olliver, Richard King.

1312 Burley. William Batten gentleman, John Warne, the heir of Thomas Tarver, William Bampton, Christopher Garrard, Christopher Lyne, Joseph Coffin.

1313 Godshill and Linwood. Lord Robert Brooke, Richard Goodridge, Ambrose Bradshawe, William Miller, Ogden Rooke, John Webb esquire, John Weekes gentleman, Edmund Okden, the heir of John Brewen, John Stent, Henry Good, Henry Rooke, lady Cooper widow.

1314 Canterton and Fritham. Jonathan Rivett gentleman, Edward Acton, the widow Elliott, Henry Read, Richard Archer junior, the heir of Benjamin Edwards, Richard Edwards, Stephen Brownejohn, the heir of Benjamin Edwards, Richard Edwards, William Easton *alias* Meux, George Venner gentleman, Edmund Perkins gentleman, John Emblin.

1315 London Minstead. Thomas Browne gentleman, the heir of Francis Raunger, John Chater, Thomas Cowdry, the heir of John Roberts.

1316 Bartley Regis. Sir John Mill Bt., Richard Goddard esquire, Edward Hamond, Robert Richbell gentleman, Thomas Lovell, Thomas Knapton gentleman.

1317 Lyndhurst. Bartholomew Bulkley gentleman, Anthony Wiseman, Thomas Graunte, James Elcombe, Edward Bright, William Gautlett, John Morris, Thomas Pearce, John Buckle, William Bright, George Rodney esquire.

1318 Jurors for the lord king. John Drew, John Barnes, Christopher Scovell, James Plowman, Christopher Bidlecombe, Alexander Purcas, Clement Morris, George House, Richard Rowe, Thomas Gretnam, Joseph Brokenshaw, John Buckle, John Moone, John Flight, William Gaine, Robert Shepheard, Charles Lyne, Richard Ghost, Henry Ghost, Henry Robbins, John Emblin, William Pynson. Sworn.

m.17

1319 It is presented by the foresters and other ministers of the forest and the twelve jurors, and proved by the verderers, that William Hancock yeoman, recently of Lyndhurst, on the 7th May 1667 in various places in the East Bailiwick had cut and lopped oak and beech trees under colour of browsewood, containing 50 colefires worth 30s, more for his own advantage than for necessary forage for the king's beasts. ‹£15. Value £1 10s›.

1320 That George Rodney, recently forester of the In Bailiwick, on the 7th May 1667 had cut and lopped various oak and beech trees under colour of browsewood, containing fifty six colefires work 28s. ‹£15. Remitted as before›.

1321 That Thomas Venner, recently underforester of Fritham

Bailiwick, on the 7th May 1667 had cut and lopped the branches of oak and beech trees containing twenty seven colefires worth £12 10s. ‹Writ to his heir›.

1322 That John Saunders, recently underforester of Godshill Bailiwick, on the 7th May 1667 had cut and lopped various oak and beech trees containing ten colefires worth £5. ‹Fine £50 and value›.

1323 That Thomas Fitzjames, recently forester of Battramsley Bailiwick, on the 7th May 1667 had cut and lopped the branches of oak and beech trees containing sixty five colefires worth £32 10s. ‹£100. Remitted as before›.

1324 That Ralph Carter, recently underforester of the East Bailiwick, on the 7th May 1667 had cut and lopped various oak and beech trees containing fifteen colefires worth £7 10s. ‹£40. Remitted to £10. Paid›.

1325 That William Rossiter, recently underforester of the South Bailiwick, on the 7th May 1667 had cut and lopped various oak and beech trees containing fifty four colefires worth £27. ‹£100. Remitted as before›.

1326 That Thomas Frye, recently underforester of Linwood Bailiwick, on the 7th May 1667 had cut and lopped various oak and beech trees containing fifty one colefires worth £26 10s. ‹£100›.

1327 That Edward Bright, recently underforester of the East Bailiwick, on the 7th May 1667 had cut and lopped various oak and beech trees containing twenty one colefires worth £10 10s. ‹£40. Remitted to £10. Paid›.

1328 That William Pawlett gentleman, recently underforester of the North Bailiwick, on the 7th May 1667 had cut and lopped various oak and beech trees containing thirty eight colefires worth £19. ‹£80. Remitted as before›.

1329 That George Bright, recently underforester of Burley Bailiwick, on the 7th May 1667 had cut and lopped various oak and beech trees containing forty nine colefires worth £24 10s. ‹£100. Remitted as before›.

1330 That John Sparrow, recently forester of the South Bailiwick, on the 7th May 1667 had cut and lopped various oak and beech trees containing thirty four colefires worth £17. ‹Writ against his heir›.

1331 That Arthur Oxford, recently forester of Fritham Bailiwick, on the 7th May 1667 had cut and lopped various oak and beech trees containing one hundred and one colefires worth £50 10s. ‹As above›.

1332 That Nicholas Barling, recently underforester of Battramsley Bailiwick, on the 7th May 1667 had cut and lopped various oak and beech trees containing seven colefires worth £3 10s. ‹As above›.

1333 That Edward Talbott, recently underforester of the North Bailiwick, on the 7th May 1667 had cut and lopped various oak and beech trees containing twenty seven colefires worth £13 10s. ‹£100›.

1334 That Hugh Pyball yeoman, recently of Linwood, on the 1st August 1667 was hunting with a gun loaded with powder and shot at Pinnick in the bailiwick of Linwood, and had shot at a deer with the intention of killing a beast of the king. ‹£5›.

1335 Hugh Pyball yeoman of Linwood acknowledges to owe the king £20. On condition that Hugh Piball will appear at the next court of the justices in eyre held for the New Forest to answer to them for as much as will be charged against him on behalf of the king, and he will not withdraw from the court without permission.

1336 Which all and each thing is signed and sealed by the verderers, foresters, regarders, agisters, and all other ministers of the forest, and the jurors, following the form of the statute.

1337 [Signatures]. Thomas Knollys, Philip Leigh [verderers]. Edward Hamon, William Pococke, Nicholas Lambert, Ogden Rooke, Richard Edwards, William Batten, Thomas Edwards, Thomas Fisher, William Fisher, Richard Combs, James Barrow, Thomas Lovell [regarders].

E32/174

m.18

1338 ‹New Forest in the county of Southampton›. Court and Pleas called the Swainmote held at Lyndhurst on the 9th June 1668 before the foresters, verderers, regarders, agisters, and all other ministers of the forest as here appear underwritten

1339 Keeper and Warden. Charles lord St. John.
Lieutenant. [Blank].
Steward. William Pawlet esquire has appeared.
Bow Bearer. Henry Bromfeild esquire has appeared.
Riding Forester. Thomas Bacon esquire has appeared.
Rangers. Thomas Urry and Robert Rheade gentlemen have appeared.

1340 Burley. John Neale esquire, forester.
Battramsley. Thomas Fitzjames esquire, forester, has appeared.
Fritham. [Blank].
Linwood. Sir Adam Browne Bt., forester.
Godshill. Sir John Penruddock, forester.
In Bailiwick. George Rodney esquire, forester.
East Bailiwick. Sir John Mill Bt., forester.
North Bailiwick. William Pawlett esquire, forester.
South Bailiwick. Richard Norton esquire, forester.

1341 Verderers. Thomas Knollis esquire and Philip Leigh esquire have appeared.
Verminer. [Blank].

1342 Regarders. William Batten gentleman, James Barrow, Thomas Lovell, Thomas Edwards, Thomas Fisher, William Fisher, James Osey, Edward Hamond, William Pocock, Nicholas Lambert, Richard Edwards, Ogden Rooke. Sworn.

1343 Agisters. Richard Rowe, William Bright, William Pocock, and William Stride have appeared.
Riders. John Stote and James Bayly have appeared.

1344 Names of the underforesters.

Burley. George Bright and John Woods.

1345 Battramsley. John Taplin has appeared.

1346 Fritham. Thomas Venner has appeared.

1347 Godshill. Edward Penruddock gentleman, John Saunders, and George Harrison have appeared.

1348 Linwood. [Blank].

1349 In Bailiwick. John Davis has appeared.

1350 East Bailiwick. Edward Bright and Ralph Carter have appeared.

1351 North Bailiwick. Moses Waldron and William Lansdale have appeared.

1352 South Bailiwick. William Rossiter has appeared.

1353 Woodward [of the forest]. William Horne esquire has appeared.
Woodward of Minstead. Robert Sope has appeared.

1354 Names of the vills, and the reeve and four men of each vill.

Vill of Exbury and Lepe. Francis Lesson reeve. Thomas Warne, John Willmott, John Mores, and David Wiseman.

1355 Vill of Holbury and Langley. Richard Lambert reeve. James Wakeford, Nicholas Bernard, Ferdinand Symons, and Christopher Frampton.

1356 Vill of Buttsash and Hardley. Gabriel Butler reeve. Henry Nash, Richard Crosse, William Hayward, and Thomas Gaton.

1357 Vill of Pilley and Warborne. Arthur Watts reeve. James Plowman, Christopher Lewis, Timothy Longe, and John Carter.

1358 Vill of Battramsley and Wootton. William Samber reeve. John Toms, Robert Frye, John Spelt, and John Chase.

1359 Vill of Baddesley. John Pope reeve. Kimberlin King, William Henning, Richard Plowman, and Thomas Wright.

1360 Vill of Brockenhurst and Brookley. Richard Draper reeve. John Smith, John Pilledon, John Hall, and John Bisse.

m.18d

1361 Vill of Godshill and Linwood. Thomas Randoll reeve. Hugh Harrington, John Scovell, John Hyde, and Hugh Pyball.

1362 Tithing of Burley. John Tiller reeve. Christopher Bidlecombe, Anthony Robbins, Anthony Fish, and William Small.

1363 Vill of Canterton and Fritham. Richard Hurst reeve. Richard Bassett, John Deale, Richard Iremonger, and John North.

1364 Vill of Minstead. John Perrier reeve. John Burden, Nicholas Stride, John Starks, and John Bowne.

1365 Vill of Lyndhurst. John Rasbridge reeve. John Harding, John Morris, Thomas Paie, and Richard Gascoine.

1366 Vill of Bartley Regis and London Minstead. William Rogers junior reeve. Robert Over, Robert Hiscock, Thomas Score, and John Purcas.

1367 Names of the Freeholders of the New Forest.

Exbury and Lepe. John Willmott, Matthew Wilson, John Flight, John Moone, William Cowdry, Benjamin Ackeridge, John Clement gentleman, Richard Cole, the heir of Stephen March, Richard Compton esquire, Benjamin Whithead, Richard Cole, William Cole, the heir of George Lesson, Henry Bromfeild junior gentleman, Nicholas Stronge, the heir of John Pittis, Richard West.

1368 Buttsash. John Crooke esquire and James Osey gentleman.

1369 Hardley. The heir of John Pittis gentleman, William Bond, the heir of Edmund Cole, Robert Shepheard, Moses Hebbart, Adam de Cardonell, John Steptoe gentleman, John Brooke, Richard Auley, John Steptoe, William Crosse, Charles Line, Thomas Edwards, Richard Combes.

1370 Pilley and Warborne. Henry Bromfeild esquire, William Slaun gentleman, John Carter, John Drew, John Rickman, Richard Arnold, James Plowman, John Carter, Christopher Chaplin, Thomas Boate, Timothy Long, William Hale, William Rasbridge, Arthur Watts.

1371 Baddesley. Henry Phillpot esquire, John Drew, sir Henry Worsley Bt., William Colebrooke, William Haines, Richard Sampson.
[Four names appear to have been omitted due to a scribal error].

1372 Battramsley and Wootton. Richard Ghost, sir Henry Titchborne Bt., Edward Scott senior gentleman, the heir of Henry Tulse gentleman, Henry Goddard gentleman, sir William Mew Bt., John Edwards, John Chase, Peter Penny, William Scott, William Burrard, Thomas Edwards.[1]

[1] *? recte* Roberts.

1373 Brockenhurst and Brookley. William Knapton gentleman, Margaret Smith, Richard Draper, John Atwood, Richard Rare,[1] Henry Williams, Thomas Burton, Thomas Gretnam, William Purdue, the heir of Nicholas Helliar, Bernard Knapton gentleman, John Oliver, Richard King.

[1] *recte* Rowe.

1374 Burley. William Batten gentleman, John Warne, the heir of Thomas Tarver, William Bampton, Christopher Garrard, Christopher Line, Joseph Coffin.

1375 Godshill and Linwood. Lord Robert Brooke, Richard Goodridge, Ambrose Bradshaw, William Miller, Ogden Rooke, John Webb esquire, John Weeks gentleman, Edmund Okden, the heir of John Brewen, John Stent, Henry Good, Henry Rooke, the lady Cooper widow.

1376 Canterton and Fritham. Jonathan Rivett gentleman, Edward Acton, the widow Elliott, Henry Rhead, Richard Archer, William Easton *alias* Meux, George Venner gentleman, Edmund Perkins, John Emblin.

1377 London Minstead. Thomas Browne, the heir of Francis Ranger, John Chater, Thomas Cowdrey, the heir of John Roberts.

1378 Bartley Regis. Sir John Mill Bt., Richard Goddard esquire, Edward Hamond, Robert Richbell gentleman, Thomas Lovell gentleman, Thomas Knapton gentleman.

1379 Lyndhurst. Bartholomew Bulkley gentleman, Anthony Wiseman, Thomas Grante, James Elcombe, Edward Bright, William Gautlett, John Morris, Thomas Pearce, John Buckle, William Bright, George Rodney esquire.

1380 Jurors for the lord king. John Drew, William Rooke, George Cole, William Rogers, Clement Morris, William Olding, William Gaine, William Scott, Richard Ghost, Joseph Coffin, Alexander Purcas, James Elcombe, James Phillipps, Richard Rowe, Henry Bright. Sworn.

m.19

1381 It is presented by the foresters and other ministers of the forest and the twelve jurors, and proved by the verderers, that John Rittear yeoman, recently of Beaulieu, on the [blank] day of the 20th year of Charles II, at Woodfidley in the East Bailiwick had taken and carried away to Hythe *(Heeth)* two cartloads of wood worth [blank]. ‹Fine 20s. Ferdinand Knapton understeward. Fine 3s for the court›.

1382 That Joan Younges widow, recently of Beaulieu, on the [blank] day of May 1668 at a place called the Rocks in Burley Bailiwick had cut green *aquilentas* growing there. ‹Presenters 3s 4d each›.

1383 That Thomas Tunbridge yeoman, recently of Lyndhurst, on the [blank] day in the 20th year of the reign in Park Grounds in the In Bailiwick had a gun loaded with a *brace of slugs* with intent to kill the king's beasts. ‹£20›.

1384 That Robert Hiscock yeoman, recently of Minstead, on the [blank] day of May 1668 in the North Bailiwick had cut and lopped the branches of oaks to the value of about £5, and he had taken and carried them away. ‹£50 and the value. Paid £2 15s›.

1385 That William Thorne yeoman, recently of Lyndhurst, on the [blank] day of May 1668 had inclosed with fences a lane in the In Bailiwick so that the king's subjects were unable to go and to return. ‹Fine 20d paid›.

1386 That George Hastings esquire, Thomas Burgan, and [blank] Gatherill, yeomen, all recently of Hinton, on the 28th October 1667 in a place close to Everley Cross in Burley Bailiwick had hunted with two greyhounds, and had put to flight, chased, and driven to death a pricket, and they had taken and carried away the flesh. ‹Hastings £10 paid. Burgan £15 remitted›.

1387 ‹Recognizance›. George Hastings esquire, recently of Hinton, acknowledges to owe the king £30. Thomas Burgan yeoman of Northington acknowledges to owe the king £20. On condition that George Hastings will appear at the next court of the justices in eyre for the New Forest to answer to them for as much as will be charged against him on behalf of the king, and he will not withdraw from the court without permission.

1388 ‹Recognizance›. Thomas Burgan yeoman, recently of Northington, acknowledges to owe the king £30. George Hastings esquire, recently of Hinton, acknowledges to owe the king £20. On condition that Thomas Burgan will appear at the next court of the justices in eyre for the New Forest to answer to them for as much as will be charged against him on behalf of the king, and he will not withdraw from the court without permission.

1389 Which all and each thing is signed and sealed by the verderers, foresters, regarders, and all other ministers of the forest following the form of the statute.

1390 [Signatures]. Thomas Knollys, Philip Leigh [verderers]. James Barrow, Thomas Lovell, William Batten, Thomas Edwards, Thomas Fisher, William Fisher, James Osey, Edward Hamon, William Pocke, Nicholas Lambert, Ogden Rooke, Richard Edwards [regarders].

E.32/174

m.20

1391 **‹New Forest in the county of Southampton›. Court and Pleas called the Swainmote held at Lyndhurst on the 14th September 1669 before the foresters, verderers, regarders, agisters, and all other ministers of the forest as here appear underwritten**

1392 Keeper and Warden. Charles lord St. John.
Lieutenant. [Blank].
Steward. William Pawlett esquire has appeared.
Bow Bearer. Henry Bromfeild esquire has appeared.
Riding Forester. Thomas Bacon esquire has appeared.
Rangers. Thomas Urry gentleman and Rober Reade have appeared.

1393 Burley. John Neale esquire, forester, has appeared.
Battramsley. Edward Seamer esquire, forester, has appeared.
Fritham. Sir Robert Howard, forester.
Linwood. Sir Adam Browne Bt., forester.
Godshill. Sir John Penruddock, forester.
In Bailiwick. George Rodney esquire, forester, has appeared.
East Bailiwick. Sir John Mill Bt., forester, has appeared.
North Bailiwick. Sir Thomas Clifford, forester.
South Bailiwick. Richard Norton esquire, forester.

1394 Verderers. Thomas Knollis esquire and Philip Leigh esquire have appeared.
Verminer. [Blank].

1395 Regarders. William Burrard gentleman has not appeared. Henry Lovell, James Barrow, Thomas Lovell, Thomas Fisher, Thomas Toomer, Edward Hamond, William Pocock, Nicholas Lambert, Richard Edwards, Ogden Rooke, William Moone, Andrew Elliott. Sworn.

1396 Agisters. Richard Rowe, William Bright, William Pocock, and William Stride have appeared.
Riders. John Stote and James Bayly.

1397 Names of the underforesters.

Burley. George Bright has appeared.

1398 Battramsley. John Taplin, John Bushell, and Edward Bright.

1399 Fritham. John Lewin gentleman and George Duke gentleman.

1400 Linwood. Henry Adams.

1401 In Bailiwick. Thomas Grante, John Troth, Philip Pocock, and John Spencer.

1402 Godshill. Edward Penruddock gentleman, John Saunders, and George Harrison.

1403 East Bailiwick. Edward Bright, Ralph Carter, and Nicholas Bright.

1404 North Bailiwick. John Carey gentleman and Robert Read gentleman.

1405 South Bailiwick. William Rossiter and Thomas Carter.

1406 Woodward of the forest. Bernard Knapton gentleman has appeared.
Woodward of Minstead. Ellis Weeks.

1407 Names of the vills, and the reeve and four men of each vill.

Vill of Exbury and Lepe. John Flight, reeve, is dead. Robert Dray, Luke Nash, and John Willmott have not appeared. Henry Stevans.

1408 Vill of Holbury and Langley. Richard Lambert reeve. Nicholas Bernard, James Wakeford, John Mabley, and Robert Warne are sworn.

1409 Vill of Buttsash and Hardley. John Scarle reeve. Charles Lyne, John Brooke, James Osey, and John Parker are sworn.

1410 Vill of Pilley and Warborne. John Carter reeve. Timothy

Longe, Edward Reeves, Martin Saunders, and Christopher Chaplin.

1411 Vill of Battramsley and Wootton. John Leggatt, Peter Penny, John Smith, Robert Frye, and Thomas Lane.

1412 Vill of Baddesley. Henry Pocock reeve. John Pope, Thomas Cozens, James Studly, and Henry Corbin.

1413 Vill of Brockenhurst and Brookley. Thomas Goodall reeve. Richard Knapton, William Furner, Richard Stoy, and John Forde.

1414 Vill of Godshill and Linwood. Henry Cozier, Henry Bradshaw, John Scovell, William Curtis, and Giles Bussey.

1415 Vill of Burley. William Ady reeve. Hugh Tiller, Stephen Reeks, Edward Pitt, and Anthony Fishe.

m.20d

1416 Vill of Canterton and Fritham. Richard Hurst, Richard Iremonger, John Deale, William Dutton, and Edward Rattee.

1417 Vill of Minstead. Robert Soph reeve. Drue Penton, Christopher Stride, Edward Wright, and Robert Hobbs.

1418 Vill of Lyndhurst. James Elcombe reeve. John Morris, John Batcheler, William Thorne, and Edward Stride.

1419 Vill of Bartley Regis and London Minstead. Robert Hiscock reeve. Philip Page, Matthew Woolfe, John White, and George Barlin.

1420 Names of the Freeholders of the New Forest.

Exbury and Lepe. John Willmott, Matthew Wilson, John Flight is dead, John Moone is dead, William Cowdry, Benjamin Ackeridge, John Clement gentleman, Richard Cole, the heir of Stephen March, Richard Compton esquire, Benjamin Whithead, Richard Cole, William Cole, the heir of George Lesson, Henry Bromfeild junior, Nicholas Strong, Nicholas Rogers clerk.

1421 Buttsash. John Crooke esquire and James Osey gentleman.

1422 Hardley. The heir of John Pittis gentleman, William Bond, the heir of Edmund Cole, Robert Shepheard is dead, Moses Hebbart, Adam de Cardonnell gentleman, John Steptoe gentleman, John Brooke, Richard Auly, John Stepto, William Crosse, Charles Lyne, Thomas Edwards, Richard Combes.

1423 Pilley and Warborne. Henry Bromfeild esquire, William Slaun gentleman, John Carter, John Drew, John Rickman is dead, Michael Quint, James Plowman, John Carter, Christopher Chaplin, Richard King gentleman, Timothy Longe, George Johnson gentleman, William Rasbridge, Arthur Watts.

1424 Baddesley. Henry Philpott esquire, John Drew, sir Henry Worsley Bt., the heir of John March, William Walton, Thomas Fisher, sir Henry Worsley Bt., William Colebrooke, William Haines, Richard Sampson.

1425 Battramsley and Wootton. Richard Ghost, sir Henry Titchborne Bt., Thomas Wansey, the heir of Henry Tulse gentleman, Henry Goddard gentleman, sir William Meux Bt., John Edwards, John Chase, Peter Penny, Edward Scott junior, William Burrard gentleman, Thomas Roberts.

1426 Burley. William Batten gentleman, John Warne, the heir of Thomas Tarver is dead, William Bampton, Christopher Gerrard, Christopher Lyne, Joseph Coffin.

1427 Brockenhurst and Brookley. William Knapton gentleman, Margaret Smith, Richard Draper, John Atwood, Richard Rowe, Henry Williams, Thomas Burton, Thomas Gretnam, William Purdue, the heir of Nicholas Hollier, Bernard Knapton gentleman, John Olliver, Richard King.

1428 Godshill and Linwood. Lord Robert Brooke, Richard Goodridge, Ambrose Bradshawe, William Miller, Henry Sex, John Webb esquire, John Weeks gentleman, Edmund Okden, the heir of John Brewen, John Stent, Benjamin Good, Henry Rooke, lady Cooper widow.

1429 Canterton and Fritham. Jonathan Rivett gentleman, Edward Acton, John Cooke, Ann Rooke, Edward Yeoman, Richard Archer is dead, William Eaton *alias* Meux, George Venner gentleman, Edmund Perkins gentleman, John Emblyn, the heir of Henry Read.

1430 London Minstead. William Olding, the heir of Francis Ranger, John Charter and Henry Charter, Thomas Cowdry, Philip Dore gentleman.

1431 Bartley Regis. Sir John Mill Bt., Richard Goddard esquire, Edward Hamond, Robert Richbell gentleman, Thomas Lovell gentleman, Thomas Knapton gentleman.

1432 Lyndhurst. John Guill, Anthony Wiseman, Thomas Graunte, James Elcombe, Edward Bright, William Gautlett, John Morris, Thomas Pearce, John Buckle, William Bright, George Rodney esquire.

1433 Jurors for the lord king. John Drew, William Bright, Edward Welch, Henry Tovey, Richard Cole, Albin Knapton gentleman, Thomas Gretnam, John Harvey, Edward Yeoman, Nicholas King, Bartholomew Clement, Joseph Coffin, James Randoll, Henry Rooke, Thomas James, Clement Morris, George House. Sworn.

m.21

[The following presentments, **1434–1448**, omit the usual phrase 'and proved by the verderers' *(et convictus per viridarios)*, instead blank spaces have been left. The usual subscription 'that all and each thing is signed and sealed by the verderers etc.' has also been omitted].

1434 It is presented by the foresters and other ministers of the forest and the twelve jurors, [blank], that William Rossiter, recently underforester of the South Bailiwick, on the 9th April 1668 had cut and lopped the branches of both oak and beech trees under colour of browsewood, containing fifty colefires worth £25, more for this own advantage than for the necessary forage of the king's beasts.

1435 That William Pawlett esquire, recently forester of the North Bailiwick, on the 9th April 1668 had cut and lopped the branches of both oak and beech trees containing forty eight colefires worth £24.

1436 That John Lewin, recently underforester of Fritham Bailiwick, on the 9th April 1668 had cut and lopped the branches of both oak and beech trees, containing thirty colefires worth £15.

1437 That George Rodney esquire, recently forester of the In Bailiwick, on the 9th April 1668 had cut and lopped the branches of both oak and beech trees, containing thirty colefires worth £15.

1438 That Thomas Carter, recently underforester of the South Bailiwick, on the 9th April 1668 had cut and lopped the branches of various oak and beech trees, containing thirty one colefires worth £15 10s.

1439 That Ralph Carter junior, recently forester of Battramsley Bailiwick, on the 9th April 1668 had cut and lopped the branches of various oak and beech trees, containing seven colefires worth £3 10s.

1440 That Edward Bright, recently underforester of the East Bailiwick, on the 9th April 1668 had cut and lopped the branches of various oak and beech trees, containing twenty two colefires worth £40 *(xl li.)*.[1]

[1] Apparently in error for £11 *(xi li.)*.

1441 That Edward Talbott gentleman, recently underforester of the North Bailiwick, on the 9th April 1668 had cut and lopped the branches of various oak and beech trees, containing twenty two colefires worth £40.[1]

[1] Apparently in error for £11.

1442 That John Saunders and George Harrison, recently underforesters of Godshill Bailiwick, on the 9th April 1668 had cut and lopped the branches of various oak and beech trees, containing six colefires worth £3.

1443 That George Bright, recently underforester of Burley Bailiwick, on the 9th April 1668 had cut and lopped the branches of various oak and beech trees, containing forty six colefires worth £23.

1444 That Thomas Venner, recently underforester of Fritham Bailiwick, on the 9th April 1668 had cut and lopped the branches of various oak and beech trees, containing nineteen colefires worth £8 10s.[1]

[1] Apparently in error for £9 10s.

1445 That Ralph Carter, recently underforester of the East Bailiwick, on the 9th April 1668 had cut and lopped the branches of various oak and beech trees, containing sixteen colefires worth £8.

1446 That Henry Adams, recently underforester of Linwood Bailiwick, on the 9th April 1668 had cut and lopped the branches of various oak and beech trees, containing twenty two colefires worth £11.

1447 That John Taplin, recently underforester of Battramsley Bailiwick, on the 9th April 1668 had cut and lopped the branches of various oak and beech trees, containing eight colefires worth £4.

1448 That Thomas Fitzjames, recently forester of Battramsley Bailiwick, on the 9th April 1668 had cut and lopped the branches of various oak and beech trees, containing fifty two colefires worth £26.

1449 [Signatures]. Thomas Knollys, Philip Leigh [verderers]. James Barrow, Thomas Lovell, Richard Edwards, William Burrard, Henry Lovell, Thomas Fisher, Thomas Toomer, William Pocock, Nicholas Lambert, Ogden Rooke, William Moone, Andrew Elliott [regarders]. [A deleted signature appears to be that of Edward Hamond].

E.32/176 [English except for heading]

m.1

1450 ‹New Forest in the county of Southampton›. The Forest Eyre of the New Forest opened at Lyndhurst on the 15th September 1670, and adjourned to Monday the 19th September at Winchester Castle before Aubrey earl of Oxford, chief justice in eyre of all forests, chases, parks, and warrens south of the Trent.

1451 The 19th September 1670. It is ordered by the court that John . . . undersheriff be summoned to attend on Wednesday next.

The vill of Lyndhurst for not coming in full, £10. South Baddesley £10 for the same. Godshill and Linwood because they have not appeared, £20. Holbury and Langley for the same, £20.

Upon every Freeholder not appearing, 40s.

Ordered by the Court that the Verderers bring their Swainmote Rolls tomorrow morning, in such sort as they will stand and abide by.

1452 Henry Browne for taking an oak of timber and carrying it away. To pay the value of the tree ‹10s› and to answer for £5 the value of the cart, horses, and oxen. Fined for the offence ‹£4›, and process immediately to bring him in. ‹£10 10s paid Master Reinold›.

m.2

Arthur Oxford a forester for cooperage timber. ‹Pardoned›.
Arthur Oxford for cutting browsewood. ‹Pardoned›.
Arthur Oxford, 13th February 1660, one oak etc. ‹Pardoned›.

Thomas Amyes, 11th August 1660, for a timber oak 10s., the cart and horses £5, and £5 for the fine, process immediate. ‹£10 10s›.

Arthur Oxford, 13th February 1660, a beech. ‹Pardoned›.

1453 Swainmote Roll 14th September 1661.

Hugh Line, 13th Charles, dug up 1000 turves from the king's soil. Fined £2. Process immediate.

Roger Russell, 13th Charles, for carrying away 1 load of wood to the value 5s. Fined £2 10s.,[1] 13s 4d.[1]

[1] Deleted.

John Hetheridge, 18th November 1660, for cutting and lopping boughs to the value of £3. Fined £30. ‹£30 5s›.

William Coghill, 13th Charles, for digging 1000 turves. Fined £2.

1454 Edward Amy. Neither day nor year in the presentment, for which each of the presenters is fined 3s 4d because they have presented less than fully.

Richard Rooke. Neither day nor year. The same rule.

Henry Rooke. Neither day nor year. The same rule.

John Wort, 13th Charles, for digging and carrying away 5000 [turves], drawn with four horses worth £6, and fined £10.

Thomas Mislin, 13th Charles, for digging 9000 turves for several persons and carrying it away. Fined £18.
Alice Harding, 13th Charles, for digging 1000 turves and carrying them away with four horses worth £4. Fined £2.

m.3
1455 Thomas Tarrant, 13th Charles, for carrying away 1000 turves with four horses worth £5. Fined £2.

James Baker. Neither day nor year. The presenters fined 3s 4d.

John Spenser. For the like 3s 4d.

George Foxe, 12th Charles, the same rule.

1456 William Rossiter, 13 Charles II, for lopping great boughs to the value of £7 by colour of browsewood containing fifteen colefires. Fined £100 and to enter a recognizance of £30 not to offend.

Clement Odway for seventeen colefires of great boughs to the value of £9. Being dead, his heir to answer £9 and a *scire facias* to make him attend.

Thomas Venner, 13 Charles II, fifteen colefires to the value of £7. Dead, the same rule.

Arthur Oxford gentleman, 13 Charles II, great boughs containing fifty nine colefires to the value of £25. Dead, the same rule.

1457 John Lewin, 13 Charles II, great boughs by colour of browsewood. Seventeen colefires to the value of £8. Fined £100 and to be bound in a recognizance of £300 not to offend.

George Rodney esquire, 13 Charles II, cut great boughs by colour of browsewood. Twenty two colefires value £10. Fined £100 and to be bound as above.

Robert Reade gentleman, 13 Charles II, cut great boughs by colour of browsewood. Sixty one colefires value £25. Fined £100 and the like recognizance.

William Paulett, 13 Charles II, cut great boughs by colour as before. Twenty three colefires value £10. Fined £100 and recognizance.

Edward Bright, 13 Charles II, twelve colefires value £5. The same.

m.4

1458 Edward Talbatt, 13 Charles II, sixty two colefires value £25. The like rule.

Robert Andrews, 16th September 1660, for hunting with a gun and killing a buck. Fined £25 and a £100 recognizance for good behaviour in the forest.

Henry Buckle, 12 Charles II. No day.

James Parkins, 12th April 1661, for hunting with a greyhound. Fined £5.

James Parkins, 8th May 1661, for the like. Fined £5.

Thomas Pickfatt, 13th February 166, for hunting with dogs and killing a deer. Fined £25.

Robert Thorne, 13th May 1661, for he had in his hand a gun with intent to kill. Fined £1.

Nicholas Rolph, 13th May 1661, the like offence. Fined £1.

Alexander Cattle, 13th May 1661, the like offence. Fined £1.

Mary Moore widow, 13 Charles II, for five thousand turves, carried away with four horses value £4. Fined £1.

1459 September 20th afternoon. A proclamation that all foresters and officers of the forest do not leave without permission. Other persons who are not witnesses and have no business may leave.

1460 Swainmote Roll 14th September 1662.

Arthur Oxford, 13 Charles II, for rooting out a moor-fall beech. No value and the party dead. The presenters fined 3s 4d each.

Arthur Oxford, 13 Charles II, for rooting up a stub fourteen feet high. The party dead. The same rule.

m.5
Henry Rooke, 13 Charles II, for taking an oak of timber cut down by a person unknown. Fined 13s 4d.

Clement Hobbs, 16th January 1662, for cutting the limb of an oak value 3s. Fined £1 10s.

Emanuel Coit, 3rd December 1661, for cutting an oak value £1. Fined £10.

1461 William Loukes, 28th February 1662, for making and hedging a purpresture of half an acre, and laid it to a house newly built where no house was before. Fined 6s 8d and seized into the king's hand.

Edward Buckle, 10th February 1662, for cutting boughs and

bushes. Fined 13s 4d.

Moses Waldron, 13 Charles II, caused two oaks for firewood to be [converted] for colewood. No rule.

John King, 14 Charles II, hunted with a gun and shot at a male deer. Fined £2.

1462 Swainmote Roll 14th September 1663.

Edward Amye, 12th January 1663. For no offence, no sum, and no place, the presenters fined 3s 4d each.

Henry Cusier, 12th January 1663, for cutting various holms containing [blank] loads and [blank] value. Fined £1.

Richard Slye,[1] 17th August 1663, for keeping ten sheep to the surcharging and nuisance of the forest. Fined 6s 8d. ‹Paid Reinild›.

[1] *recte* Stoy.

William Miheel, 17th August 1663, for keeping three sheep to the surcharging [of the forest]. Fined 3s 4d.

m.6

1463 Henry Goddard gentleman, 17th August 1663, for putting twenty sheep in the forest. Fined 6s 8d. Paid Samuel Reinold.

Richard Smith, 17th August 1663, for putting eight sheep in the forest. Fined 6s 8d. ‹Paid Reinold›.

William Parry, 17th August 1663, for putting seven sheep in the forest. Fined 6s 8d.

Thomas Browne, 17th August 1663, for putting two sheep in the forest. Nothing. No rule.

1464 Bernard Knapton, 17th August 1663, for putting in fourteen sheep. Fined 6s 8d. ‹Paid Samuel Reinold›.

Lukenor Mill, 17th August 1663, for putting in six sheep. Fined 3s 4d. ‹Paid Reinold›.

Arthur North,[1] 21st August 1663, for putting in eight sheep. Fined 5s. ‹Paid Samuel Reinold›.

[1] *recte* Watts.

Edward Rainer,[1] 21st August 1663, for twelve sheep. Fined 6s 8d.

[1] *recte* Reeves.

Roger Holiar, 21st August 1663, for putting two hundred sheep. Fined £5.

1465 Christopher Cord, 21st August 1663, for eight sheep. Fined 3s 4d.

John Drew, 21st August 1663, for thirty sheep. Fined 6s 8d. ‹Paid S. Reinold›.

Richard Smith, 21st August 1663, for five sheep. Fined 3s 4d. ‹Paid Reinold›.

Richard Saunders, 23rd July 1663, for hunting and chasing the king's deer with dogs. Fined £5.

George Hastings, 23rd July 1663, for hunting with dogs and chasing deer. Fined £5. Reduced by the lord chief justice to £2 10s. Paid Samuel Reinold.

m.7

1466 Ralph Hastings, 23rd July 1663, for hunting and chasing with dogs. £2 10s. Paid Samuel Reinold.

[Blank] Gatherhill, 23rd July 1663, for hunting with a gun and shooting at a buck. No rule. The presenters fined 3s 4d each for the uncertainty.

John Saunders, 23rd July 1663, for hunting and chasing with dogs. Fined £2 10s.

Henry Hastings and George and Ralph Hastings, John Saunders, and Richard Saunders, for chasing and killing a deer. No year. The presenters fined 3s 4d each.

1467 Arthur Oxford, April 1663, for cutting the boughs of trees for sixty seven colefires, value £33 10s. Dead. *Scire facias* against his heir for £33 10s.

George Bright, April 1663, for cutting boughs. Forty eight colefires value £24 under colour of browsewood. Fined £120 and committed to the marshal until he pay his fine. ‹Remitted, his and Mr. Neale's to £100›.

Thomas Fitzjames, April 1663, for cutting thirty six colefires value £19. Fined £100. Remitted by my lord, all his fines to £20. Paid Reinold.

William Pawlett esquire, April 1663, for colefires to the value of £28. Fined £150. Remitted by my lord. ‹Totally remitted›.

m.8
1468 Wednesday 21st September. Swainmote Roll 14th September 1664.

Ordered that the agisters and woodwards bring in their account by tomorrow morning. Ordered that the foresters and all other officers of the forest attend tomorrow morning to give an account whether they have taken their oath to be true to the forest.

Ordered that process be made out against all the persons presented in this roll, but no process is to ensue until further order.

1469 Swainmote Roll 14th September 1665.

Henry Hastings and George Hastings, 3rd August 1664, for having had two greyhounds in the forest, but it not appearing whether they were loose or leashed, the presentment discharged.

George Rodney, 10th July 1665, for a moorfall beech taken and sold, value 12s. Fined £1 4s. All his fines remitted by my lord to £10. Paid Reinold.

William Waterman, 10th July 1665, for a green beech cut and carried away value £4. Fined £40.

George Rodney, 10th July 1665, for cutting boughs. Fourteen colefires value £7. Fined £50. ‹Remitted as above›.

Nicholas Clement, 10th July 1665, for cutting fifty four tons of timber value £32 4s. The party dead, *scire facias* against the heir, but no process without my lord's further direction. Bernard Knapton produced as a witness to prove that there was a sale of this coppice wood. The court, unless you produce the king's grant it is to no purpose. ‹Paid Reinold £32 4s›.

m.9

1470 Nicholas Clement, 11th July 1665, for cutting four and a half tons value £2 10s. The same rule. ‹Paid Reinold £2 10s›.

Thomas Wiat, 10th July 1665, for a purpresture and enclosing one acre. Fined 13s 4d and to be seized into the king's hand.

[Blank] Wist[1] widow. Void for no Christian name. The offence for enclosing ninety pole and setting up a house and fodder house. The presenters fined 3s 4d each, and the thing to be seized into the king's hand.

[1] *recte* Wyatt.

1471 The court being informed by my lord warden that there are diverse records concerning the forest in the hands of John Hildasly of H. Ordered he brings in all the records, rolls, and memorandum into this court.

Nicholas Durrant, [blank], for erecting a cottage in Bulslade. Fined £1 and to be seized into the king's hand.

William Hooker, 5th June 1665, for cutting four oaks of timber value £5 5s after they were seized. Fined £40.

John Aldridge, 10th June 1665, a parcel of wood consigned to him. No value set of the wood. The presenters fined 3s 4d.

1472 Swainmote 14th September 1666.

Nicholas Clement and William Knapton, 8th March 1666, the

boughs of various trees to blank value and also the wood. The presenters fined 3s 4d.

1473 Swainmote 9th November 1666 adjourned to 20th November following.

William Pawlett, 10th July 1666, for cutting
m.10
oaks and branches. Thirty five colefires value £2 10s. Fined £50. ‹Remitted as above›.

Sir Adam Browne Bt., 10th July 1665, for cutting boughs by colour of browsewood, seventeen colefires value £5. ‹Remitted to £10. Not paid›.

Thomas Fitzjames, 10th July 1655, for cutting boughs, Forty four colefires value £4. Fined £40. ‹Remitted as above›.

John Neale, 10th July 1665, for cutting boughs. Thirty nine colefires value £8. Fined £50. Eight colefires unlawful value £8. ‹All his and George Bright's [fines] remitted to £100. Paid Reinold›.

William Rossiter, 10th July 1665, for cutting boughs. Twenty seven colefires value £4. Fined £40. ‹All his fines remitted to £50. Paid Reinold›.

1474 Arthur Oxford, 10th July 1665, cutting boughs. Sixty nine colefires value £5. Dead. *Scire facias* against the heir for £5.

Thomas Venner, 10th July 1665, boughs. Seventeen colefires value £1. The same rule.

Ralph Carter, 10th July 1665, cutting boughs. Twelve colefires value £1 10s. Fined £15.

George Rodney, 10th July 1665, cutting boughs. Seventeen colefires value £2 10s. Fined £20. ‹Remitted as above›.

Nicholas Barling, 10th July 1665, cutting boughs. Seven colefires value £1. Dead. *Scire facias* as above.

John Sparrow, 10th July 1665, for cutting boughs. Twenty one colefires value £2 10s. *Scire facias* as above.

1475 Swainmote Roll 9th June 1668.[1]

[1] Date incorrectly altered from 14th September 1667.

William Hancock, 7th May 1667, cutting boughs.
m.11
Fifty colefires value £1 10s. Fined £15.

George Rodney, 7th May 1667, cutting boughs. Fifty six colefires value £1 8s. Fined £15. ‹Remitted as above›.

That all officers of the forest convicted as aforesaid enter recognizance not to offend etc.

Thomas Venner, 7th May 1667, cutting boughs. Twenty seven colefires value £12 10s. *Scire facias* as above.

John Saunders, 7th May 1667, cutting boughs. Ten colefires value £5. Fined £50.

1476 Thomas Fitzjames, 7th May 1667, cutting boughs. Sixty five colefires value £32 10s. Fines £100. ‹Remitted as above›.

Ralph Carter, 7th May 1667, cutting boughs. Fifteen colefires value £7 10s. Fined £40. ‹Remitted all his fines to £10. Paid Reinold›.

William Rossiter, 7th May 1667, cutting boughs. Fifty four colefires value £27. Fined £100. ‹Remitted as above›.

Thomas Frye, 7th May 1667, cutting boughs. Fifty one colefires value £25 10s. Fined £100.

Edward Bright, 7th May 1667, cutting boughs. Twenty one colefires value £10 10s. Fined £40. ‹Remitted to £10. Paid Reinold›.

William Pawlett, 7th May 1667, cutting boughs. Thirty eight colefires value £19. Fined £80. ‹Remitted as above›.

1477 George Bright, 7th May 1667, cutting boughs. Forty nine colefires value £24 10s. Fined £100. ‹Remitted as above›.

John Sparrow, 7th May 1667, cutting boughs. Thirty four colefires value £17. *Scire facias* as above.

Arthur Oxford, 7th May 1667, cutting boughs. One hundred and one colefires value £50 10s. *Scire facias* as above.

m.12
Nicholas Barling, 7th May 1667, cutting boughs. Seven colefires value £3 10s. *Scire facias* as above.

Edward Talbott, 7th May 1667, cutting boughs. Twenty seven colefires value £13 10s. Fined £100.

Hugh Piball, 19 Charles II, for hunting with a gun and shooting at a deer. Fined £5.

1478 Swainmote Roll 9th June 1668.

John Ritiar, 20 Charles II, for taking two cartloads of wood. Mr. Knapton, understeward, fined £1.

Joan Young widow, 20 Charles II, for cutting green trees to a [blank] value. Presenters 3s 4d.

1479 Swainmote 9th July 1668.[1]

[1] This appears to be an incorrect and unnecessary heading.

Thomas Tunbridge, 20 Charles II, for having a gun charged with powder and bullet with intent to kill a deer. Fined £1.

Robert Hiscock, 20 Charles II, for cutting boughs of oak to the value of £5. Fined £50. ‹Remitted to £2 15s. Paid Reinold›.

William Farne,[1] May 1668, for enclosing a lane with a hedge that they could not pass, but being long time lane. Fined 1s 8d. Paid Samuel Reinold.

[1] *recte* Thorne.

George Hastings and Thomas Burgin, [blank] Gatherhill for killing a pricket with dogs. George Hastings fined £15. Thomas Burkin fined £15, remitted upon his petition. ‹George Hastings remitted to £10. Paid Reinold›.

1480 Master Ferdinand Knapton bound in a recognizance of £100. With condition that he attends the court tomorrow with the original conviction, and not to depart the court without permission.

m.13

1481 It is ordered by this court that William Israll and William Hancock of Southampton be sent for by the messenger that attends this court to answer matters of misdemeanour, and that they attend this court tomorrow morning.

1482 Ordered that William Tulse esquire, Henry Goddard, and William Slaun, being duly elected regarders of this forest, being summoned to take the oath of regarder did refuse to do so. This court orders that they take the oath of regarder at the next county court upon penalty of £20.

1483 Ordered of Master John Read, being named a regarder and wishing to be discharged, that he attends that service during this justice seat and then is discharged.

1484 21st September afternoon. It is ordered by this court that lord Broke upon payment of 3s 4d fines may amend the several claims put in by him at this justice seat. ‹Paid Reinold £1›. The like rule for my lord keeper and others. ‹3s 4d paid Reinold›.

1485 Thursday 22nd September 1670. It is ordered by this court that sir Robert Jason and master Carew shall amend their three claims, numbers 21, 22, and 26, paying 13s 4d each. ‹Never amended›.

1486 George Carew, William Israell, and William Hancock examined and acknowledged that they followed the directions of Master Knapton and transcribed the indictments with blanks. Master Knapton brought to answer concerning his neglect. It is ordered by this court that master Ferdinand Knapton be fined £100 and turned out of office.

m.14

1487 Thursday 22nd September 1670. Memorandum that the king's counsel attends the lord chief justice in eyre this afternoon to advise concerning the amendment of the Swainmote Roll for 21 Charles II.

1488 Sir John Norton sworn to the place of woodward.

1489 It is ordered by the court that his majesty's warrant concerning cutting down 30 tons of timber shall be enrolled by the clerk of the eyre, and the original returned to the lord warden.

1490 That all warrants and orders that are sent from the king to the lord chief justice in eyre shall be enrolled by the clerk of the eyre.

1491 The Swainmote Roll of 21 Charles II delivered by order of the court to the lord warden. To be returned again by him in court.

1492 Afternoon. Upon the first reading of the Swainmote Roll of 22 Charles II, the insufficiency thereof being discovered, the court thought fit to reject the same. It is therefore ordered that the verderers do bring in their roll tomorrow morning to be read for the court to proceed upon. The court orders that the regarders do attend the verderers this night.

1493 Charles Rex to the Commissioners of the Treasury. Warrant for timber for Lyndhurst. Whereas it has been represented to us that there is a necessity for a further quantity of timber to be supplied for repairs of our house at Lyndhurst and the bridges thereunto belonging, over and above the 45 tons already allocated for that purpose. Our will and pleasure is that you forthright give order to our Surveyor General of our woods this side of the Trent, or to the woodward of the New Forest, to
m.15
assign and mark out as many timber trees as may contain 30 tons of timber more, and cause the same to be fallen and cut down within or close by the ground that there be no loss or waste of timber, and taking care that all the bark, tops, boughs, and offal wood not servicable to this use are to be sold and disposed of for our best benefit and advantage, this to be accounted for upon oath in the Exchequer before the end of Michaelmas term next. Given at Whitehall on the 27th May 1669. By his majesty's command, Ashley, T. Clifford.

m.16
1494 Friday 23rd September 1670. Richard King and the rest of the regarders make affidavit in court. Henry Blomefeild, one of the

verderers, makes affidavit in court. Master Knowles also makes affidavit. These affidavits are made in relation to the order made last night for bringing in the Swainmote Roll 22 Charles II.

1495 Ordered that the foresters attend the grand jury and give to them the evidence they have against any persons mentioned in the Swainmote Roll of 22 Charles II, and then the court will proceed thereon. And the verderers are discharged from bringing in the Swainmote Roll mentioned in the order made last night, it appearing to this court that the parties proceded against and convicted were never summoned or had notice thereof whereby they might have made their defence.

1496 The claim of sir Orlando Bridgman Kt. and Bt., lord keeper of the great seal of England, was this day read. Serjeant Maynard desires they should produce their patent. Master Strad desires until this afternoon to bring it in, which is ordered accordingly.

The petition of Robert Hiscock was read, and ordered thereupon that the presentment be produced in the afternoon.

Claim No. 61 of the bishop of Winchester was read. The king's counsel desires to have time to consider it and the patent to be brought in.

m.17
Ordered that my lord keeper's patent be enrolled. Ordered that the bishop of Winchester's patent be enrolled and remain in court during the eyre upon the demand of the king's cousel.

1497 Upon the petition of the inhabitants of Holbury and Langley, the fine of £20 set upon the vill because their four men and reeve the first day of the session ‹ordered by the court›, be remitted to 40s to be paid in court. Paid Samuel Reinold.

1498 Claim No. 62 of the bishop of Winchester was read. The king's counsel desires as above.

1499 James Fifeild being a bailiff appointed to attend the grand jury and neglecting his duty, fined 20s.

William Curtis, bailiff, sworn to attend the grand jury.

A process against Joseph Stockman esquire of Borford in Wiltshire.

1500 Saturday 24th September. The original indictment ‹against Robert Hiscock› being brought into court, and it appearing that the value was 5s and not £5, it is ordered that the fine of £50 formerly set be remitted to 50s. ‹50s fine, 5s value›.

1501 Ordered that process is immediately taken out against those that are fined for unlawful hunting with dogs, guns, and such like.

By the presenters his lordship declares that it is process to issue out against verderers, regarders, all other officers, and the jury.

The regarders roll read. Delivered to the Swainmote 27th June 1670 ‹. . . you ought to have followed the words of the last Roll›.

1502 The sheriff makes a return upon the *venire, non est inventus,* which being an improper return upon those writs is was delivered back to the sheriff to be amended, for it should be *nihil habet in balliva*

m.18

etc. quod attach . . . potest, and when appears that return a *capias* issued. If the sheriff returns that he hath a freehold, after that goes a *distringas*.

A *venire facias* against Henry Philpott esquire of Pylewell. A *venire facias* against James Harding labourer of Lyndhurst.

1503 Afternoon. Sir George Cary presented upon the regarders roll for having inclosed and ploughed 30 acres to the value of £10 while having the custody of New Park. Sir George Carew appears and pleads not guilty and he petitions that it is inquired into by the forest officers, and a special justification for the ploughing, and time until Monday to put in that plea. Also to alter that plea of not guilty.

1504 Ordered upon the motion of master Strode that a claim of William Kroley, an infant, and a claim of John Read, be received paying for each claim a sum of 6s 8d. ‹Paid Reinold 13s 4d›.

1505 Monday 26th September 1670. George Hastings gentleman, there being a *capias* against his appearing in court, is handed over into custody and delivered by a fine. Remitted to £10 and his recognizances discharged. ‹Remitted as above›.

The petition of the regarders and jurors being read, his lordship is pleased to remit their fines of 3s 4d each.

Henry Philpot, being a freeholder, pays his fine. ‹Paid Reinold £2›.

Sir George Cary appears upon his presentment and puts himself in the mercy of the court. Fined £10. ‹Paid Reinold £10›.

A *venire* against William Chamberlin esquire of Milton. Discharged having a colourable license thereof. Fined but 7s and the license delivered up. ‹7s paid Reinold›.

A *venire* against Arthur Poor of Breamore.

A *venire* against James Franks, glover, of Fordingbridge.

m.19
1506 The petition of the inhabitants of Lyndhurst is read.

The petition of John Clement the heir of Nicholas Clement is read. He engages to pay £34 14s.

Ordered that my lord warden's two claims be received.

Ordered that sir John Norton's patent for woodward be enrolled.

1507 Ordered that James Oviat gentleman ‹discharged› of Tatchbury, Andrew Elliot gentleman of Fritham, Philip Purcivall gentleman of Ringwood, John Rooke of Blashford, and John Hobby of Ashley in the parish of Ringwood, do appear at the next county court and take the oath of regarder upon the penalty of £20 each. The same rule for Henry Goddard. William Slaun and William Tulse discharged.

1508 Upon reading the petition of the inhabitants of Lyndhurst, the fine of £10 is remitted to £5.

Richard Edwards, being presented by the grand jury for erecting a malt kiln, places himself in the mercy of the court. He is fined 40s and the malt kiln to be demolished. ‹£2 paid Reinold›.

Alice Harding's petition read. The value and also the fine remitted to 20s. ‹£1 paid Reinold›.

Ordered that my lord warden have liberty to withdraw his two claims and to amend his claims.

Ordered that sir John Penruddock have liberty to put in his claims for the fine of 20s. ‹£1 paid Reinold›.

1509 Thomas Tomour gentleman appointed regarder in place of James Oviat who is discharged. Master Tomour to be sworn at the next county court upon penalty of £20.

m.20

1510 Master Neale and master Bright's fine remitted to £100. To be paid this night.

A *venire* against James Freake and Charles Barnes.

The petition of John Saunders is read. [Fine] remitted to £25.

Thomas Fitzjames' petition is read. All his fines remitted to £20 to be paid this night by engagement of Henry Fitzjames esquire.

The petition of the inhabitants of South Baddesley. Remitted to 40s. ‹£2 paid Reinold›.

Thomas Lovel presented by the grand jury for three acres of coppice wood value 5s. Places himself in mercy etc. Fined £1. ‹£1 paid Reinold›.

1511 Presentment that no forester is to cut down ashes except such trees as have been previously branched or lopped.

Ordered that Thomas Morflin having only an estate for 99 years within the forest, and being returned a freeholder, be discharged of his fine of 40s for non appearance. That the fine for cutting turves be respited until his claim is heard.

Ordered that the woodward do forthwith take care that the prison of the forest be repaired.

m.21

1512 Ordered upon the motion of master Riley that the twenty four claims in master Knapton's hand be received upon the fine of 20s each. ‹£24 paid Reinold›.

Ordered upon the motion of George Stroud that the claims of Edward Cary be received upon the fine of 20s. ‹£1 paid Reinold›.

Ordered that my lord keeper's patent, the bishop of Winchester's patent, and the woodward's patent be delivered out by the clerk of the eyre, they bringing the same to his office in Michaelmas term next or when he calls for them to be enrolled.

1513 25th September 1670. Whereas James Oviat merchant, coming to attend this court on behalf of his father, and being here present was named a fit person to be a regarder. Upon the petition of James Oviatt that by reason of his employment as a merchant he cannot conveniently attend the duty and office of regarder, it is therefore this day ordered by the court that James Oviatt be wholly and absolutely discharged from the office of regarder of this forest.

1514 Tuesday 27th September 1670. Upon reading the petition of William Colbrock, Thomas Fisher, Christopher Chaplin, and John Chair, freeholders, having been fined 40s each. Ordered that their fines be remitted to 40s for all. ‹£2 paid Reinold›.

John Wort, his petition read, his fine of £10 remitted to 40s. ‹£2›.

Ambrose Bradshaw discharged.

George Rodnye's petition read, his several fines remitted to £10.

m.22

1515 John Lewin's petition read. His fine remitted to £8 recognizance.

Sir Adam Browne's petition read. Remitted to £10.

William Rossiter and the groom keeper of South Bailiwick petition read. Remitted to £50 to be paid this noontime. Henry Blomefeild engages for the money and a recognizance of £300.

John Wilmott's petition read. He is discharged.

Richard Eaden's petition read. Discharged.

Edward Bright and Ralph Carter, underkeepers of the East Bailiwick, their petition read. Remitted to £10 each. Sir John Mills bound in their surety in a £300 recognizance.

1516 Robert Read's petition read. Remitted to £5. John Cary enters a recognizance of £300 for their good behaviour. ‹£5 paid Reinold›.

Ordered that for the future all keepers shall give security for themselves and their underkeepers to my lord warden for their good behaviour.

William Waterman's petition read and laid aside.

The fine of Robert Hooker to be respited until my lord warden's claim is heard.

Arthur Wilson's petition read and laid aside. Afterwards discharged. ‹£2 paid Reinold›.

Charles Line's petition read and laid aside. Afterwards Lyne discharged.

Richard Come's petition read. He is discharged.

The court adjourns until the 23rd March 1671 to Winchester Castle.

m.23
1517 Memorandum. That Mr Reinold received of Thomas Knowles esquire, one of the presenters, £1 16s. 8d.; of Mr Leigh another presenter, 10s; of William Olding, 6s 8d.

[*m.24–27* are blank]

m.28

1518 The Clerk of the Iter's Patent Inrolled

To all Christian people to whom these presents shall come, I, Aubrey de Vere, earl of Oxford, chief justice in eyre, send greetings. Whereas king Charles II by his letters patent under the great seal of England dated at Westminster the 27th June 1660 have given and granted unto me Aubrey de Vere the office of chief justice and justice in eyre of all his majesties forests, chases, parks and warrens on this side of Trent, and keeper of the beasts of all the said forests etc., together with all fees, regards, profits, commodities, privileges, jurisdictions, authorities, pre-eminences, advantages and emoluments due, accustomed, or belonging, or before that time with the said office had used or enjoyed, with power to hear and determine all causes of forest etc., and to ordain, make, and constitute all and all manner of officers in the said forests etc., or other officers appertaining to the office of chief justice. To have hold and exercise the said offices by myself or my sufficient deputy or deputies during his majesties pleasure.

m.29

Now know ye that I, the earl of Oxford, have ordained, constituted, and appointed sir John Shaw of Colchester in Essex to be clerk of the iter for all the forests etc., and to have, receive, and enjoy all the fees, regards, profits, commodities, privileges, and advantages to the said office; to have, hold, use, exercise, and enjoy the said office by himself or his sufficient deputy or deputies, for and during such time as the said sir John Shaw shall well, faithfully, and honestly behave himself in the said office. In witness whereof I have hereunto set my hand and seal the 14th November 1667. Oxford.

E.32/182

m.1 [English]

1519 The Grand Jury of the Justice in Eyre's Seat for the New Forest held at Winchester on the 19th September 1670

(1) We present sir Steven Fox or his assignees for having an inclosure of about 20 acres, a dwelling house, and a decoy pond, in the East Bailiwick, newly erected and enclosed to the prejudice of the forest.

(2) We present that the foresters have not kept the Commoners' cattle out of the forest during the fence month because from time out of mind the Commoners have had common of pasture for their cattle throughout the fence month, this under consideration of a fixed annual rent called Month Money received and accepted by his majesty and his predecessors.

(3) We present that summons have not been issued to offenders by the Lyndhurst Court in accordance with former custom, whereby many have been convicted unheard.

(4) We present that it is a great offence and nuisance to the forest that the making of charcoal wood is permitted for it leads to the destruction of the woods, covert, and herbage.

(5) We present that the cutting of ash and holm in summer time by the keepers, under the pretence of browse, is very much leading to the destruction of the vert and greenhew of the forest.

m.2 [English]

1520 We present that Richard Gauntlett gentleman of Plaitford, with various other persons unknown to the jurors, on the 5th August 1665 at Bentley Coppice had unlawfully killed two male deer by means of an unlawful engine called a buckstall. ‹Robert Andrews›.

1521 We present that Charles Barnes gentleman of Charlton, Wiltshire, and Robert Pope of Melchet, Wiltshire, on the 17th September 1665 at Holm Hill in the North Bailiwick had carried a gun worth 5s, and had unlawfully killed a rascal deer.

1522 That Richard Edwards yeoman of Bramshaw on the 15th September 1661 in the North Bailiwick had erected on his own land a dwelling house and malt kiln, containing by estimate four perches, and ever since has carried on the trade of maltster, but by what warrant we know not. ‹Robert Andrews. Fine 40s. Let it be thrown down›.

1523 That the said Richard Edwards on several occasions between the 15th September 1661 and the 15th September last had taken timber for his malthouse from the king's demesne soil in the North Bailiwick [Entry deleted].

1524 We find the first three presentments to be true, but we doubt the evidence of the last presentment, this being a thing so public that we desire to hear the testimony of the keepers and regarders before we find it proved.

m.3

1525 It is presented that lord Henry Saunds of Mottisfont on the 12th August 1668 in the South Bailiwick with four greyhounds had put to flight, chased, and driven to death a buck, and had carried away the flesh. ‹A true bill. Thomas Carter›.

m.4

1526 That Thomas Lovell of Bartley Regis on the 20th October 1668 on his land had cut a coppice containing 3 acres, and had carried away wood worth 5s. ‹A true bill. John Carey and Robert Read, sworn›.

m.5 [English]

1527 Henry Browne gentleman of Brockenhurst on the 20th October 1668 had cut a coppice of 8 acres on his land in Battramsley Bailiwick, worth 5s. ‹John Bushell, E[dward] Bright, John Taplin›.

m.6 [English]

1528 William Chamberlayne esquire of Milton on the 20th October 1668 had felled timber trees worth 7s in his wood at Burcomb in Linwood Bailiwick. ‹Henry Davis›.

m.7 [English]

1529 Arthur Poore of Breamore on the 4th July 1668 at Amberslade in Linwood Bailiwick was hunting with three greyhounds with the intention of harming the deer. ‹Henry Davis›.

m.8 [English]
1530 That James Freake gentleman, Charles Barnes husbandman, Charles Burt and William Burt butchers, and Richard Spiller awlblade maker, all of Fordingbridge, on the 27th February 1668 had hunted the king's beasts with two greyhounds at Rushmore Pound in the North Bailiwick. ‹John Carey. A true bill›.

m.9
1531 Henry Phillpott esquire of Pylewell on the 4th June 1668 at the Pitts had caused to be cut upon the king's soil eighty young oaks, two ash trees, many thorns, and a grove, worth £80, and had carried them away. ‹William Rossiter›.

m.10
1532 James Harding labourer of Lyndhurst on the 20th October 1669 had harboured William Syne, recently of Lyndhurst, knowing him to be a common offender of venison. The foresters of Lyndhurst Bailiwick had entered his house and had found guns and other engines to harm the king's beasts. ‹George Rodney, Thomas Grant, John Buckley, sworn›.

m.11
1533 Joseph Stockman esquire of Barford in Wiltshire, claiming to be an underwoodward in the Franchises outside the bounds of the forest, on the 31st May 1669 did interfere with deer browsing.

m.12
1534 The jury for the lord king present on oath that Henry Phillpott of Pylewell in September 1668 had inclosed with fences and ditches an acre and a half of the king's waste in a place called Pooles within the South Bailiwick, and had cut down four timber trees worth 20s, without permission. ‹William Rossiter, sworn›.

m.13
1535 That John Goddard gentleman of London on the 20th October 1668 had cut his wood in Bartley Regis, called Lambs Coppice, containing ten acres, and had carried away the wood to the damage of the forest. ‹John Carey and Robert Reade, sworn›.

m.14

1536 That John Mills of Bury on the 20th October 1668 had cut his coppice containing two acres in Bartley Regis in the North Bailiwick. ‹John Carey and Robert Reade›.

m.15

1537 William Stanley gentleman on the 20th October 1668 had cut his coppice called ?Qumpfeilds Coppice and Newlands Coppice in Langley containing twelve acres. ‹Nicholas Bright, Ralph Carter, Edward Bright›.

m.16

1538 William Signe, recently of Bartley, on the 8th May 1668 at Rockram in the North Bailiwick had taken a sore. ‹Robert Read›.

E.32/178 [English]

[Affadavits made by the Regarders and by the Verderers]

m.1

1539 Richard King, William Batten, William Burrard, Christopher Garrett, Abraham Olding, Thomas Lovell, Henry Lovell, James Barrow, Richard Edwards, Richard Warne, William Moon, regarders of the New Forest, make oath that the foresters having instruction from Mr. Pawlett the steward of the forest to bring in the names of all those in their bailiwicks who put beasts to pasture and took turbary and wood in the forest, at the Swainmote Court held at Lyndhurst on the 19th August 1670 in pursuance of those instructions returned the names of very many people for putting in cattle and cutting turves and taking fuel, and immediately upon the foresters presenting these names, the steward Mr. Pawlett did cause the regarders to present them, telling the regarders that those who had right of common as well those who had no rights must be presented, and that it would be a strong thing to their right in relation to their claim, and no harm to them. Whereupon the regarders did cause their foreman to affirm the papers you produced to them not knowing it was any prejudice to the parties presented. Richard King, one of the deponents, said that because of the steward's persuasions he caused his own name to be put in amongst the rest for cutting three thousand turves for fear that he should loose his right of turbary, although this deponent had not cut any turves that year. And they further say that the parties presented were not attached nor had any summons to appear, and did not make any defence. Other persons who having notice that they were being presented, namely William Knapton and Edward ?Spiney, who having notice that they were presented did appear, and before being convicted they offered to make their defence and produce witnesses to prove their right, but Mr. Pawlett refused to have them saying they must be laid at the Justice Seat. [Signed] Richard King, Richard Warne, Abraham Olding, William Batten, James Barrow, Thomas Lovell, William Burrard, Christopher Garrett, Henry Lovell, and Richard Edwards.

m.2

1540 Henry Bromfield esquire, one of the verderers of the New Forest, makes out that on the 19th August 1670 at the Swainmote

Court held at Lyndhurst, there were many presentments brought in by the foresters of persons for cutting fuel turves and putting cattle into the forest, and were the same day convicted by the regarders and petty jury without any attachment or summons given to the parties presented. That Mr. Pawlett did then affirm it to be the law, and that provision would be made at the justice seat to the parties so presented and convicted. [Signed] Henry Bromfield.

m.3

1541 Thomas Knollys esquire, one of the verderers of the New Forest, makes out that there was no attachment granted by him, or any other verderer, of any of the persons presented at the Swainmote Court held on the 19th August 1670 for taking fuel turves or putting cattle into the forest, and that he sat judicially in court when the presentments were brought in by the keepers, and that the persons mentioned to be offenders were the same day convicted by the regarders and petty jury there empanelled and sworn. Mr. Pawlett, the steward, then affirmed it to be according to law. [Signed] Thomas Knollys.

E.32/177

[The Regarders' Roll]

m.1

1542 Charles II to Charles Powlett, Lord St. John, warden of the New Forest; Greeting : We command you that you cause to come all and each regarders that they appear at our court of pleas of the said forest, called the Swainmote, to be held on the 9th June at Lyndhurst, to be sworn. Before the 27th day of the same month, they will make their regard of the said forest. They will go through the said forest to view, enquire, and present all transgressions and matters which are contained in the Chapters of the Regard. If any of the regarders do not attend, their default shall be recorded in the verderers' rolls, and in full court the verderers may have other free and honest men, dwelling within the forest, chosen as regarders to make up the number of twelve for the said regard. Witness, Aubrey, earl of Oxford, chief justice in eyre, the 10th May 1670.

m.2 [English]

1543 Chapters and Articles of the Regard containing particulars of such things as are to be done, viewed, inquired, and presented by the Regarders of the New Forest.

(1) First they are to perambulate the metes and bounds of the Forest and present the same at the Swainmote that according to custom it may be delivered at the next Justice Seat.

(2) They shall survey the old assart and purpresture lands previously granted by the late kings James and Charles I to several persons in fee farm by patent, and shall inquire and present the names of the persons who hold the said lands, and what tenements and closes they hold, and how many acres of pasture, meadow, and arable, the yearly rent, and details of rents paid over the previous six years so that his Majesty may be aware of his revenue and whether any rents have been unpaid or concealed.

(3) They are likewise to inquire and present all other old and new purprestures made in the Forest, especially since the last justice seat, to the prejudice of the Forest; and by whom they were made or are continued, the value of the land and in what places, whether within

or without the king's demesne lands, and if within the yearly value of the land and of the crop if under cultivation.

(4) What townships or parishes within or without the Forest, and what persons have used any common of pasture within the king's lands at any time since the 25th April 1660, and with what beasts and with what number, and who have overcharged the said common.

(5) And what erections, houses, cottages, mills, cowhouses, hog-sties, walls, pales, stiles, rails, hedges or ditches, have been made or erected since the said 25th April, or being made or erected previously have been continued since that date.

(6) And what incroachments or enclosures have been made of the king's land, and by whom and where, and the yearly value of such incroachments.

(7) They are likewise to view, inquire, and present all old and new assarts, and in what places they were made, the number of acres, by whom asserted, whether cultivated and the value of the crops. If the assart was in the king's demesne woods, the yearly value of the land asserted and the value of the timber and underwood destroyed and taken away.

(8) They are likewise to view all woods and coverts within the Forest, both within and without the demesne, and to inquire and present what wastes, destructions, or spoils have been made since the said 25th April, and by whom made and by what warrant, and the number of tons of timber and how many loads of dead or decaying trees or of underwoods, have been cut down and by whom, and who carried them away and with what carts or horses, and the value of the said timber and wood, and the damage that any such waste has brought to the king's inheritance.

(9) They shall likewise view, inquire, and present all common, public, and particular nuisances made or continued since the said 25th April, and by whom and by whose default they were made or continued either in not repairing bridges, obstruction of highways, digging of marlpits or other pits, or of turves, or of setting fire to the heath, fern, gorse, or bushes, and the damage occasioned to the king's inheritance or to the king's subjects living in or about or travelling through the said Forest.

(10) They shall likewise inquire whether the king's hedges, or the hedges or ditches upon the lands of any subject within the Forest, are kept according to the Assizes of the Forest. Also what new hedges or inclosures have been made since the said 25th April, and where and by whom, and how much the same is to the prejudice of the Forest.

(11) They are likewise to inquire and present the defaults, negligences, and insufficiencies of the foresters and woodwards and their underkeepers, deputies and servants, and whether they commit, consent to, or conceal any vert or venison offences.

(12) They shall likewise view, inquire, and present all aeries of hawks in the king's demesne woods, and who does take them away, and what persons shoot, kill, or destroy with guns, nets, or other engines or devices, any fowls of warren, or other fowls privileged there as pheasant, partridge, heathcock, heathhen or heathpult, duck and mallard, and such like wild fowls.

(13) They shall likewise view, inquire, and present all ports and creeks lying within the Forest, and what ships or boats may arrive there to carry away any charcoal, timber, or wood out of the Forest, and the names of such persons as do the same, and what quantities of wood, timber, and charcoal have been carried away since the said 25th April.

(14) They shall likewise inquire and present what persons keep alehouses without the license of the lord chief justice in eyre, or other house suspected to harbour hunters, and what persons do keep crossbows, or other bows and arrows, guns, nets, buckstalls, or other engines for the destruction of deer, or hounds, bloodhounds, greyhounds, and other unlawful dogs to hunt and destroy the king's game.

(15) They shall likewise view, inquire, and present whatsoever persons that keep such dogs as are allowed to be within a forest such as mastiffs and house dogs, but which have not been expeditated and lawed according to the Assizes of the Forest.

m.3

1544 The presentments of the Regarders made at the King's

Court called the Swainmote held at Lyndhurst on the 27th June in the 22nd year of Charles II [1670]

1545 The Perambulation of the Forest made by the Foresters and Regarders in the presence of William Powlett esquire, the Steward, and Sir Robert Dillington Bt., and Philip Leigh esquire, Verderers of the Forest.

The perambulation begins at Milton Bridge, and thence by the River Avon to the wooden aqueduct which crosses the Avon, where the ditch begins which formerly bounded the lands of the canons of Breamore and now divides Parsons Mead, Weremead, and other fields, and so to the beginning of Hale Hedge, and by the same hedge leaving Barnefarne on the right hand, straight by Helclose to Hellcorner, and from thence by the same hedge to Weldclose Corner; and thence by the public road leading to the Forest as far as Millersford where a post has been placed, and thence northwards towards a small valley called Woolmer Bottom as far as Woolmer post, and thence to a bush called Wynnyatesbush growing in the common road of Markeway. Thence going up the Markeway as far as Tittebrooke, thence to Churchstele, and thence to the horse road called Holloway, and from thence direct to Horewithey where stands a now decayed post marking the Forest from the lands of Richard Compton and Giles Ayres. Thence to Hedgeford *alias* Hedgefeild, and by the hedge to an old lane called Blindlane, and along the length of the same lane towards the north side of Bramshaw church, and by the broader way which extends to Plaitford as far as the bridge, thence in a direct line across enclosed fields to the ford of Burnford, thence by the small stream to Brookebridge, and by the same stream to Bircheford near to Birchenwood, and by the same stream to Shavewater, and going up the same stream to Wittensford, and from thence to Cadnambridge, and by the same stream to Markeford. Thence to Horemore, and from thence to where the common road makes a right-hand turn to a certain oak called Markeoake, and thence to the corner of a hedge which divides the Forest and a field called Cirkins, and thence along the same hedge and adjacent ditch direct to a boundary post erected in the middle of the common road, and thence to the stream called the Bourne which crosses the same road, and by the stream until it reaches the end of the ditch which separates the manor of Bisten Bartley from the liberty of the warden of Winchester.

1546 Thence by a hedge from Goomescorner to Pridhayes Corner, and thence across the green near Nashurst to Otterslane *alias* Coxlane, thence along Otterslane and direct, including Halfepenny Hurst within the Forest, by the road to the ford in the small valley opposite Buskets Corner, thence to a boundary oak almost decayed by age, thence to Pottersford and to the western side of Fletswood *alias* Fletchwood, thence by the road to a boundary post put in the place of a beech formerly called Diked Beech, and thence by the road which runs by the woods to a ditch called Langeley Ditch, and thence by the king's road as far as the place known as John of Farrindons Close, now waste but showing traces of old enclosures, and thence by a road winding from the left to a square piece of land called Riding Foresters Booth. Thence direct to the corner of Ipsleys Croft *alias* Iplers Corner where there is a boundary post, and thence by the road leading across the large green to the top of Applemore Hill, and thence by an old road, now almost disused, to the top of another hill called Horestone Hill, anciently Strayhup, and thence direct by an old bank to the corner of Butsashlane, and by that streeet past Butsash Farm as far as Carbuts Close, and by the western edge of that close to an ash growing midway along the hedge, and from thence across the middle of the close to the corner of the hedge on the east side of the close, and from thence by the said hedge to the spring where the great ditch begins, and by that ditch to Butsbridge, from thence following the river by Walemore to the sea, and by the sea to Mell Lane Lake, thence going up the river to Sheepwash Ford.

1547 Thence to the corner of Ferney Hill Ground, crossing a hollow valley to the great ditch which excludes Cadland Common, and from thence to the old spring called Marked Well adjoining the king's road leading from Fawley to Southampton, and thence by the same road to Cadland Pound in the direction of Fawley, thence to the end of a now closed lane called Forsters Lane, and from thence by the ditch which separates the lands of Shablands and Whitelands to the road which leads to Fawley common, and thence along the south-west hedge of the common to its far corner, and thence by the old bank and ditch to Preests Croft Corner, and by the same hedge and ditch to Newmans Wood, and by the corner of the same wood following the hedge and double ditch to Newlands Corner, and by the same hedge to Horlands. Thence by the dry ditch which encloses Langley Wood, now waste, to the west side of a square field enclosed by hedges, and continuing by the hedge of the field as far as Forster Lane, going the length of that road to Ironmell Hill, thence to Whitfeild Lane, and thence to Hoe Lane, thence direct to the marsh called Dark Water from the opposite corner of Leape Meadow, from thence by the end of the said marsh to the sea, and thence continuing by the sea to the boundary post of Sharpricks.

1548 From thence to the ditch called Deersditch, and from the north side of the said ditch to the king's road adjacent to Pylewell House and where a boundary post must be placed, and from the west side of the said house to the road called Shotslane, and thence by a ditch as far as Pratstile, and from there by the ditch of Lockland, where a boundary post is newly erected, as far as the lane called Postlane, and thence from the west side of the lane to the Claypitts, and thence to another pit called Gravell Pitts, and thence by the same ditch called Deersditch across the king's road which leads from Walhampton to Beaulieu, thence to a road called Towns Lane. Then along that road to the south side of a house belonging to the vicarage of Boldre, and thence by Furzy Hill Lane to Lymington Haven *alias* Bolder Water, and across the Haven to the road called Deerelane, and along that road across the king's road which leads from Lymington to Bolder Bridge, and so by the lane to Gally Hill. Thence by the road leading from Lymington to the ditch of Battramsley, and by the said ditch by the road adjoining the north-east corner of a wood called Tuckingmell Coppice, thence by the small lane next to the wood as far as the ditch of Battramsley at New Croft Corner *alias* Newlands, following the ditch as it crosses the west part of Scotts Common, thence to the bridge called Huckbridge *alias* Breggehuch, thence going up the river to the double ditch, turning to the north of East Streete Close to the king's road leading from Battramsley to Sway, and by the same double ditch to East Streete Corner *alias* Cole Corner, and thence by the same double ditch going by the north side of Retresetmere *alias* Fetmore Pond and near the gate of North Sway, and by the hedge from North Croft as far as Stamford, thence going up the stream at the end of the vill of Stamford, and thence across the little valley called Bulslades Bottom to the boundary post.

1549 From thence to Birdpond, thence direct to Kitlegutter, and by that gutter to Fox Hole on the west side of a great ditch called Whiteditch, thence going down the ditch to the stream, and by the stream to Boundway Ford *alias* Carpenters Ford, and thence by the boundway to the Bound Oak, thence to a place called Elcombegrave and marked by a boundary post, and thence by a road to the king's road leading from the Avon river to Milton. Thence from the boundary post west to Brownescroft *alias* Ferneycroft, and across that croft by the ditch next to the king's road, and from thence by the ditch which separates the common of Ossemsley from the Forest, formerly called Crowchford Croft *alias* Croxforcroft, and thence by way of Withenden, thence by the road to Marbrade Deep *alias* Burypeere. Thence by the hedge of East Close to the beginning of Rowditch, and from thence to Blackditch where there is a boundary post, and from thence by the king's road to Haythorne-slade, and by the same to Divells Den, and from thence ascending to Eversley Cross, and from thence to Whitelimeborough. From thence to the north-east end of Lackams Ditch, and along the same to the crossroad which leads from Shirley to Everley Cross, and from thence to Brickenedborough where there is another boundary post, and from thence to the boundary post of Lugdenborough *alias* Foxberry, and from thence direct to Alisborough *alias* Brownelease-borough.

1550 From thence direct by the crossroad leading from Burley Beacons across Greene Moor to Knavesborough, and from there going down to the hedge which separates the lands of Richard Compton and the lands of the Warden of the Forest for the time being, thence to Greene Shade of Buricombe *alias* Bircombe, from thence to Linford water, from thence by the hedge to Highwood Barrs *alias* Oviatts Barres where is a boundary post. From thence to Wickenstake near to the head of the marsh called Little Whitemore where there is another boundary post, and going down a little valley called Rodenbottome to Illbridge upon Docken Water, and thence to Markingborough upon Gorles Downe *alias* Gorleyhill, and so across Gorley Hill to the Pitts, and from thence to Charlesford *alias* Coliarsford, thence to Abbotts Well, and by the valley called Gawsley Bottome to Blesford *alias*
m.4
Bisford, thence going up the stream to a curtilage, anciently belonging to Robert Ernes now Bulkley, and through the middle of the said curtilage and adjoining garden as far as the king's road, now disused, which used to lead between Fritham and Fordingbridge, and from thence to the Butt, and thence to Gileswell, and thence to

the stream which descends to the Avon river, thence going up the same river to the bridge of Milton where the perambulation of the Forest begins.

[English]

1551 ‹1st Article›. We present that we have perambulated the metes and bounds of the said Forest, which are mentioned above.

‹2nd Article›. We present that we have examined the copies of the Assart Lands by Richard Gaynes and Thomas Grant, the receivers of the rents of these lands, and have ascertained the rents and present occupiers of those lands.

‹3rd Article›. We present Thomas Butler and Giles Tarver of the bailiwick of Battramsley for erecting and continuing since the Act of Indemnity each of them a cottage on the freehold land of Nicholas Lambert of Battramsley.

We also present Nicholas Durrant of the said bailiwick for erecting and continuing a cottage and enclosing twelve luggs of ground since the 25th April 1660.

As for other cottages and inclosures mentioned in this article, we refer to the several presentments of the Foresters or Keepers.

‹4th Article›. We present Nicholas Bayly and the widow Gregory, both of the liberty of Beaulieu, for keeping or depasturing two hundred sheep within the Forest at most times of the year, which they and many others of that liberty do under pretence of their charter.

1552 ‹5th Article›. We present a double rail of about 9ft. high which has very recently been made (by order) almost around the New Park, which said rail have consumed a ‹great› number of timber trees and wood. It is so ill set up that it is believed it cannot last more than seven years before it falls down, and if it should be repaired or set up again, it will prove a very great prejudice to the timber and wood of his majesty.

‹6th Article›. As to the matters of this article we refer to the several presentments of the Foresters or Keepers.

‹7th Article›. We present Henry Phillpott of the South bailiwick for the felling of a coppice containing about 8 acres at Norly Farm, and cutting down about 20 timber trees about four years ago, whether with license or without we do not know. As to the rest of the matters or things contained in this article we refer to the several presentments of the Foresters or Keepers.

1553 ‹8th Article›. We present that there has been both before and since the 25th April 1660 great destruction and spoil made in the king's woods and coverts, but who made the same we do not know, saving only that the greatest spoils have been made by the Foresters or Keepers by their unlawful browsing in the winter, more for their own benefit and advantage than for the preservation of his majesty's deer. As to what number of trees and their value, and by what warrant they have been cut down and carried away, or to whose use converted, we refer to the several presentments of the Foresters or Keepers.

We present that his majesty has various demesne woods within the Forest, namely:—
In the South bailiwick: Hollands Wood decaying, Ironshill Wood decaying, New Coppice very prosperous, Stubby Coppice and Stockley Wood prosperous, Litten Wood prosperous, Norley Wood very prosperous, Balmer (Barmoore) Wood, Little Salisbury, and Pignal decaying.
In East bailiwick: Denny Wood decaying, Woodfidley prosperous, New Coppice and Ashurst (Ashers) Wood very prosperous, and Kings Coppice likewise prosperous.
In the North bailiwick: East Linwood and Holmhill the greatest part decaying, Malwood partly decaying, Rockram and Little Eye Woods very prosperous.
In the Inn bailiwick: Old Lodge Wood and Costicles very prosperous, Gritnams Wood and Annsleys Bank very prosperous.
In Fritham bailiwick: Eyeworth Wood and Studley Wood very prosperous, Anses (Anstees) Wood and Bentley Coppices very prosperous, Bolderwood and Bratley Wood very prosperous, Ocknell Coppice prosperous, and Ocknell Wood decaying.
In Godshill bailiwick: Godshill Wood very prosperous, Island Thorns Wood very prosperous, and Crockhills Wood likewise prosperous.
In Linwood bailiwick: Linwood Wood decaying, Poleaks Wood,

Roe Wood, and South Wood prosperous.
In Battramsley bailiwick: Wootton Coppice, Broadley Coppice, and Chamberlains Corner very good young timber and prosperous, Mountaine Wood, Cocken Banke or Brow likewise prosperous young timber, Rhinefield Wood, Sandis Wood, Hurst Hill Wood, and Watracksley Wood decaying.
In Burley bailiwick: Ridley Coppice very prosperous with young timber, Anderwood, Sheerwoods, and Oakley prosperous. Cardinalls Hatt and Cockroad Wood prosperous. Shabden, High Croft, and another wood called the Trees, good, young, and prosperous.

1554 ‹9th Article›. We present Richard Hinning of the South bailiwick for carrying two loads of turves to Annanias Hall of the same bailiwick, who has erected a cottage upon the Forest since the Act of Indemnity, and has no right as we conceive.

We also present Edward Reeves of the same bailiwick for carrying a load of turves to John Badcock's house in Old Lymington, which house is newly erected and has no right as we conceive.

We also present the said Edward Reeves for carrying a load of turves to a newly erected house in Lymington belonging to Bartholomew Bulkley gentleman, which house has no right as we conceive.

As to the other things contained in this article, we refer to the several presentments of the Foresters or Keepers.

1555 ‹10th Article›. We present that various enclosures have been made previously in New Park, but we do not know by whom they were made, with the exception of sir George Carey Bt., the keeper of the New Park, whom we present has since the Act of Indemnity enclosed a field making two grounds containing about 30 acres, and which have since been sown with several crops of corn to the value of about £10 by John Carey gentleman who now lives in the said Park, all of which enclosures are now laid common in the Park. ‹Fine £10›.

We also present the said John Carey for digging a marlpit within the Forest for the improvement of the said ground enclosed by sir George Carey.

We present that about 22 acres of the Forest situated near Beaulieu were inclosed by the order of master Richard Cromwell during the late rebellious times, which made a decoy and is now continued by master John Jenings.

We present that about 100 acres of land have been recently inclosed at Home Hill by order of the Lords Commissioners of his Majesties Treasury, and are intended for the growth of wood.

As to the other matters contained in this article we refer to the several presentments of the Foresters or Keepers.

m.4d
1556 ‹11th Article›. As to this article, as we have come so recently into office, we have nothing further to present.

‹12th Article›. We know of no hawks within the woods of the Forest. As to the killing or destroying of pheasants, partridges, heathcocks, or other protected fowls, we refer to the Foresters or Keepers who can best supply such information.

‹13th Article›. We present that Beaulieu Haven and Bolder Water leading to Lymington are fit places for carrying timber, wood, and charcoal out of the Forest, but what persons or what quantity has been carried or imported from thence we do not know, but we believe that the greatest part of the timber, wood, and charcoal is imported from Redbridge which is 2 miles from the Forest.

1557 ‹14th Article›. We present Nicholas Masters and Richard Stote, both of the bailiwick of Battramsley, for keeping alehouses.

We present Martin Sanders of the South bailiwick and Sarah Wilcox widow of the Inn bailiwick for keeping alehouses.

The other alehouses are presented by the Foresters or Keepers.

We know of none who keep crossbows or guns except for the Foresters or Keepers, who pretend to keep them in his Majesties service.

‹15th and last Article›. We present John Bushell and John Taplin, Foresters or Keepers of the bailiwick of Battramsley, for each keeping a mastiff dog not expeditated.

We also present Edward Bright senior, one of the Foresters of the East bailiwick, for keeping a mastiff dog not expeditated.

We also present Thomas Carter, one of the Foresters of the South bailiwick, for keeping a mastiff dog not expeditated.

1558 [Signatures]
William Batten, William Burrard, Richard King, Richard Warne, Thomas Lovell, John Drew, Richard Edwards, Henry Lovell, James Barrow, Abraham Olding, William Moon, Christopher Garrett.

C.99/54

1559 Grant to George Merreil and Thomas Ely made 22nd December 1608

Lands and properties granted to George Merreil and Thomas Ely of London in consideration of the sum of £1015 19s, and subsequent to an inquest held at Romsey on the 20th July 1608 before sir Edward Grevill and Othone Nicholson esquire. Dated at Westminster the 22nd December 1608.

Five messuages, fourteen cottages, and eighty three closes, containing 332ac. 2r. 28p. of arable, meadow, pasture, gorse, moor, and woodland, situated in various villages and in the possession of Anthony Battyn gentleman and his tenants. These comprise four messuages, eleven cottages, and seventy one closes, containing 288ac. 2r. 8p. in Burley in the possession of Anthony Batten, Thomas Robins, Robert Bishop, Peter Warne, Henry Carter, Peter Hinton, John Ayles, Thomas Lacy, Richard Ade, Thomas Phelips, John Burgis, William Saunders, Henry Fisher, Thomas Coffyn, John Etheridge, Robert Cooke, Richard Stephens, William Rogers, Thomas Randall, Richard Ford, William Goldwyer, John Beddlecombe, and Simon Younge. Paying annually 24s. Also a messuage, two cottages, and nine closes, called by the names of Cox Closes, Hickes, South Close, Palmers, and Stephens, containing 26 acres of meadow, pasture, and arable land in Fritham in the possession of Anthony Batten and his tenants, namely John Emlyn, Thomas Tarver, John Musklewhite, and John Hobbes. Paying annually 6s. 8d. Also a cottage and three closes, one called Dorehayes, another Lukes Meade, and the third one adjoining the cottage, containing 8ac. 26p. of arable, meadow, and pasture in Lyndhurst and in the possession of John Elcombe, Margaret Brice, and Thomas Smith as tenants of Anthony Batten. Paying annually 2s. 6d. Which said five messuages, fourteen cottages, and 322ac. 2r. 28p. are after payment of the said annual rent of 33s. 2d. and after all other deductions of a net annual value of £40 15s.

1560 A messuage, twelve cottages, a water mill and watercourse, with gardens and fifty closes containing 284ac. 2r. 30p. of arable, meadow, pasture, gorse, and woodland in Burley and other places. These comprise a messuage, seven cottages with gardens, and thirty one closes containing 249ac. 1r. 20p. in Burley in the possession of William Battyn and his tenants, namely John West, the widow Awner, Peter Hinton, Robert Cooke, Martin Sanders, Robert Wattes, Henry Olliver *alias* Scowrser, Robert Warne, Henry Croker, John Burges, Richard Pytt, Hugh Deane or Thomas Coffyn, Oliver Etheridge, Thomas Randall, Henry Fisher, Ann Lyne, Henry Rogers, and Henry Lyne. Paying annually 17s. 4d. Also five cottages, the water mill, and sixteen closes of arable, meadow, pasture, and gorse, of which six are called Buttleshorne Meadows and the other ten are called Buttleshorne *alias* Bisthorne Closes, together containing 135ac. 1r. 6p., held by various tenants of William Battyn. Paying annually 19s. 8d. Which said messuage, twelve cottages, water mill, and fifty closes, after payment of the annual rent of 37s. and all other deductions, have a net annual value of £35 10s.

1561 A cottage and five closes of pasture, of which one is called Whitehead Close, another Turke Crofte, another Longe Close, and the other two Ferleys Groundes, together containing 26ac. 39p. in Burley and other places and in the possession of John Wagge. Which after payment of the annual rent of 3s. 10d. and all other deductions, has a net annual value of £5.

1562 A cottage and 46 acres of meadow, pasture, arable, and woodland, in various parcels in Burley, called by the names of Ashengrove, Estfeild, Brome Close, the Warde, Burchins Grove, and the More, and in the possession of William Rogers. Which after payment of the annual rent of 4s. and all other deductions, has a net annual value of £10.

1563 13ac. 2r. 37p. of pasture and gorse in three closes, one of which is divided into two, in Burley and other places, and in the possession of William Biddlecombe senior. Which after payment of the annual rent of 8d. and all other deductions, has a net annual value of 55s.

1564 A cottage and 38ac. 2r. 13p. of arable, pasture, and woodland, in seven closes in Burley and other places, in the possession of John Welsted, Christopher Garrett, John Kellaway, and Roger Ales. Which after payment of 5s. 4d. annual rent and all other deductions, has a net annual value of £8.

1565 A messuage and two cottages, and 42ac. 2r. 18p. of meadow, pasture, arable, and woodland, in various places in Bramshaw. These comprise a messuage, 18ac. 1r. 22p. of arable, meadow, pasture, and woodland in eight closes called Berchaies, Magetes Garden, and Olding, and 9ac. 3r. 5p. of pasture in three closes in the possession of John Strugnell for which is paid 4s. 6d. annually. Also a cottage, 12ac. 31p. of pasture and woodland in four closes, one of which is called Wimbleton and the other three Stanchers, in the possession of John Bannister for which is paid 8d. annually. Also a cottage, 2ac. 1r. 7p. of pasture called Pynhornes, in the possession of Richard Pinhorne for which is paid 4d. annually. Which said messuage, two cottages, and 42ac. 2r. 25p., after payment of the total annual rent of 5s. 6d. and all other deductions, have a net annual value of £9.

1566 A messuage and 53ac. 3r. of meadow, pasture, and arable, inclosed in separate parcels in the forest and in the possession of Michael Caule. These comprise 19ac. 22p. in three closes called Pincherdons. A messuage, 16ac. 26p. in four closes belonging to the messuage. 11ac. 1r. 22p. in three closes called Southcloses. 6ac. 3r. 4p. in a close called Buddle. Which messuage, 53ac. 3r., after payment of the total annual rent of 6s. 2d. and half a pound of pepper and all other deductions, have a net annual value of £8 15s.

1567 A cottage and 33½ac. of pasture, arable land, and wood, in eight closes, of which one called Brandes contains 6ac. 1r. in Fritham and is in the possession of Andrew Hobbes. Which after payment of 2s. 11d. annual rent and all other deductions, have a net annual value of £7.

1568 Five cottages and 50ac. 3r. 17p.[1] of meadow, pasture, and arable land in various parcels of Fritham. This comprises 7ac. 12p. of pasture in three closes called Hone. A cottage and 5ac. 2r. 20p. of meadow in two closes, and a piece of pasture called the Grove. A cottage, 5ac. 3r. 13p. of meadow, pasture, and arable land, in three closes called Coxe Closes and Coxe Meade, in the possession of John Barry and paying 2s. 11d. annually. A cottage, 7ac. 3r. 30p. of meadow in three closes in the possession of Roger Reade paying 1s. 9½d. annually. Two cottages, 20ac. 29p. of meadow and pasture in five closes called Brandes Home Meade, Stoney Hayes, and Potters, in the possession of John Reade, paying 1½d. and half a pound of pepper annually. 4ac. 2r. 33p. of pasture called Hone in the possession of Henry Scovell, paying 6d. annually. 4ac. 2r. of pasture similarly called Hone, in the possession of Francis Spencer, paying 6d. annually. Which five cottages, 55ac. 3r. 17p., after paying a total annual rent of 5s. 10d. and half a pound of pepper and all other deductions, have a net annual value of £7.

[1] *Recte* 55ac. 3r. 17p.

1569 A messuage and 63 acres of pasture, arable, and woodland in Bartley in the possession of sir George Wrothesley. This comprises a messuage, 26ac. 3r. 12p. of arable land, pasture, and wood, in four closes in the possession of William Webster. 9ac. 3r. 3p. of pasture and arable land in three closes near Havers Lane. 26ac. 1r. 36p. of pasture and woodland in three closes called Havers and Havershill. Which messuage and 63 acres after paying 4s. 2d. annually and all other deductions, have a net annual value of £8 15s.

1570 Two messuages, three cottages, and five stables, gardens, and orchards, and 58ac. 3r. 27p. of meadow and pasture in Lyndhurst in the possession of William Browne gentleman. These comprise a messuage and 6 acres in three closes called the Parrock, Barne Close, and Cauntes [?Canutes] Meade. 8ac. 1r. 32p. of pasture and arable land in three closes called Newlandes. 3ac. 7p. of meadow called Grove Meade. 2ac. 3r. 19p. of pasture called Buttes Close *alias* Edwardes. 8ac. 3r. 25p. of pasture called Pinhornes. 5ac. 23p. of meadow in two closes called Orcharde Close *alias* Gardiners and Strides Meade. 2ac. 1r. 34p. of pasture called Willhayes. A cottage, 3r. 29p. of pasture, in the possession of Philip Stride called Little Vearinges. 1ac. 12p. of pasture called Foordes Acre. A messuage, 11ac. 35p. of pasture and meadow called Great Veringes. A cottage, 8ac. 3r. 11p. of pasture and meadow in the possession of Bartholomew Beach. A cottage with garden and orchard in the possession of Philip Waterman. A parcel of land called Hemp Plott. Which two messuages, three cottages, and 58ac. 3r. 27p. of land after paying 23s. 10d. annually and all other deductions, have a net annual value of £9.

1571 30ac. 34p. of pasture and arable land in Burley in the possession of Thomas Lyne or his assignees, of which 15ac. 2r. 30p. lies in five closes jointly called Androwes in the possession of Felicity Hunt, also 11ac. 1r. 20p. of pasture called Whitehall and also in the possession of Felicity Hunt, also 3ac. 24p. of pasture called Ferley in the possession of John Ayles. Which 30ac. 34p. of land, after paying 1s. 5d. annually and all other deductions, has a net annual value of £6 5s.

1572 A cottage and 46 acres of pasture in four closes called Wootton Closes in Wootton in the possession of Robert Westbury. Which after payment of 3s. 9d. annually and all other deductions has a net annual value of £6 5s.

1573 28 acres of pasture and gorse in various parcels in Burley in the possession of Christopher Lyne or his assignees. Of which 6ac. 3r. 7p. of pasture lies near the land of Richard Ade and abuts upon the forest, also 19ac. 3r. 11p. of pasture between two lanes in the possession of Robert Odbere, also 1ac. 1r. 25p. of gorse lying between the land of William Goldwyer and of William Beddlecombe. Which 28 acres, after payment of 2s. 8d. annually and all other deductions, has a net annual value of £4.

1574 A messuage and three cottages and 85 acres of meadow, pasture, and arable land in various places in the forest and in the possession of various persons. Of which 43ac. 3r. 19p. of pasture and arable land lies in Lyndhurst in five closes, of which four are called Norlandes and the other Lyfeild, and are in the possession of John Elcombe senior and for which is paid 4d. annually. Also a messuage, three cottages, 28ac. 2r. of meadow, pasture, and arable land in Lyndhurst in the possession of John Elcombe junior, a messuage, 5ac. 1r. 24p. of meadow and pasture near Sowthe Grene, a cottage, 1ac. 11p. of meadow called Wolles, and 7ac. 2r. 18p. of pasture and arable land in two closes called Parke Closes, with the residue in various places in Lyndhurst, for which are paid 11s. 11½d. annually. Also 2ac. 3r. of pasture and arable land in Lyndhurst called Peakes in the possession of Richard Peake and paying 4½d. annually. Also 9ac. 3r. 34p. of meadow and pasture in Fritham in the possession of Vincent Mist, of which 2ac. 25p. of pasture is called Widnalls, 4ac. 2r. 39p. is called South Close, the residue comprising a separate close of meadow, for which are paid 3s. 4d. annually. Which messuage, three cottages, and 85 acres, after payment of 16s. 10d. and all other deductions, have a net annual value of £16 17s. 6d.

1575 A cottage with garden and orchard containing 1 acre called Little Howe, situated in Bartley and in the possession of John Andrews, which after payment of 1½d. annually and all other deductions, has a net annual value of 5s.

1576 6ac. 2r. 18p. of pasture in Linwood in the possession of John Aynell, which after payment of 6d. annually and all other deductions, has a net annual value of £1.

1577 Two cottages, 33ac. 1r. 12p. of pasture, arable, and woodland in various places in the forest and in the possession of various men. It comprises a cottage, 17ac. 2r. 25p. of woodland in Minstead called Harmans Grove lying near Clayehill in the possession of William Hobbes and paying 5s. annually. Also 2ac. 2r. of pasture called Glashay in Lyndhurst in the possession of William Bunckley paying 2s. 6d. annually. Also a cottage and garden, 13ac. 27p. of pasture and woodland in Hardley in the possession of Thomas Brooke, of which a parcel is called by the names of Howe, Baldhill, Blackhill, Little Crofte, Bredleys, Cobbes, Park Litten, and Three Stitches, the residue lying in separate closes, paying 4s. 8d. annually. Which two cottages and 33ac. 1r. 12p., after the payment of 12s. 2d. annually and all other deductions, have a net annual value of £4 3s. 4d.

1578 7ac. 2r. of meadow called Tanners More lying between Brodestone Coppice and Winchbury Meade in the bailiwick of Godshill in the possession of John Good, which after payment of 1d. annually and all other deductions, has a net annual value of £1 5s.

1579 123ac. 2r. 30p. of meadow, pasture, and arable land called Blackmansleys in Brookley in the bailiwick of Battramsley in the possession of Thomas Sowthe gentleman, which after payment of 3s. 9d. annually and all other deductions, has a net annual value of £6 13s. 4d.

1580 A messuage, two orchards, and four closes of arable, meadow, and pasture, called Northhaye, the Grove, Bynney, and the Parrock, together containing 23 acres in Bartley Regis in the possession of Thomas White, which after payment of 1s. 10½d. and all other deductions, have a net annual value of £3 6s. 8d.

1581 A messuage and five closes of meadow, pasture, arable, and woodland, containing 12ac. 17p. in Minstead in the possession of Richard Stephens, which after payment of 6d. annually and all other deductions, has a net annual value of £2 10s.

1582 Two closes of woodland and pasture containing 16 acres in Wootton in the possession of Richard Chickford, which after payment of 9d. annually and all other deductions, have a net annual value of £4.

1583 A messuage, 47ac. 2r. of meadow, pasture, and arable land, in various places in Battramsley in the possession of Hugh Darvall, which after payment of 10s. annually and all other deductions, have a net annual value of £6 5s.

1584 A messuage and 4ac. 3r. of meadow and pasture called Gawens Land lying in Brook in the parish of Bramshaw, in the possession of Gabriel Greene gentleman, which after payment of 6d. annually and all other deductions, has a net annual value of £1.

1585 A cottage and 8ac. 3r. 24p. of pasture, arable land, and gorse in various parcels in Buttsash and Hardley in the possession of Francis Hopkins, which comprise a close called Croft, a cottage and two closes called Frost Croft, a close called Stubby Croft, a close called Dereditch, and two parcels of arable land in the meadows called the Estfeildes, and which after payment of 3d. annually and all other deductions, have a net annual value of £1 5s.

1586 Two cottages, a garden, and 21ac. 1r. 20p. of meadow, pasture, and arable land in various parcels in Hardley and in the possession of Richard Wadmore, which after payment of 3s. 8d. annually and all other deductions, have a net annual value of £3 6s. 8d.

1587 Two cottages and 21ac. 2r. 20p. of meadow, pasture, and arable land in various parcels in Hardley in the possession of John Yates, which after payment of 2s. 8d. annually and all other deductions have a net annual value of £3 6s. 8d.

1588 A cottage and 11ac. 31p. of pasture and arable land in various places in Hardley in the possession of John Harris, which after payment of 1s. 6d. annually and all other deductions, has a net annual value of 10s.

1589 A cottage and 16ac. 3r. of pasture, arable, and woodland in various parcels in Buttsash and Hardley and in the possession of various men. It comprises 2 acres in Northfeild called Strawbery Acre in the possession of John Osmond for a rent of 1s., also 7ac. 1r. of pasture, arable, and woodland in various parcels in Hardley in the possession of John Hall for a rent of 1s. 6d. Also a cottage, 6ac. 1r. of pasture and arable land in five separate parcels in Hardley in the possession of Edmund Brice for a rent of 2s. 11d. Also 1ac. 2r. of heath in Hardley called Horestone in the possession of John Withers for a rent of 1d. Which cottage and 16ac. 3r. after payment of 5s. 6d. annually and all other deductions have a net annual value of £2 5s. 6d.

1590 A messuage, cottage, and 30ac. 2r. of meadow, pasture, arable, and woodland in various parcels in Hardley and Buttsash in the possession of various men. Of which 11ac. of pasture, arable, and woodland in various places in Hardley is in the possession of Stephen Bound for a rent of 3s. 8d. 29ac. 2r. are in sixteen separate parcels in Hardley and Buttsash in the possession of Thomas Lyne of Ringwood for a rent of 5s. 11d. Which messuage, cottage, and 30½ acres after payment of the said 3s. 8d. and 5s. 11d. annually have a net annual value of £5 10s.

1591 A cottage and 40ac. 28p. of pasture, meadow, arable, and woodland in fifteen parcels in Hardley in the possession of John Hopkins, which after payment of 7s. 8d. annually and all other deductions has a net annual value of £5.

1592 23ac. 2r. 17p. of pasture in various parcels in Langley and the East bailiwick, in the possession of various men. Of which 9ac. 3r. 35p. of pasture are in two closes called Preistes Crofte in the possession of William Rixon for a rent of 1s. Also 12ac. 1r. 29p. of pasture also called Preistes Croft in the possession of William Yelman for a rent of 1s. 8d. Also 1ac. 33p. of pasture called Est Gore Acre in the possession of John Gretham for a rent of 1d. Which 23ac. 2r. 17p. after payment of the said rents of 1s., 1s. 8d., and 1d. annually and all other deductions, have a net annual value of £2 13s.

1593 A messuage, five cottages, and 61 acres of pasture, gorse, heath, and woodland in various parcels in Buttsash in the possession of Thomas Richardes. It comprises a parcel called by the various names of Buttesashe Furzie Hoe, Buttockes Greene Croft, Frostes Croft, Sandy Hoe, and Leten Acres, with the residue in various parcels, which together after a payment of 2s. annually and all other deductions, have a net annual value of £6 5s.

1594 A cottage and half a messuage and 5ac. 3r. 29p. of meadow, pasture, and arable land in various places and in the possession of various men. It comprises a close of pasture containing 1ac. 27p. in Buttsash called Kinges Land in the possession of Edward Harvy for a rent of 1d. Also a close of 1ac. 2r. of arable land in Buttsash called Longlandes in the possession of Philip Yateman for a rent of 1d. Also half a messuage, 3ac. 2r. 21p. of meadow and arable land in Brookley and Ober in the possession of John Purdue for a rent of 2d. Which messuage, half messuage, and 5ac. 3r. 29p. after payment of the said annual rents and all other deductions have a net annual value of 16s. 2d.

1595 A messuage, a cottage, and 26ac. 1r. 32p. of meadow, pasture, gorse, and woodland in various parcels in possession of various men. It comprises a messuage, cottage, and 24 acres of gorse and woodland in various places in Buttsash and Hardley, of which a parcel is called by the names of Fordes, Pipes, Seacroft, Seavers Feild, and Anslade, and the residue in various parcels, in the possession of Augustus Brett for a rent of 1s. 8d. Also a parcel of 2r. of woodland abutting Andrewes Meade, and a close of pasture of 1ac. 3r. called Frost Close in the possession of Alexander Wadmore for a rent of 2d. Which messuage, cottage, and 26ac. 1r. 32p. after payment of the separate rents of 1s. 8d. and 2d. and all other deductions, have a net annual value of £3 12s. 11d.

1596 A messuage, cottage, and 45ac. 3r. 7p. of pasture, arable land, gorse, and woodland in various parcels in Hardley in the possession of various men. It consists of a messuage, cottage, and 44ac. 3r. 7p. of pasture, arable, woodland, and gorse in the possession of Nicholas Withers for a rent of 6s. 8d. Also a parcel of 1 acre called Cox Lane in the possession of Stephen Warwick for a rent of 2d. Which messuage, cottage, and 45ac. 3r. 7p. after payment of the rents of 6s. 8d. and 2d. and all other deductions, have a net annual value of £5 1s. 3d.

C.99/50

1597 Grant to Thomas Ely and George Merreill made 27th May 1609

Land and properties granted to Thomas Ely and George Merreill of London in consideration of the sum of £766. Dated at Westminster the 27th May 1609.

Two messuages and two cottages, with gardens and orchards, and 71 acres in Exbury and Lepe. This comprises a messuage with garden, orchard, and 30 acres of meadow, pasture, arable, and woodland in the possession of William Cowche paying 10s. 2½d. annually. Also a messuage with garden, orchard, and 16 acres of meadow, pasture, and heath called Henslowes Tenement, recently in the possession of William Henslowe and now in the possession of William Cowche, paying 8s. 6d. annually. Also a cottage with garden, orchard, and 9 acres of meadow, pasture, and woodland, in the possession of Ralph Webbe as tenant of William Cowche, paying 7¾d. annually. Also a cottage with garden, orchard, and 10 acres of meadow, pasture, arable, and woodland in the possession of Richard Stephens or John Hunnyman, paying 7¾d. annually. Also 6 acres of meadow, pasture, and arable land called Grenes in the possession of Richard Stephens or Thomas Burton, paying 2s. 8d. annually. Which two messuages, two cottages, with gardens, orchards, and 71 acres, after payment of total rents of £1 2s. 8d. and all other deductions, have a net annual value of £10.

1598 A cottage, barn, and 9ac. 1r. of meadow, pasture, arable, and woodland in Lepe in the possession of Richard Moone. This comprises a cottage, barn, garden, and courtyard containing 1ac. 2r. situated between Lepe and the sea. Also 3ac. 2r. called Downe Crofte. Also 2 acres called Suthwick. Also 3r. in a close called the East Feild between the land of Richard Whordon and the Lordes Land. Also 2r. in Haxland between the lands of Thomas Orchard and West Fashron. Also 1 acre of meadow between the lands of John Cole and John Hailes. Which cottage, barn, and 9ac. 1r. after payment of an annual rent of 3s. 6d. and all other deductions, have a net annual value of £1 5s.

1599 A cottage with garden containing 1r. in Leape in the possession of John Moone, paying 6d. annually, and with a net annual value of 5s.

1600 Three cottages and 8 acres of meadow, pasture, and arable land in London Minstead in the possession of John Hillars. It comprises a cottage, garden, orchard, and 4½ acres in the possession of Thomas Hobbes paying 11½d. annually. Also a cottage with garden and 1 acre in the possession of Richard Hobbes paying 6d. annually. Also a cottage with garden and 2½ acres in the possession of John Gates paying 4d. annually. Which three cottages and 8 acres after payment of total annual rents of 1s. 9½d. and all other deductions, have a net annual value of £1 5s.

1601 A cottage with barn, stable, and 9½ acres of pasture, arable, and woodland in Lepe in the possession of Robert Cole. It comprises the cottage, barn, and stable lying between the lands of John Cole and Hugh Cole. Also 1¾ acres between the land of John Cole and the king's road. Also 2 acres in a close called Northover. Also 5½ acres in a close called Long Meade. Paying an annual rent of 2s. for the 9½ acres, with a net annual value of £1 5s.

1602 A cottage, a barn, and 20 acres of pasture, arable, and woodland in Lepe in the possession of John Humber. It comprises the cottage, barn, and courtyard containing 4½ acres lying between the Lordes Landes and the king's road. Also 2 acres in a close called Tabers. Also 2¾ acres between the lands of John Newberry and Hugh Cole. Also 1¼ acre adjoining the land of John Cole. Also 2 acres between the land of George Paulett and the Lordes Land. Also 1½ acres between the Lordes Land and the little lane. Also 1 acre in Haxland Feild between the Lordes Land and the lands of Alice Moone and William Ricardes. Also ¾ acre between the lands of Thomas Barton and Mary Rakyns. Also ½ acre between the lands of John Rookeley and Reginald Sanders. Also ½ acre in Eastfeild between the lands of Thomas Orchard and Richard Whordon. Also ¼ acre between the lands of Alice Moone and William Ingram. Which 20 acres after payment of an annual rent of 1s. 4½d. have a net annual value of £3.

1603 A cottage and barn, 20¾ acres of meadow, pasture, and arable land in Lepe in the possession of John Newbery. It comprises a cottage and barn and 3 acres between the king's road and the

Lordes Lande and the land of George Tailor. Also 6 acres called Appledore Crofte. Also 4 acres being a moiety of the meadow called Wetmeade. Also 1 acre between the lands of John Cole and Thomas Orchard. Also 2 acres called Compe. Also ¾ acre in Haxland Feild between the Lordes Land and the land of Richard Stephens, with the residue being a moiety of a close called Heathie Downe and containing 4 acres. Which 20¾ acres after the payment of 2s. 6½d. annually have a net annual value of £2.

1604 A cottage and half acre in Lepe in the possession of Alice Cole widow paying 2d. annually, with a net annual value of 3s. 4d.

1605 A cottage with 1¼ acres in Lepe in the possession of Thomas Cole, comprising a cottage and orchard containing ¼ acre lying between the land of Richard Whordon and the king's road. Also ¾ acre of meadow between the lands of William Cole and William Ingram, and the residue ¼ acre in Haxland Feild between the lands of William Cole and John Rookeley. Which after payment of 1s. annually has a net annual value of 3s. 4d.

1606 A cottage and 1ac. 20p. of meadow and arable land in Lepe in the possession of William Cole. The 20p. is garden to the cottage, ¾ acre is meadow between the land of Thomas Cole and the king's road, and the remaining ¼ acre is in Haxland Feilde between the lands of Thomas Cole and William Ingram. Which after payment of 1s. annually have a net annual value of 6s. 8d.

1607 Two cottages, two barns and stables, and 37 acres of meadow, pasture, and arable land in Lepe in the possession of John Hailes. A cottage, barn, stable, garden, orchard, and courtyard containing ½ acre lie between the king's road and the land of Richard Stephens. The other barn and ¼ acre of land are between the land of George Tailor and the king's road. The other cottage and ½ acre of land are situated between the land of John Cole and the little lane. Also 5 acres called Seaclose, 2 acres of marsh between the Lordes Land and the land of Robert and John Cole, ¾ acre in Northover between the lands of John and Robert Cole, ¼ acre in Corney Downe between the land of John Cole and the land in the possession of Matthew Miles, 2 acres called Morecrofte, 2½ acres called Pynnockes, ½ acre in East Feild between the lands of Richard Whordon and John Cole, 2 acres called Stanckford, 1 acre of meadow joining the Lordes Land, 5 acres called Parsons Crofte, 7 acres called Prattes Croft *alias* Pier Trees, ½ acre called Wormes near the land of Alice Moone, 2 acres called Pere Tree Perockes, and 6 acres which are a moiety of the meadow called the Great Wett Meadowe. Which after a payment of 4s. 10d. have a net annual value of £5.

1608 A cottage and 1 acre of land in Lepe in the possession of Nicholas West or Alice West. The cottage and half an acre are between the king's road and the land of Richard Moone, and the other half acre in Worleche, which after payment of 6d. annually have a net annual value of 5s.

1609 20½ acres of meadow, pasture, arable, and woodland in Exbury in the possession of Thomas Haward. Of which 5 acres are called Avons, another 3 acres are called Aldergrove, another 3 acres are called Staffordes, 4 acres are called James Crofte, 3 acres are called Dowle, 2 acres are in Exbury Feild, ¾ acre are called Brownes Perock, 1 acre in Burnt Oakes near the land of Richard Whordon, and the remaining ¾ acre lies between the lands of Richard Stephens, West Fashron, and the Lordes Lande. Which after payment of 7s. 10½d. and one pound of pepper annually have a net annual value of £3.

1610 A messuage, barn, stable, and 41ac. 3r. 20p. of meadow, pasture, arable, and woodland in Lepe in the possession of John Cole. Whereof the messuage, barn, stable, and garden contain ½ acre situated between the king's road and the land of Richard Moone. Another 1 acre, formerly harbour, between the land of George Pawlett and the lane called Worliche Lane. Another 3 acres called Hoskins Close. Another ¾ acre called Hoskins Meade, 2 acres between the lands of Robert Coles and John Hailes, 1 acre of meadow lying on the west side of the road called the Cawsey Waye, and 1 acre of meadow on the east side of the said road. Another 1 acre is in Northover between the lands of John Hailes on the west and east sides, ¼ acre between the lands of John Hailes and the Cawseway, another 1½ acre in the Eastfeild between the lands of John Hailes and Richard Whordon, another ½ acre between the land of John Hailes and the Lordes Land, another 1r. 20p. in Haxland Feild between the Lordes Land and the land of William Ingram, another 2½ acres are closes lying near the Lordes Land, 1 acre in Bunney, ½ acre in Drindes [?Druides] Crofte, 2 acres in Stanckford, 1 acre between the lands of master Trumblefeild and Richard Whordon, ¾ acre called Newclose Meade, 5 acres called Newclose Coppice, 3 acres called Shorte Landes, 5½ acres called Corney Downe, 4 acres called Shortbromes, 3 acres called Glascroft, 5 acres called Looselades, 1 acre of marsh between Darkwaters and the lands of George Tailor and Richard Whordon, another ½ acre between the lands of Hugh Cole and Richard Stephens, another 4 acres are a parcel of land called Pinnockes and an adjoining coppice, ½ acre among the lands of George Taylor, another ½ acre among the lands of John Humber, the remainder being ½ acre lying between the lands of John Newbery and Thomas Orchard. Which 41ac. 3r. 20p. after payment of 6s. 2½d. annually have a net annual value of £6 5s.

1611 One acre of meadow in Lepe in the possession of William Hailes paying 1d. annually and with a net annual value of 3s. 4d.

1612 A cottage with garden, orchard, and small meadow in Lepe and containing 1 acre. Also 3½ acres of pasture, arable, and woodland called Bryan Saltern, and ½ acre adjoining a parcel of land called Sealand in Exbury, in the possession of Samuel Coleman or William Coleman, paying 10d. annually and having a net annual value of 16s. 8d.

1613 A messuage and 17½ acres of meadow, pasture, arable, and woodland in Exbury in the possession of Thomas Barton. Whereof the messuage and garden, orchard, and courtyard, contain ¾ acre, and another parcel contains 10p. between the Lordes Land and the king's road. Another 3 acres are called Worm Crofte, another 7 acres are called Inchmary, 3 acres called Wyrre, 1 acre in Exbury Field between the lands of Richard Stephens and Richard Whordon, 1 acre in Exbury Field between the lands of John Symondes and West Fashion, ¾ acre between the lands of West Fashion and Richard Stephens, and 1 acre between the land of William Ricards and the Lordes Land. Which pays 4s. 3½d. annually and has a net annual value of £2 10s.

1614 A messuage, cottage, and 36½ acres of meadow, pasture, arable, and woodland, in Exbury in the possession of William Ricarde. Whereof the messuage, garden, orchard, and courtyard contain 3 acres lying between the land called the Lordes Landes and the king's road. Another 1 acre of meadow lies between the land of Thomas Barton and the king's road, 5½ acres called Vowles Crofte, 2½ acres called Bonney, 1 acre of woodland in Bonney among the land in the possession of Matthew Miles, 3 acres called Seaford, 1 acre between the lands of John Hailes and Hugh Cole, 1¼ acre in Bonney between the land of West Fashion and the Lordes Landes, 1 acre in Haxland Feild between the land of Mary Rawkins and the Lordes Landes, 1 acre in Haxland between the land of William Kinge and the Lordes Lande, another 1½ acre among the Lordes Land, another 1½ acre in the same place between the land of West Fashion and the Lordes Land, another ¼ acre in the same place between the lands of John Symondes and Mary Rawkins, another ½ acre in the same place between the land of Richard Stephens and the Lordes Land, another 2 acres called Bromey Close, another 6½ acres called Shord, another 1 acre which is the courtyard of the said cottage at Shord, 3½ acres called Inchmery, and the remaining 1 acre in Inchmary between the lands of Richard Stephens and Hugh Cole. Which 36½ acres after payment of 8s. 8½d. annually has a net annual value of £2 10s.

1615 A cottage, garden, and 2½ acres of arable land in Exbury in the possession of John Palmer, paying 9d. annually and having a net annual value of 6s. 8d.

1616 A messuage, cottage, barn, and 28½ acres of meadow, pasture, arable land, moor, and woodland, in Hardley in the possession of William Osey. Of which the messuage, cottage, barn, garden, orchard, and courtyard together contain 2 acres lying between the land of Thomas Stronge and the high road leading through the village of Hardley. Another 1 acre is in the meadow called the Southfeild, another 5 acres called Flowders, 2 acres called Cobmore, 1 acre called Cropenpole, 2 acres called Lammas, 2 acres called Ashelden Crofte, 1 acre called Newcrofte, ½ acre in Little Howe, 1 acre abutting the east side of Coblane, 1 acre of coppice on the north side of Lytton Lane, 4 acres of coppice called Longhow, 2 acres called Redcrofte, another ½ acre are coppice lying at Lammas, also 5 acres of arable and woodland in various parcels in the Eastfeild. Which 28½ acres after payment of 9s. annually have a net annual value of £3.

1617 A messuage, cottage and 25¾ acres of meadow, pasture, arable, and woodland in Lepe in the possession of Edmund Barnes and Alice his wife. Of which the messuage and 8 acres comprising the garden, orchard, and courtyard, are situated between the Lordes Land on the east and the king's road on the west, 1 acre is called Little Wolley, 2 acres at Morestiles, 5 acres are meadow and coppice called Bakers Mead, 3 acres are called Campe, ½ acre is in Worlech. The cottage with orchard, garden, and courtyard adjoining, containing 2 acres, is situated between the land of John Palmer on the west and the Lordes Land on the east. Another 1 acre is coppice between the lands of West Fashion and John Rookeley, 1 acre is in Pinnockes, and another 2 acres are in Haxland Feild. Which 25¾ acres after payment of 6s. 10½d. annually have a net annual value of £3.

1618 A messuage, cottage, and 29½ acres of meadow, pasture, arable, and woodland, in Exbury in the possession of John Symondes. Of which 1½ acres are the garden, orchard, and courtyard of the messuage, lying between the lands of Hugh Cole, Alice Kent, and Katherine Finche. Another ½ acre in Fillettes between the lands of Mary Rakyns and Richard Stephens, ¾ acre at Groveland End, ½ acre in Densale, ½ acre at Haxland Gate, 1 acre in Haxland Feild, 1 acre in Exbury Feild, 1 acre in Wollers Meade, 5½ acres called Glascrofte, 3 acres of coppice at Water Lane, 5½ acres called Netherblacland, 3¼ acres called Sumpters Crofte, and another 8 acres of coppice with the cottage lying between the land called Bramley Crofte and the king's road. Which 29½ acres after payment of 4s. 10d. annually have a net annual value of £3 15s.

1619 A cottage and 5 acres of pasture and arable land in Buttsash in the possession of John Pynnock, paying 4d. annually with a net annual value of 5s.

1620 Two messuages, three cottages, and 59 acres of meadow, pasture, arable, and woodland, in Exbury and Lepe in the possession of Hugh Cole. Of which a messuage, two cottages, and 27 acres of meadow, pasture, arable, and woodland are in Exbury, whereof the messuage, garden, and courtyard contain 2¼ acres lying between the lands of Richard Stephens and John Symondes, also 1 acre in Woody Croft, 1½ acres called Churche Close, 3 acres called Blage Deanes, 3 acres called Buttinesford. One of the cottages, garden, courtyard, together containing 1¼ acres is situated between the lands of Richard Stephens and Mary Coleman, another 3 acres in three separate parcels in Densale, the other cottage and courtyard containing 2 acres called Shord, another 1¼ acres in Haxland, 2¾ acres in two separate parcels in Haxland Feild, another 2 acres in separate parcels in Inchmary, another ½ acre in Bonnye, 3½ acres called the Wett Mead, and coppice between the lands of William Ricard and Thomas Orchard. In Lepe are 32 acres, of which 3½ acres together with a cottage, garden, and courtyard containing 2 acres are situated between the Lordes Landes and the king's road, another 1½ acres called Dereibought, 3 acres called Compe, ¾ acre in Haxland Feild, 3 acres called Yardcrofte, 6 acres called New-crofte, 2 acres called Bridgmans, 1 acre of coppice lying at Ground-leys Well, another 5 acres are a close at the same place, another 5 acres are called Loselades, and 1 acre is a parcel of meadow lying between the lands of John Cole and Robert Cole and the king's road. Which 59 acres after payment of £1 1s. 2½d. annually have a net annual value of £7 10s.

1621 Two cottages and 31¾ acres of meadow, pasture, arable, and woodland in Exbury and Lepe in the possession of Thomas Orchard. Whereof a cottage and 12 acres consisting of garden, orchard, and courtyard is situated between the land of Richard Whordon and the Lordes Land, ½ acre in the Estefeilde between the land of John Humber and the Lordes Land, 1 acre of meadow between the land of Matthew Miles and the Lordes Land, ½ acre of meadow between the lands of Richard Younge and John Hailes, 5 acres called Seafordes, ¾ acre in Haxland in the possession of Reginald Saun-ders, ¾ acre in Haxland Feild, another 3 acres in Haxland between the lands of West Fashion and John Symondes, ½ acre at Haxland among the Bushie Hilles, 1 acre between the lands of William Kinge and John Hayles, 2½ acres between the land of William Kinge and the Lordes Land, 2 acres called Blackland, 1 acre of coppice between the land of Alice Moone and the Lordes Land, ½ acre near the land of John Cole, ½ acre in Short Broomes, ½ acre near Gatwood Howse, and the other cottage and ¾ acre of meadow in Lepe between the land of Alice Moone and the king's road. Which 31¾ acres after payment of 4s. 4½d. annually have a net annual value of £4 10s.

1622 A cottage and 14 acres of pasture, gorse, and heath in Exbury and Lepe in the possession of William Kinge *alias* French or Thomas Barton, paying 1s. annually with a net annual value of £1 15s.

1623 A cottage and 12½ acres of pasture and arable land in Exbury in the possession of Mary Rakyns or Thomas Coleman. Whereof the cottage and 1½ acres, with garden and courtyard, is situated between the land of Thomas Haward and the land called Boughton, 1 acre called Cattesden, 3½ acres in four parcels in Exbury Feild, 1 acre in Densale, 2 acres in four parcels in Haxland Feild, ½ acre in Haxland Close, 1 acre in Rowland, and 1 acre in Fillettes between the lands of Hugh Cole and John Symons. Which 12½ acres after payment of 2s. 5½d. annually has a net annual value of £1 10s.

1624 A messuage, barn, orchard, garden, and 44¾ acres of meadow, pasture, arable, and woodland in twelve closes in Baddesley and Boldre in the possession of Henry Whitehead and the widow Martell as tenants of Christopher Wheler, paying 4s. 4d. annually and with a net annual value of £6 5s.

1625 A messuage, two cottages, and the lands called Bunie Start Coppice and Brode Croft, and various other lands in sixteen parcels together containing 76 acres of meadow, pasture, gorse, heath, and woodland, in various places in Exbury, Hardley, and Lyndhurst in the possession of West Fashion, for which paying annually for the land in Exbury 7s. 7d., in Hardley 3s., and in Lyndhurst 4s. 2d, together having a net annual value of £12 10s.

1626 A messuage, cottage, and 30¼ acres of meadow, pasture, arable, and woodland in South Baddesley in the possession of John Emery. Of which the messuage, garden and orchard is called Eston Towne. Another parcel of meadow and coppice called Rymead and Rymead Coppice, and a parcel of land called the Perock adjoining the coppice, are situated among the lands of sir George Philpott. Another parcel is called Westfeild, another is called Newton Meadowe, another is called Py Leaz, another Forest Close, another Sprolls Parock, and another two parcels are called Stone Parock. Which 30¼ acres after payment of 1s. 8d. have a net annual value of £4 10s.

1627 A messuage, two cottages, and 76¾ acres of meadow,

pasture, arable, and woodland in Buttsash in the possession of sir William Webb. Of which one of the cottages and two closes are called Kitches, another parcel is called Andrewes Mead, another Longlandes, another Perrye Crofte, another White Crofte, the residue being in various places in Buttsash. Which pays 3s. 4d. a year, with a net annual value of £12 10s.

1628 A cottage and close of pasture and woodland containing 17 acres in Burley in the possession of Richard Lyne gentleman, paying 8d. a year with a net annual value of £2 5s.

1629 A cottage and 20¾ acres of meadow, pasture, arable, and woodland in Exbury and Lepe in the possession of John Rookeley, of which a parcel is called Haxland, another parcel Bunny Coppice, another parcel Bunny Meade, another parcel Suffrance Crofte, and the remainder in various places. Paying 4s. 1½d. annually, with a net annual value of £2 10s.

1630 12 acres of meadow, pasture, arable, and woodland called Barnibies and West Close in Lyndhurst and Linwood in the possession of William Beconsawe. Paying 2s. 6d. annually, with a net annual value of £2.

1631 Closes called Newland Furzey and Northey, and a coppice called Northey Coppice, which together contain 22½ acres in Bartley in the possession of Robert White. Paying 1s. 10½d. annually, with a net annual value of £4 10s.

1632 A cottage and six closes of meadow, pasture, and arable land together containing 8¼ acres in London Minstead in the possession of John White. Paying 1½d. annually, with a net annual value of £1 10s.

1633 Two cottages and 25¼ acres of pasture in Baddesley in the possession of Thomas South senior, of which 3ac. 10p. are a close of pasture adjoining one of the cottages, another 11ac. 1r. 20p. are the close Crockett, the other cottage with two closes of pasture, one of which contains 8 ac. 3r. 28p. and the other 1 ac. 3r. 12p., are situated at Slipford. Paying an annual rent of 3s. 10d., with a net annual value of £2 10s.

1634 Two closes of pasture and woodland called Esterley Wotton and Chamberlens which contain 92 acres in Baddesley in the possession of John Wallers. Paying annually 8s. 4d., with a net annual value of £12 10s.

1635 29 acres of meadow called Wichbery *alias* Winchbury Meades in the bailiwick of Godshill in the possession of lady Dorothy Morison widow, paying annually 1s., with a net annual value of £10.

1636 A messuage and seven closes of pasture which together contain 19ac. 2r. 13p. in Newtowne and Baddesley in the possession of Thomas Cheverton, of which the messuage and two closes are called Homested, another close adjoins Fowles Meade, another close is called Bromey Close, another close is called Pickett Close, and the other two closes are called Greencloses. Paying annually 1s. 6d., with a net annual value of £3 6s. 8d.

1637 A cottage and close of meadow called Morris Pickes in Lyndhurst, also another cottage and parcel of pasture called Trumps in Minstead, together containing 5½ acres and in the possession of John Morris. Paying 1s. 2½d. for the land in Lyndhurst and 2d. for the land in Minstead, with a net annual value of 18s. 6d.

1638 A cottage and parcel of pasture, divided into two parts, called Dowles and containing 1ac. 2r. 30p. in Exbury in the possession of Walter Sheperd. Paying annually 2d. with a net annual value of 7s. 6d.

1639 Three cottages and the land called Rockleys, Cops Acre, Nichams, Pylewell, Bewen, Seacristes, and How Meade, together containing 19ac. 3r. 14p. of pasture, arable, and woodland in various places in Baddesley and Sharprick, in the possession of Richard Cole, paying annually 1s 5½d., with a net annual value of £3 6s. 8d.

1640 A messuage, two gardens, and five closes called Southwood, Longe Acre, the Parock, and the Westfeild, and a coppice called Py Leaz Coppice, together containing 12 acres of meadow, pasture, arable, and woodland, in Baddesley in the possession of John Dale, paying annually 2d., with a net annual value of £2 5s.

1641 Two cottages and land called Newton Perock, Slipp, Eston

Towne, Newtowne Close, Hares Bridge Close, Downes, and Newtowne, which together contain 18¾ acres of meadow, pasture, arable, and woodland, in Baddesley in the possession of Thomas South senior, paying annually 2s., with a net annual value of £2 5s.

1642 A cottage and two parcels of land, one of pasture called Hobrians and the other of woodland, together containing 4 acres, in Haxland Closes and in Exbury, in the possession of Mark Mathew and James Horsey, paying annually 4d., with a net annual value of 10s.

1643 1ac. 1r. 28p. of land called Parsonage Barne Close in Exbury in the possession of Laurence Washington, paying annually 1d., with a net annual value of 5s.

1644 A messuage and closes of arable land, meadow, pasture, and woodland, one of which is called Cokley Feild, another Backside Close, another Prates Croft, another Bushie Close, another Southwood, another Pitchdepe Coppice, another Freshwater Meade, and another Jepsons Perock, together containing 19ac.3r.14p. in Baddesley in the possession of Robert Over, paying annually 1s. for Bushie Close and 1s. 6d. for the rest, with a net annual value of £3 6s. 8d.

1645 Three cottages and seven closes of pasture and meadow called Sturgions together containing 15ac. 3r. 30p. in Minstead in the possession of Elizabeth Mizley, or any other person acting as guardian of John Cooke an infant, paying annually 6s. 8d. with a net annual value of £2 5s.

1646 A cottage, garden, and courtyard, and several closes of meadow, pasture, arable, and woodland, of which one is called Gutt Meade, another Yard Crofte, another Nottes Crofte, another Upper Wett Meads, and a moiety of Heathie Downe, together containing 18 acres in Lepe and in the possession of George Taylor, paying 2s. 6½d. annually, with a net annual value of £3 6s. 8d.

1647 A messuage, cottage, and closes of meadow, pasture, arable, and woodland, called Sansome and Rookeleys, together containing 6 acres in South Baddesley in the possession of William Purdue, paying annually 1s. 6d. with a net annual value of £1.

1648 A messuage, cottage, and 82ac. 13p. of meadow, pasture, arable, and woodland, in thirteen separate closes lying in Bartley in the possession of Robert Lambe, of which the messuage and twelve closes of meadow, pasture, arable, and woodland contain 78ac. 1r. 38p. inclosed by the forest, and the cottage and other close contain 3ac. 3r. of pasture called Nicolls, paying annually 9s. 4d. for the messuage and twelve closes and 7d. for the cottage and close, with a net annual value of £18.

1649 Two cottages and 31ac. 18p. of meadow, pasture, and arable land in ten separate closes in Bartley in the possession of John Milles esquire, whereof two small closes adjoining one of the cottages contain 3ac. 2r. 35p., another three closes of pasture and meadow adjoining the other cottage contain 13ac. 1r. 7p., and the other five closes of meadow, pasture, and arable land contain 14ac. 16p. called Feelinges and are on three parts inclosed by the forest, in the possession of Thomas Sh ... as tenant of John Milles, paying annually 2s. 1d., with a net value of £4.

1650 Two messuages and 96½ acres of meadow, pasture, gorse, heath, moor, arable land, and woodland in various places in the possession of John Hale, George Rowe, and of others, whereof a certain part is called Sandyland, another parcel called Aldershare More, and the residue in separate parcels dispersed in the forest, paying annually 11s. 1d., with a net annual value of £7 10s.

[In addition to the above lands, the grant also includes land in the forest of Chippenham *alias* Pewsham in the county of Wiltshire.]

C.99/55

1651 Grant to John Foyle made 29th May 1609

Land and properties granted to John Foyle of Shaftesbury in consideration of the sum of £228 8s. and subsequent to an inquest held at Hartley Row in the county of Southampton on the 12th January 1609 before sir Edward Grevill' and Othone Nicholson esquire. Dated at Westminster the 29th May 1609.

Twenty two messuages, eight cottages, and 680 acres in Brockenhurst and Brookley in the possession of Alban Knapton gentleman.
Comprising Home Meadow, Home Close, Long Close, Sollandes, Sollice Coppice, White Pitts, White Pitt More, Ashley Meadow, Asheleaz, Pigsmore Meadow, Pigsmore Long Land, Ten Acres, Long Furlong, Pettie Furlong, Twelve Acres, and Culverheyes in Siblis messuage.
The Backside, Wantons, and Watcombe are in Palmers Meadow.
Pilgrims Pond Close, Paine Dowe, Palmers Closes, and Palmers Meadow in the possession of Stephen White.
Fonthilles messuage in the possession of Anthony Balsh.
Rabitsley, Aldermore Howen near the road from Brockenhurst to Battramsley, Conigre, Fonthill Close, Burnardes, Highwodes, Pond Close, Tydy Close, Tydy Iland, and Tydy Meadow lying in Trenchardes messuage in the possession of Mary Harvy widow.
Well Close, Well Perock, Barn Close, Barn Perock, and Broad Croft lying in another messuage, with two closes called Barnard and Lettis, in the possession of John Harding.
A messuage with closes called Hickes More, Hickes, Hickes Meadow, Haslettes, Upper Haslettes, Lower Haslettes, in the possession of Nicholas Rogers.
Knightes Mill in the possession of Richard Knight.
Another messuage and a close called Claylandes in the possession of John Downer.
Ayshelachmore with a messuage and four closes in the possession of Thomas Michell.
Queeneslachmore divided into two closes in the possession of Roger Coward.
A moiety of Knowles messuage comprising Pond Close, Toles Croft, Colmans Coppice, Wheathill, Norlandes Close, Gis Coppice,

Fishers, and the Gore divided into various closes. Which moiety contains 46 acres in the possession of John Furner.
Another messuage with the Backside, Northlandes, Black Acre, and Buttes in the possession of Agnes Imberley widow.
Another messuage with closes called The Upper Close, Lower Close, Norclose *alias* Norleaze, Roydons Meadow, Rowdens Hill, and Rowdens Dale, in the possession of William Furner.
Shepperdes messuage, Lyttle Lettys, Tutmans, Red Medowes, and Northlandes Close in the possession of John Wren.
Another messuage with the Backside and various closes called Spring Whethels, Upper Whethells, Lower Whethilles, and Wayghtons Perock in the possession of Dorothy Lewes widow.
Eatons messuage comprising Gill Croft, Greene Close, and two closes in Northland in the possession of Alice Andrewes widow.
Milwardes messuage comprising Great Milwardes, Cock Meade, and Milwardes Meades in the possession of Thomas Ames.
Oylett messuage comprising Corner Close, Colesettley, and Stoney Landes in the possession of Alice Stephenson widow.
Rookleys messuage comprising the Backside with various closes called Sewyers More, Trades, and Peake Closes in the possession of Tristram Elmes.
Saddlebowes messuage comprising Upper Saddlebowes, and Lower Saddlebowes, in the possession of Peter Attwood.
A close called Marlepooles in the possession of Edmund Browne.
Various closes called Colehayes Meadowes, Milhaines, Colehayes Groves, and Colehaies Feildes in the possession of Alice Andrews widow.
Warnes messuage comprising the Backside with two closes in Brodeland in the possession of Nicholas Tagge.
Another close in Northlandes in the possession of Elizabeth Burt widow.
Another messuage with various closes called Crickettes, Peny Crofte, and Stonyland in the possession of Joyce Bowden widow.
Another messuage with two closes called Welhead and Church Close in the possession of Henry Baker.
Also seven other cottages with gardens in the tenure of John Jones, Hugh Clerke, John Beaumonte, John Gretnam, Giles Rabbett, Thomas Hancock, and John Jourd.

1652 Two cottages and 47 acres in Brockenhurst, Brookley, Battramsley, and Wootton in the possession of William Tulse gent-

leman.
Comprising a close of meadow in Brookley in the possession of Nicholas Tagge.
Two closes near to Wide Lane Greene.
Another close of pasture near to Widemore.
Another close of arable land in the possession of William Atwood called Broadland.
Another close of arable land called Broadland.
Another close of pasture called Obberground.
In Wootton a close of pasture called Wootton Ground.
Another close in the possession of Nicholas Roughe.
In Battramsley a cottage and three closes of pasture, arable, and woodland in the possession of Richard Parnell.
In Brockenhurst a close of meadow in the possession of William Attwood.
Another close of arable, pasture, and woodland, called the Gore.
Another close of pasture in the possession of John Purdue.
Two closes of arable and pasture called Buttes in the possession of William Attwood.

1653 A cottage and 35½ acres in various places in Brockenhurst in the possession of John Story and William Tulce.
Comprising Colmans Coppice, a cottage, and two closes of meadow in the possession of John Story and John Furner.
A close within the land of the widow Lewys.
A close of pasture adjacent to the land of the widow Andrewes.
A close called Newlandes.
A close of pasture called Woodes Close.
A parcel of land in the possession of John Purdue.

1654 A messuage, four cottages, and 70 acres in Brookley, Brockenhurst, Wootton, and Lyndhurst, in the possession of Lewis Emberley.
Comprising a close of pasture in Brookley in the possession of Tristram Elmes.
A parcel of woodland near to Wyde Lane.
A cottage and close of arable abutting the lane from Widelane Greene to Brookley Bridge.
A cottage and meadow near to the Ashe.
Three closes of pasture in the possession of Richard Roffe.
A close of arable lying between the lands of William Monday and

John Hobbes.
A close of arable in the possession of Richard Roffe.
Another close of pasture in the possession of Tristram Elmes.
Two closes of arable and pasture between Wideland and Munckes in the possession of Tristram Elmes.
A close of pasture between Great Munckes Lane and Little Munckes Lane in the possession of Tristram Elmes.
Another close of pasture called Furzy Trendlye in the possession of Richard Roffe.
In Wootton a close of pasture in the possession of Richard Carter.
A cottage and three closes of pasture in the possession of John White.
In Brockenhurst a cottage and two closes of pasture and arable in the possession of Lewis Emberley.
A close of pasture within a close a part of which is called Lampacre in the possession of Richard Roffe.
A close of pasture near to Cowleaz in the possession of Richard Roffe.
In Lyndhurst a close of meadow called Ford Meade in the possession of James Pocock.

1655 A messuage, cottage, and 16½ acres in Brookley and Brockenhurst in the possession of William Adam *alias* Adams.
Comprising in Brookley a close of pasture called Broadland.
Another close of pasture called Obber Landes.
Meadow near Mockes Lane containing ½ acre.
In Brockenhurst a messuage and four closes of arable, meadow, and pasture containing 7 acres.
A parcel of meadow near Milhaine.
A parcel of meadow called Fishers.
A parcel of pasture called Milheard.
A parcel of land called Stonyland.
A close of pasture near Brockenhurst church.

1656 6¼ acres of pasture and arable in Brockenhurst in the possession of Nicholas Tagge.

The above twenty two messuages, sixteen cottages, and 855½ acres after paying an annual rent of 18s. 11d. and all other deductions have a net annual value of £36 10s.

1657 A cottage, 29 acres and 2 perches of meadow, pasture, arable, and woodland, in Brookley and Brockenhurst in the possession of Alexander Paynton. Comprising a cottage, 1ac. 3r. 34p. of pasture in the possession of Humphrey Elmes.
1ac. 11p. of pasture called Brodelandes.
3ac. 3r. 30p. of pasture called Huntes Crofte.
2ac. 1r. 27p. of pasture and woodland called Obber Ground.
6ac. 3r. 39p. of pasture and meadow called Mockes.
8ac. 1r. 29p. of arable and pasture called Bassettes.
3r. of pasture called Millardes.
The residue in various parcels in Brookley and Brockenhurst.
Which said cottage and 29ac. 2p. after payment of 2s. annually and all other deductions have a net annual value of £5 10s.

1658 Five messuages, two cottages with barns, gardens, and orchards, and 68ac. 3r. 8p. of land in various places in the possession of tenants of Albany Knapton gentleman.
Comprising four closes of pasture, one being called Grigges and the other three Knightes, together containing 5ac. 1r. 16p. in Brookley and Brockenhurst and in the possession of John Uphill.
Three messuages and 33 acres in Mill Street, Brookley and Brockenhurst and in the possession of John Draper and his assignees. Of which one messuage with orchard and parrock contains ½ acre in Brockenhurst. Another messuage with 2 acres adjacent and a close of meadow in Milstreete called Reeves. Another messuage and courtyard containing 3½ acres in Brockenhurst called Knightes. A close of arable and meadow containing 6½ acres in Brookley called Mockes. A close of gorse, one of broom, and adjacent coppice called Clarkes, which together contain 15 acres and are the residue of the premises in the possession of John Draper.
Two closes of pasture, one called Sorehaies and the other Stonyland, together containing 6ac. 3r. 32p. in the possession of Edmund Browne in Brockenhurst.
Another messuage, barn, garden, and orchard called Knightes Standinge, with meadow, pasture, and arable land, together containing 15 acres in Brockenhurst in the possession of Richard Draper. Of which two parcels are called Fower Acres and Three Halfes, two closes are called Upper Groundes, another parcel is called Redmeade, another close Soles Coppice, another parcel called Wheat Hilles Parrock, and another close Battymores.
Another messuage and four closes of pasture together containing 8½

acres in the possession of Thomas Cooke, the tenant of William Lyon, and comprising the remainder of the said five messuages, two cottages, and 68ac. 3r. 8p. Which after payment of an annual rent of 2s. and all other deductions has a net annual value of £8 17s.

C.66/1790

1659 Grant to Edward Savage and Andrew Mundey made 2nd June 1609

Land and properties granted to Edward Savage of Bradley in the county of Southampton and Andrew Mundey of Grove Place in the same county in consideration of the sum of £557 18s. 4d. Dated at Westminster the 2nd June 1609.

Five messuages, forty five cottages, a water mill, 1,888 acres by the perch of 16½ft., meadow, pasture, arable land, woodland, gorse and heath, of assarts and purprestures and other lands, in Haywood, Pilley, Warborne, Baddesley, Newtowne, Battramsley, Brookley, Brockenhurst, and Lyndhurst, and other places in the New Forest and recently in the occupation of sir Richard Mill'.

1660 A messuage with garden, orchard, and courtyard, the water mill, and 450 acres of meadow, pasture, arable land, gorse and heath, and woodland, in 24 closes called Haywood *alias* Haywood Farm *alias* the manor of Heywood and Boldre, of which the parcels are called Haywood Meade, Culverclose, Millclose, Cowleaze, Whiteclose, Mill Copse, Howhay Croft, Heath Close, Beanfeild, Shipfeild Copse, Shipfeild, Brodefeild, Radley, Picked Close, Churchfeild, Church Hill, and Churchmeade, paying annually 14s.

1661 Two messuages and twenty eight cottages with gardens and courtyards, and 472ac. 24p. of meadow, pasture, arable land, gorse and heath, and woodland in Pilley and Warborne of which the parcels are called Pilley Farm in the occupation of Martin Carter, Barbers Grove, Steres Crofte, Coopers Crofte, Mackes Hall, Peny Croft, Longe Close, Bromehills, Bolderbridge Close, Cole Crofte, Greate Rodscombe, Little Rodscombe, Twelve Acres, Furzie Close, Sparborowes, Bromehill, Longe Close, Kidneis, Bolderbridge Meades, Little Darneford, Colecrofte, Beane Perocke, Stockhouse, Shallowe, Costers Crofte, Barley Close, Bull Meade, Ferney, Roscombe Downes, Pylewell Ground, Longland, Rodscombe Ould Land, Bull, Bushie Close, Great Close, Wareborne Ferne, Twelve Acres Feild, Dumpalls, Longland, Twelve Acres, and Parock, paying 12s. annually.

1662 Two cottages and 74ac. 24p. of meadow, pasture, gorse and heath, arable land, and woodland, in Newtowne and Baddesley in various parcels known as Threshars, Popes Close, Damerfeild, a coppice near Whiskers, Hares Meade, Slipps, Brode Close, and Heath Hills, paying annually 1s. 8d.

1663 A messuage, six cottages, and 470ac. 1r. 34p. of meadow, pasture, gorse and heath, arable land, and woodland, in Battramsley, of which the parcels are called Richardinges, Downe Furlonge, Newcroft, Zowters Coppice, Comon Close, Gillons, le Common, Woodfoldes, Rye Parock, Homefeild, le Grove, Hetherlongland, Furtherlongland, Corner Coppice, Greene Close, Meare Close, Pookes Coppice, Horsdeale, Meere Close and Highcroft, Beane Close, Bolderbridge Close, Pallmers Wood, Wheatparocke, Poole Croft Wood, Rye Close, Summer Close, Aldermead, Moory Landes, Jennettes, Shallowe Close, Pitt Close, Heath Closes, Pookes, Bushy Close, Little Poole Crofte, Aldermead, Emlandes More, Blosses Parocke, Shill' Meade, Gally Hill, Danes Meade, Crokers, Ponde Heath, Plecke, and Furzye Close, the residue in various places in Battramsley and in Battramsley bailiwick, paying £2 10s. 6d. annually.

1664 A messuage, six cottages, 365ac. 2r. 18p. of meadow, pasture, gorse and heath, arable land, and woodland, in Brookley, of which the parcels consist of Brookley Ferme, Picknells, Longe Close, Brodelandes, Obberhill, Obbermockes, Trenley, Fernehills, Colliers, Sowclose, Weare Meade, Burnardes, Pepps, Bushe Mockes, Wildlane Coppice, Shepheardes, Truckes, Pikes, Holmes, Milwardes, Frogbridge Lowen, and Setley Closes, the residue in various places in Brookley and in Battramsley bailiwick, paying £1 10s. 6d. annually.

1665 Two cottages with gardens, orchards, and courtyards, and 15ac. 2r. 31p. of meadow, pasture, gorse and heath, arable land, and woodland, in Brockenhurst, the parcels comprising Churchclose in the occupation of Thomas Russell, also Churche Close in the occupation of Humphrey Elmes, Cooke Croft, Hickes in the occupation of Arthur Loade, Barnehaies, and Foxdens, the residue in various places in Brockenhurst and the South bailiwick, paying 6d. annually.

1666 A cottage and 35ac. 3r. 38p. of meadow, pasture, arable land, and woodland, in Lyndhurst, the parcels comprising Dickmans, Birchingclose, Brodeclose, and Westclose, paying 14s. 6d. annually.

Which five messuages, forty five cottages and 1,888 acres after payment of the total rents of £6 3s. 8d. and all other expenses have a net annual value of £139 9s. 7d. as determined by the inquest held at Romsey on the 20th July 1608 before sir Edward Grevill' and Othone Nicholson esquire, and upon the oath of John Hopkins and other good and true men.

1667 The aforementioned properties are now or recently in the occupation of sir Richard Mille, sir William Oglander, sir George Philpott, sir Ambrose Button, John Gooky, Richard Elmes, John Long, John Shepheard, Margaret Uphill, Katherine White, John Elmes, John Atlane, Jonathan Silver, William Saunders, Edmund Reeves, Richard Wheeler, William Luke, Richard Whittington, Edward Wavell, Martin Godard, Henry Lyon, William Lyon, Elizabeth Burt, [Blank] Pratt, John Martell, Thomas South, sir John Mewis, Richard Worsley esquire, Hugh Darvall, William Weston esquire, Edward Lewen, Martin Carter, Thomas Martell, Thomas Corbyn, Thomas Sleyhound, John Castell, William Turner, John Wavell, Thomas Read, Richard Knowles, John Daye, Robert Flight, Richard Hall, Francis Wale, John Maller, John Tucker, John Gally [Blank] Foxe, Sibil Martell, John Gastard, Peter Aldred, Thomas Kinge, Richard Knowles, John Eston, Agnes Smith, William Atwood, Thomas Payne, William White, Thomas Whale, Thomas Gawpyn, Richard Parnell, Alexander Russiter, Richard Browne, Edmund Brown, John Wilmott, Joan Hobs widow, William Burton, Thomas Russell, Anne Castell, Nicholas Tagge, Roger Peckham, Richard Moore, Thomas Sowth, Thomas Love, Thomas Norton, Sibil Tutt, Thomas Russell, Humphrey Elmes, Arthur Loade, and Richard Tarver.

C.66/1995

1668 Grant to Thomas Elye and Nicholas Lucye made 13th June 1613

Assarts and purprestures, and other lands, granted to Thomas Elye and Nicholas Lucye. Dated at Westminster the 13th June 1613.

Various parcels of meadow, pasture, arable, and woodland, with a mill, various messuages and cottages, containing 557 acres within the bailiwicks of Lyndhurst, Battramsley, the South bailiwick, and the North bailiwick, now or recently in the occupation of Thomas Goddard esquire or his tenants. Of which a parcel known as Hincheslea *alias* Westfeild contains 75 acres, a parcel known as Latchmoor *alias* Blackmansley contains 24 acres. Another parcel known by the various names of Canterton, Brooke, Bramshaw, Canterton Farm, Skires Farm, Lacyes, Pypers, Kite, John Carters Haye, Milholme, Hoppettes, Wildcloses, Cole More, Smarley, Ricardes Haye, Newehaies, Hobbes his Houlde, Shave, and the waste situated in Brooke Heath, in total containing 279 acres. The residue consists of certain closes of pasture, arable, and woodland, situated in Brockenhurst, Brookley, Battramsley, Pilley, Boldre, South Baddesley, Lyndhurst, and Old Lymington, of which the parcels are known as Pinnockes, Richemondes, Collyers, Trenley, Darvelles Moore, Serchers, Haskettes, Shagges Meade, Longe Close, Manburye Close, and Brodecloses, also certain land recently held by Hugh Darvell, in total containing 179 acres.
Which premises, now or recently in the occupation of Thomas Goddard, have a net annual value of £75 after payment of an annual rent of £2 4s. 4d., namely for the premises called Hincheslea *alias* Westfeild, Blackmansley, and Latchmoor, 14s; for the premises called Canterton, Brooke, Bramshaw, Canterton Farm, Skires Farm, Lacyes, Pypers, Kite, John Carters Haye, Milholme, Hoppittes, Wildcloses, Colemore, Smarley, Ricardes Haye, Newe Haye, Hobbes his Holde, Shave, and the waste, 12s.; for the premises in Lyndhurst, 8s. 4d.; and for the remaining premises in Battramsley, Pilley, Boldre, Brockenhurst, Brookley, South Baddesley, and Old Lymington, 10s.
The above mentioned premises being the subject of an inquest held at Hartford Bridge on the 7th April 1612 before Othone Nicholson and George Mortymer, and on the oath of Christopher Lipscombe and others.

1669 Two cottages with barns and various parcels of arable land, meadow, pasture, woodland, gorse, moor, and heath, in total containing 210 acres by the perch of 20ft., of assarts and purprestures and other lands and tenements known as Rollstone which in the 11th year of Edward II [1317–8] was rented to John Foxley by Gilbert de Wigeton for a rent of £3 10s., described as having been in Rollstone and extending north to south between Holbury and Exbury. Which 210 acres by letters patent given at Westminster the 28th November 1604 were granted to sir Edward Moore and Henry Awdley esquire for a term of 40 years, paying annually £3 13s. 4d. and 3s. 4d., with a net annual value of £18 6s. 8d., as determined by an inquest held at Winchester on the 12th January 1613 before Thomas Kirkbye esquire, William Budd, and Lancelot Thorpe, upon the oath of John Crooke and others.

1670 Various parcels known as Southbaddesley *alias* the manor of Baddesley, Whiskers, and Daneford, now or recently in the occupation of sir George Philpott, paying annual rents of £4 1s. for Southbaddesley *alias* the manor of Baddesley and Daneford, and 2s. for Whiskers. Also a parcel of land called Woodhouse, of which 30 acres were formerly known as the Firma de Broell', situated in the forest of Chute and paying annual rents of 14s. and 10s. Containing in total 800 acres by the perch of 16½ft. and paying an annual rent of £5 7s., with a net annual value of £21 5s., as determined by an inquest held at Hartford Bridge on the 29th July 1612 before Othone Nicholson esquire and George Mortymer gentleman, upon the oath of Christopher Lypscombe and others.

C.99/48

1671 Grant to John Chamberlaine esquire made the 21st May 1631

A grant of land and properties made to John Chamberlaine esquire in consideration of the sum of £200. Dated at Westminster the 21st May 1631.

A close of meadow, pasture, wood and underwood, gorse and heath, now or recently in the occupation of George Staples gentleman, situated in the New Forest containing 60 acres by the perch of 16½ft., of an annual value of 2s.

1672 Two parcels called Lammas Greene and Fowle Corner in the occupation of the villagers of Hardley, containing 10 acres and worth 6d. a year.

1673 A cottage with garden and orchard adjoining in the occupation of the widow Heycrofte, containing half an acre and worth 2d. a year.

1674 A close or parcel of arable land and pasture called Preiste Crofte in the occupation of Richard Whitehead, containing 12 acres and worth 4d. a year.

1675 Eleven cottages with gardens, orchards, and an adjacent parcel of land, in the occupation of William Clewer, Thomas Thayre, John Garrison, John Buckler, Thomas Bullocke, Alice Cloade, Thomas Rennell, Elizabeth Bayly widow, John Foxe, William Hibbert, and George Hedger, situated in the In bailiwick *alias* the bailiwick of Lyndhurst, containing 6 acres and worth 2s. a year.

1676 Fifteen cottages with gardens, orchards, and an adjacent parcel of land, situated in the North bailiwick and in the occupation of Richard Wolfe, John Coffin, John Melton, Agnes Warwicke widow, Agnes Willis widow, the widow Emery, Agnes Rowden widow, William Osman, William Younge, the widow Easton, John Eldred, Thomas de Luke, Agnes Luke widow, John Kember, and Henry Morlis, containing 6 acres and worth 2s. 6d. a year.

1677 A cottage with garden, orchard, and adjacent parcel of land, situated in the North bailiwick and in the occupation of Peter Younge, and containing one acre.

1678 A cottage with garden and orchard, and a close of land containing 3 acres, situated in the North bailiwick and in the occupation of John Adams.

1679 A cottage with garden and orchard, and a close of land containing 3 acres, situated in the North bailiwick and in the occupation of John Kinge.

1680 A parcel of land containing 3 acres situated in the North bailiwick and in the occupation of William Lovell.

1681 A close containing 2 acres situated in the North bailiwick and in the occupation of John Dawson.

1682 A close or parcel of meadow called Marle Pooles containing 2 acres situated in the North bailiwick and in the occupation of Richard Kember.

1683 A cottage with garden and orchard, and an adjacent parcel of land containing 2 acres, situated in the North bailiwick and in the occupation of John de Luke.

1684 A cottage with garden and orchard, and an adjacent parcel of land containing 1½ acres, situated in the North bailiwick and in the occupation of Nicholas Spencer.

1685 The parcels of land known as Otter Lane *alias* Cox Lane containing 2 acres, situated in the North bailiwick and in the occupation of Stephen Warwicke.

1686 The parcels of land called Shave containing 20 acres and situated in the North bailiwick, in the occupation of Thomas Goddard esquire and worth 4s. a year.

1687 A cottage with garden and orchard and an adjacent parcel of land, called Crowders and containing 5 acres, situated in the bailiwick of Fritham, in the occupation of James Barry and worth 6d. a year.

1688 The closes and parcels of meadow, pasture, wood and underwood, gorse and heath, known as Burcombes and containing 30 acres, situated in the bailiwick of Linwood and in the occupation of John Mist and Richard Elliott, and worth 2s. 6d. a year.

1689 A cottage with garden and orchard, and half an acre of land, situated in the bailiwick of Godshill and in the occupation of William Waterman.

1690 A cottage with garden and orchard, situated in the bailiwick of Godshill and in the occupation of Jerome Trippacke.

1691 A cottage with garden and orchard, and a close of land containing 3 acres, situated in the bailiwick of Godshill and in the occupation of Nicholas Read.

1692 A cottage with garden and orchard, and a parcel of land containing 2 acres, situated in the bailiwick of Godshill and in the occupation of the widow Hall.

1693 A cottage with garden and orchard situated in the bailiwick of Godshill and in the occupation of William Wheeler.

1694 A cottage with garden and orchard, situated in the bailiwick of Godshill and in the occupation of Walter Williams and [Blank] Moore.

1695 Two cottages with gardens and orchards, situated in the bailiwick of Godshill and in the occupation of John Gillett and [Blank] Wheeler, with an annual value of 1s. 8d.

1696 The parcels of land known as Howse Moore containing 15 acres and situated in the bailiwick of Godshill.

1697 The parcels of water meadow lying by the Avon close to Breamore mill, containing 10 acres.

1698 The parcels of waste containing 40 acres and called Glaspitt, situated in the bailiwick of Godshill.

1699 The parcels of waste containing 12 acres and known as

Bryans Moore, situated in the bailiwick of Godshill.

1700 The parcels of meadow containing 2 acres, situated in the old course of the Avon in Godshill bailiwick, and in the occupation of William Fullford and Edward Fullford.

1701 The parcels of land containing 2 acres and situated near to Foxeholes in the bailiwick of Godshill, and worth 2s. 8d. a year.

1702 A cottage with garden and orchard situated in the bailiwick of Burley and in the occupation of Thomas Shave.

1703 A close of pasture containing 2 acres situated in the bailiwick of Burley and in the occupation of Pretesia Rogers widow.

1704 A pasture close called Collett' containing 5 acres, situated in the bailiwick of Burley and in the occupation of Anthony Robins.

1705 The parcels of land and pasture called Fowleford and containing 10 acres, situated in the bailiwick of Burley and in the occupation of John Saunders, with an annual value of 1s. 8d.

1706 A cottage with garden and orchard, and adjacent parcels of land, containing half an acre, situated in the bailiwick of Battramsley and in the occupation of John Harvey.

1707 A cottage with garden and orchard situated in the bailiwick of Battramsley and in the occupation of Gilbert Wheatland.

1708 A cottage with garden and orchard situated in the bailiwick of Battramsley and in the occupation of William Gretnam.

1709 A cottage with garden and orchard situated near to Widelane in the bailiwick of Battramsley and in the occupation of William Maybanoke.

1710 A part of a parcel of land containing 1r. situated in the bailiwick of Battramsley and in the occupation of Richard Wyatt.

1711 A close or parcel of land containing 3 acres at Wootton and in the occupation of William Davie', with an annual value of 1s.

1712 A cottage with garden and orchard at Ravensbecke in the South bailiwick and in the occupation of John Goffe.

1713 A cottage with garden and orchard situated at Pilley in the South bailiwick and in the occupation of [Blank] Marshall. Marshall.

1714 A cottage with garden and orchard situated at Pilley and in the occupation of Thomas Salter.

1715 All the parcels of waste situated between Brockenhurst bridge and the west corner of the close called Colehayes *alias* Coldhayse, containing 3 acres and in the South bailiwick.

1716 All the parcels of waste situated between the east corner of the close called Colehayes *alias* Coldhayse and the road leading from across the river at Millstreete in Brockenhurst, and from the road by the river as far as Brockenhurst mill, containing 3 acres and in the South bailiwick.

1717 All the parcels of waste called White Pitt Moore near Brockenhurst, and between White Pitt Poole *alias* Whitt Pitt Poole on the west, Goore *alias* Gore on the east, and the place called Raysford *alias* Rackford *alias* Rayford on the south, containing 3 acres and in the South bailiwick, and with an annual value of 1s.

All the above mentioned properties having a total annual value of £1 2s. 6d.

Appendix A

Lord Wardens or Keepers from the 14th to the 17th century

1343	John de Beauchamp
1360	Richard de Pembridge
1372	John de Foxle
1383	Thomas Holland, earl of Kent
1397	Edward of York, earl of Rutland
1415	Edward Courtenay, 3rd earl of Devon
1418	Thomas de Montacute, 4th earl of Salisbury
1428	Humphrey, duke of Gloucester
1448	William de la Pole, marquess of Suffolk
1450	John lord Beauchamp, baron of Powyke
1461	William Fiennes, 2nd lord Saye and Sele
1467	William Fitz-Alan, 15th earl of Arundel
1488	Thomas Fitz-Alan, 16th earl of Arundel
1524	William Fitz-Alan, 17th earl of Arundel
1544	Henry Fitz-Alan, 18th earl of Arundel
1580	? Philip Howard
1589	Charles Blount, 8th baron Mountjoy and earl of Devon
1607	Henry Wriothesley, 3rd earl of Southampton
1624	Philip Herbert, 4th earl of Pembroke, lord chamberlain (during the minority of Thomas Wriothesley)
	Thomas Wriothesley, 4th earl of Southampton
1668	Charles Paulet, lord St. John [subsequently 6th marquess of Winchester]
1676	Edward Noel [son-in-law of Thomas Wriothesley, subsequently 3rd baron Noel and earl of Gainsborough]
1687	James Fitz-James, duke of Berwick
1689	Charles Paulet, 6th marquess of Winchester [reappointed, subsequently 1st duke of Bolton]
1699	Charles Paulet, 2nd duke of Bolton

Appendix B

Forest Officers between 1487 and 1489

Lieutenant	Sir Edward Berkeley
Deputy Lieutenant	John Dudelesfold
Riding Forester	Henry Rake
Bow Bearer	Robert Moore
Rangers	Thomas Alwyn (1487–8) Thomas Fulfan (*alias* Wulfan) (1487–8) Thomas Witham (1488)
Verderers	Sir Maurice Barrow Thomas Troys
Steward	John Coke
Woodward of Minstead	John Chaplin
Woodward of Ipley	William Palmer
Foresters	
Burley bailiwick	Sir Edward Berkeley (1487) deputies: William Foule Richard Marlow Thomas Jordan
Fritham bailiwick	John Pocock
Godshill bailiwick	Richard North
Linwood bailiwick	John Bishop
Battramsley bailiwick	Henry Erlesman
South bailiwick	Richard Marke
East bailiwick	John Chaplin
In bailiwick	Peter Pocock
North bailiwick	John Pyper
Agisters	vacant

Regarders

John Andrews (1489)
John Arnewode (1488)
George Banbyrge (1488)
Peter Biddlecombe (1488)
Henry Blake (1487)
John Blake (1488)
William Blake (1489)
William Cole (1487, 1489)
William Cooke (1488)
John Cott (1488)
Reginald Dollyng (1487, 1489)
John Dudelesfold (1487)
James Ede (1487)
John Ede (1487–9)
Walter Fletcher (1487–8)
John Hammond (1488)
John Harris (1488)
Thomas Hendy (1489)
Henry Hobby (1489)
William Holcombe (1489)
Robert Holmor (1488)
William Hooker (1488)
Edmund Hussey (1487)
Thomas Jordan (1488)
Henry Knight (1488–9)
Simon Knowles (1488–9)
Maurice Leigh (1488)
John Lewen (1487–8)
Geoffrey Lorde (1487)
Richard Lorde (1488)
Thomas Lovell (1488)
Simon Marchaunt (1488–9)
John Pake (1488)
Richard Phillipps (1488)
Richard Pocock (1489)
Thomas Purse (1489)
Nicholas Rawlyne (1489)
Richard Reede (1488–9)
Charles Ringwood (1487–8)
John Romsey junior (1488)
John Romsey senior (1487–8)
Nicholas Swetyngham (1488–9)
John Syms (1488)
William Tycheborne (1488)
James White (1487)
Richard Whitehead (1488)

Forest Officers in 1622

Riding Foresters	Richard Draper Richard Gasten John Archer junior
Rangers	Edward Willoughby Robert Knapton
Verderers	George Dowce Thomas Bacon
Woodwards	William Christmas Francis Bennett
Woodward of Minstead	Michael Caule
Foresters	
Fritham bailiwick	Henry Gifford
Godshill bailiwick	Sir Thomas Penruddock
Linwood bailiwick	Henry Hastings
Battramsley bailiwick	Cuthbert Bacon
South bailiwick	Edward Cheeke
East bailiwick	John Chamberlaine
In bailiwick	Robert Cheney
North bailiwick	Oliver Twyne
Agisters	James Barry James Brockenshaw William Rogers
Regarders	William Batten of Burley William Gose of Godshill Andrew Hobbs of Fritham William Jenkins of Avon Albin Knapton of Brockenhurst William Knight of Sway Richard Knowles of Pilley Henry Lyne of Over Kingston Apfradesius Oviatt of Poulner Ambrose Ringwood of Fordingbridge Thomas Stevens of Osmansley Thomas White of Baddesley

[Information taken from Rev. A.W. Stote, Ms. Notebook, Society of Genealogists, Ac. 29232]

Forest Officers in 1634–5

Lieutenant	Sir William Uvedale
Riding Forester	Cuthbert Bacon
Bow Bearer	John Kempe
Rangers	Robert Knapton Thomas Browne
Verderers	Richard Goddard William Beeston
Steward	Robert Mason
Verminer	Henry Gifford
Woodward	Gabriel Lapp
Woodward of Minstead	Michael Caule
Foresters	
Burley bailiwick	Philip Herbert, earl of Pembroke
Fritham bailiwick	Arthur Oxford (1634) Sir John Jephson (1634–5)
Godshill bailiwick	Sir Thomas Penruddock
Linwood bailiwick	Henry Hastings
Battramsley bailiwick	Cuthbert Bacon
South bailiwick	Michael le Jeune
East bailiwick	Sir Richard Uvedale
In bailiwick	John Chamberlain (1634) vacant (1635)
North bailiwick	John Knight
Agisters	James Brokenshawe William Rogers Richard Stote
Riders	Richard Gastin (1634) Thomas Bullock (1634–5) Thomas Purdue (1635)
Regarders	John Bannister (1634–5) William Batten (1634–5) Michael Caule (1634) William Cole (1634–5) Walter Drew (1634) John Eliott (1635) William Gose (1634–5) Andrew Hobbes (1634–5)

	Thomas Hyde (1634)
	Richard Ingpen (1634–5)
	Ambrose Ringwood (1634–5)
	Edward Scott (1634–5)
	John Smith (1634–5)
	Richard Strong (1634)
	William Twyne (1634–5)
	Andrew Yelman (1635)

Forest Officers between 1660 and 1670

Lieutenant	vacant
Riding Forester	Thomas Bacon (1660–9)
	deputy : Bernard Knapton (1661)
Bow Bearer	vacant (1660–1)
	Henry Bromfield (1662–9)
Rangers	Thomas Urry (1660–9)
	Thomas Browne (1660–1)
	Robert Reade (1662–9)
Verderers	Thomas Knowles (1660–9)
	Thomas Mill (1660–4)
	Philip Leigh (1665–9)
Steward	Richard Goddard (1660–65)
	vacant (1666–7)
	William Paulet (1668–9)
Verminer	Arthur Oxford (1660–7)
	vacant (1668–9)
Woodward	Gabriel Lapp (1660–3)
	William Horne (1664–8)
	Bernard Knapton (1669)
Woodward of Minstead	Robert Soff (1660–8)
	Ellis Weekes (1669)
Foresters	
Burley bailiwick	Robert Reade (1660–1)
	John Neale (1662–9)
Fritham	Arthur Oxford (1660–7)
	vacant (1668)
	Sir Robert Howard (1669)
Godshill bailiwick	Sir John Penruddock (1660–9)
Linwood bailiwick	John Bulkeley (1660–1)

	Anthony Ashley-Cooper, lord Ashley (1663–4)
	Sir Adam Browne (1665–9)
Battramsley bailiwick	Thomas Fitzjames (1660–8)
	Edward Seamer (1669)
South bailiwick	Richard Norton (1660–9)
East bailiwick	Sir John Mill (1660–9)
In bailiwick	George Rodney (1660–9)
North bailiwick	William Paulet (1660–8)
	Sir Thomas Clifford (1669)
Agisters	Richard Draper (1660–3)
	Thomas Ford (1660–3)
	Richard Rowe (1664–9)
	William Bright (1664–9)
	William Pocock (1665–9)
	William Stride (1665–9)
Riders	John Stote (1660–9)
	Thomas Marshman (1660–2)
	James Bayly (1665–9)
Regarders	James Barrow (1660–70)
	William Batten (1662–8, 1670)
	William Burrard (1669–70)
	John Caule (1660)
	George Cole (1660)
	Richard Combes (1660–7)
	Richard Draper (1663)
	John Drew (1660, 1670)
	Benjamin Edwards (1660–4)
	Henry Edwards (1661)
	Richard Edwards (1662, 1666–70)
	Thomas Edwards (1660–8)
	Andrew Eliott (1669)
	Thomas Fisher (1662–9)
	William Fisher (1661, 1666–8)
	Christopher Garrett (1663, 1670)
	Henry Goddard (1660)
	Edward Hammond (1664–9)
	William Henvist (1661–3)
	Richard King (1670)
	Bernard Knapton (1660–2)
	Nicholas Lambard (1665–9)
	William Lane (1661)
	Henry Lovell (1669–70)

Thomas Lovell (1660–70)
Christopher Lyne (1664)
William Miller (1662–4)
William Moone (1669–70)
Abraham Olding (1670)
Robert Olding (1660–1)
William Olding (1664–5)
James Osey (1665–6, 1668)
William Pocock (1664–9)
Ogden Rooke (1665–9)
Edward Scott (1661–3)
Thomas Toomer (1669)
Thomas Turner (1660)
Richard Warne (1670)

Appendix C

Chronological Table of Forest Statutes

c.1100	**Leges Henrici** : a list of chapter headings of forest offences probably intended as a guide for forest justices or regarders
c.1184	**Assize of Woodstock** : in itself of doubtful authenticity but represents a composite of earlier forest assizes and contains a number of precepts concerning forest offences
t. Ric. I	**Assize of Richard I** : similar to earlier assizes but with additional articles
1217	**The Charter of the Forest** : a series of measures introduced to relax existing forest laws
c.1278	**Assizes and Customs** : exist in various forms and appear to be the working rules for forest administration
1287	**Assize of William de Vescy** : an extension of previous assizes
1293	**Statute 21 Edw. I, s.2** : deals with trespassers in forests, chases, parks, and warrens
1305	**Ordinance 33 Edw. I, s.5** : allowed for areas which had been disafforested to return to the forest
1306	**Ordinance 34 Edw. I, s.5** : revoked disafforestations, and laid down rules for legal procedures
1327	**Statute 1 Edw. III, s.1, c.8** : a reiteration of the Ordinance of 1306

1350	**Statute 25 Edw. III, s.5, c.7** : no forest officer to collect sustenance except by ancient right
1369	**Statute 43 Edw. III, c.4** : the king's general pardon for offences of vert and venison
1383	**Statute 7 Ric. II, c.3 & 4** : a forest jury shall give their verdict where they receive their charge; and none shall be taken or imprisoned by forest officers without indictment
1482	**Statute 22 Edw. 4, c.7** : relaxation of the forest laws to allow private woods to be enclosed after cutting for a period of up to seven years
1540	**Statute 32 Hen. VIII, c.13** : contains instructions for the drift of forests in connection with the improvement of horses
1540	**Statute 32 Hen. VIII, c.35** : forest justices to appoint deputies
1543	**Statute 35 Hen. VIII, c.17** : an Act for the preservation of woods whereby coppices must be enclosed after felling and a sufficient number of trees retained
1640	**Statute 16 Car. I, c.16** : to determine the metes and bounds of the forests
1667	**Statute 19 & 20 Car. II, c.8** : the Dean Forest Act for reafforestation and timber inclosures
1698	**Statute 9 & 10 Will. III, c.36** : provided for the inclosure of 6000 acres in the New Forest, with rolling powers of further inclosure
1754	**Statute 29 Geo. II, c.36** : an Act for preserving trees
1765–6	**Statutes 6 Geo. III, c.36 & c.48, s.1** : for the preservation of timber
1775–6	**Statute 16 Geo. III, c.30, s.27** : penalties for deer killing
1800	**Statute 39 & 40 Geo. III, c.86** : for the better preservation of timber in the New Forest and for ascertaining the boundaries
1801	**Statute 41 Geo. III, c.108** : extension of previous Act

1801–2	**Statue 42 Geo. III, c. 107, s.1** : penalties for deer killing
1808	**Statute 48 Geo. III, c.72** : established the legality of earlier New Forest inclosures, and provided for further inclosure
1810	**Statute 50 Geo. III, c.116** : to extend and amend the 1800 Act
1811	**Statute 51 Geo. III, c.94** : further extension of the 1800 Act
1812	**Statute 52 Geo. III, c.161** : gave power for the exchange and sale of forest land, and gave statutory powers to the verderers
1817	**Statute 57 Geo. III, c.61** : to abolish the offices of warden, chief justices, and justices in eyre
1819	**Statute 59 Geo. III, c.86** : for regulating common of pasture in the New Forest
1829	**Statute 10 Geo. IV, c.50** : to consolidate the laws relating to woods and forests
1849	**Statute 12 & 13 Vict., c.81** : for Commission to report upon rights or claims over the New Forest
1851	**Statute 14 & 15 Vict., c.76** : to extinguish the right of the Crown to deer in the New Forest
1854	**Statute 17 & 18 Vict., c.49** : for the settlement of claims upon and over the New Forest
1877	**Statute 40 & 41 Vict., c.121** : to amend the administration of the law relating to the New Forest
1879	**Statute 42 & 43 Vict., c.194** : to amend the 1877 Act
1949	**Statute 12 & 13 Geo. 6, c.69** : New Forest Act 1949
1964	**Statute Eliz. II, 1964, c.83** : New Forest Act 1964
1970	**Statute Eliz. II, 1970, c.21** : New Forest Act 1970
1971	**Statute Eliz. II, 1971, c.47** : Wild Creatures and Forest Laws Act. Repealed much earlier legislation

Glossary

Assart [1543]: the illegal conversion of forest land into arable

Browse, browsewood [908]: the tops or branches of trees cut by the keepers to provide winter feed for the deer, called *cablicium* in latin

Buckstall [1520]: a large net [Elisha Coles, *An English Dictionary,* 1676]

Burn beak [522]: to cut up the turf and burn as compost [James Britten, *Old Country and Farming Words,* 1880]

Colefire [322]: A measure of firewood the equivalent when burnt of a load of coals [Elisha Coles, op. cit.]

Colewood [905]: presumably wood to be burned to charcoal

Deer — the different terms used to distinguish species, sex, and age, are as follow :—

Age	*Red Deer*		*Fallow Deer*	
	Harts	*Hinds*	*Bucks*	*Does*
1 year	Calf	Calf	Fawn	Fawn
2 years	Brocket		Pricket	Tegge
3 years	Spayad	Hind	Sorel	Doe
4 years	Staggard		Sore	
5 years	Stag		Buck	
6 years	Hart			

Special terms:—

Aryder [**253**]: not identified

Dama [**708**]: in later latin this word was used for both bucks and does

Rascal [**149**]: a young, lean, or inferior deer [O.E.D.]

Soaking Doe [**94**]: a barren doe [J.O. Halliwell, *Dictionary of Archaic and Provincial Words,* 1901]

Fawsett maker [228]: fawset alternative faucet, a peg or spigot [O.E.D.]

Fence month [1519]: the fifteen days either side of Midsummer Day being the traditional time for the fawning of deer

Frith [492]: originally a sanctuary, but later a name for woodland

Fusterer [410, 624]: a saddle tree maker, i.e. the wooden supports for pack saddles [O.E.D.]

Legal terms: a problem of the forest courts was to ensure the attendance of persons living outside of the forest. This was achieved by means of various writs of attachment issued to the sheriff, these including a **scire facias** whereby a person was informed that he was to attend before the court; a **venire facias** whereby a person was to be made to attend, this being issued when a summons would be ignored; and a **capias** ordering the arrest of a named person. The procedure is described in the present documents **[1502]** that if the sheriff was unable to serve a **venire facias,** then a **capias** should be issued, and if the person concerned had property there should be a **distringas** whereby the sheriff should distrain upon the property to compel the person's appearance in court. In contrast a person living within the forest would probably have attended an earlier court and there would be a **recognizance** that he would appear at the justice seat to be sentenced. This was a bond of record testifying the recognizor to owe a sum of money to the king, this becoming void upon his subsequent appearance in court. When **sureties** were required they would each be liable for half the amount of the bond, this to be levied from their goods and lands in the event of a default.

Moorefalls [905, 972]: roots called moores. The origin of the term is obscure

Perambulation: the bounds of the forest, these being perambulated by forest officers on special occasions

Purpresture [1543]: an encroachment, usually an illegal enclosure

Scelyng [158]: ceiling, the inside planking of a ship's bottom [O.E.D.]

Social status: although not always consistent the documents usually note a person's status or occupation. Below the **nobleman** came the **armiger** or esquire, a person entitled to bear arms. Next followed the **gentleman**, a man of birth and extraction though not noble. A **yeoman** was a freeholder owning a small estate but below the rank of gentleman, and at the bottom came the **husbandman**, an agricultural labourer, and other labourers

Vagabond [23, 51]: in this context probably means leading an unsettled, irregular, or disreputable life, and without proper occupation

Index of Persons and Places

References are to entry numbers

Index of Subjects

References are to entry numbers